THE ILLUSTRATED GOLDEN BOUGH

THE ILLUSTRATED GOLDEN BOUGH

A Study in Magic and Religion

by

Sir James George Frazer

Abridged by Robert K. G. Temple

SIMON & SCHUSTER EDITIONS

SIMON & SCHUSTER EDITIONS

Rockefeller Center

1230 Avenue of the Americas

New York, NY 10020

A LABYRINTH BOOK

Printed in the U.S.A.

1 3 5 7 9 10 8 6 4 2

Library of Congress Cataloging-in-Publication Data

Frazer, James George, Sir, 1854-1941

(Golden bough)

The illustrated Golden bough : a study in magic and religion / by

Sir James Frazer : edited and abridged by Robert Temple.

p. cm.

Includes index.

1. Mythology. 2. Religion. 3. Magic. 4. Superstition. I. Temple, Robert K. G. II. Title.

BL310.F7 1996

291— dc20   96-11489   CIP

ISBN 0-684-81850-7 (hardcover)

CONTENTS

INTRODUCTION

THE GOLDEN BOUGH is one of the most influential works on social anthropology ever to be published. Written at a time when scholars were questioning the certainties of the past and seeking to explain human thoughts and beliefs, Sir James Frazer's twelve-volume masterpiece was a landmark in the study of magic and the origins of religion. What began for Frazer as an examination of the meaning of the strange and murderous priesthood of Diana in Nemi's sacred grove, grew into a far-ranging and detailed description of customs, rituals and beliefs all over the world. His work led him to the opinion that religion was man's attempt to conciliate the powers that, in Frazer's words, "control and direct the course of nature and of human life."

Frazer's work had an influence on world culture far exceeding the readership of his books. The discoveries he made about the history and development of belief entered into the currents of cultural change which swept around Darwin, the social anthropologist E. B. Tylor and other new thinkers who were his friends. Frazer's view of the history of human belief was essentially evolutionary and psychological. He described man as progressing from a belief in magic as a means of controlling his environment to religious belief, which propitiated gods and spirits; to Frazer, the logical third stage in this process was scientific thought. His work made clear

for the first time that matters of human belief are important, not so much for their content, as for their psychological significance.

He was the first person to elucidate the phenomenon of totemism and the first modern writer to take seriously the subject of taboo. Twenty-two years after the publication of the earliest version of *The Golden Bough*, Sigmund Freud published *Totem and Taboo*. Later, the psychologist Carl Jung drew on Frazer's concerns with the traditions and history of belief in his identification of the collective archetypes, which he believed to underlie human experience. Twentieth-century writers like T. S. Eliot and D. H. Lawrence were inspired by the wealth of descriptions and ideas in *The Golden Bough*.

Frazer (1854-1941) came from a well-to-do home in Glasgow, Scotland. He was educated first at the Unversity of Glasgow, at about the time when Charles Darwin's theories were being accepted and a liberalization of thought was taking place. Frazer studied the classics, philosophy and natural philosophy, continuing his studies at Cambridge University and studying law at the Middle Temple in London. In 1907, he accepted a chair of social anthropology at the University of Liverpool, but gave it up not long afterwards. Inspired by his friend William Robertson Smith's pioneering work on ancient religions, he had begun to publish articles on folklore and anthropology. He now settled down to intensive research, writing articles for the ninth edition of the *Encyclopedia Britannica*, two of which dealt with taboo and totemism. They were to become predominant in his major work.

Frazer then set about writing a book entitled *The Golden Bough*, which was published in 1890 in two volumes. This was only a first draft of the work of that title which would eventually reach its full length in 1915, with supplementary volumes still appearing as late as 1939. On a similar theme, he also wrote a little book called *Psyche's Task*, in which he concluded that superstition, which he described as "false opinion," has helped mankind by promoting respect for authority and thus preventing many forms of violence.

Although his peers did not always agree with his interpretations, Frazer's work was acclaimed in his lifetime. He received honorary doctorates from universities around the world. In 1914 he was knighted, and he was one of those rare people elected to be a Fellow of the British Academy and the Royal Society. He was part of the revolution in thinking which freed Western minds from rigid dogmas about the nature and function of belief in human culture. He took the grand view: he surveyed world history as a whole, drawing on a wealth of ethnographical material and his extensive classical knowledge. Frazer also had two exemplary characteristics: he was not afraid to change a hypothesis if he saw it to be inadequate and he had a disregard for excessive specialization.

Despite its popular reputation, *The Golden Bough* has tended to be read only by specialists due to its great length. The first person to do anything about this was Frazer's wife, Lilly. In 1924, she published *Leaves from the Golden Bough*, intended as a children's book with illustrations, omitting all theory and concentrating on folklore. The next year, Frazer himself published a single-volume abridgment of his own work, but it was still over 750 pages of small type. It is this work I have in turn abridged here.

Frazer was essentially a nineteenth-century thinker, and approaches to social anthropology have changed. His evaluation of primitive modes of thought can at times seem rather harsh and some of his views are no longer compatible with current thinking. However, *The Golden Bough* remains a vital part of our cultural history. It is a unique archive and work of literature, and Frazer's splendid prose style is a pleasure to read. In making him accessible to ordinary readers and providing illustrations, I hope that the benefits of his wisdom can be made available to the wide audience he has always deserved.

Robert Temple

Chapter One

THE KING OF THE WOOD

ART LOVERS MAY well be familiar with Turner's picture of the Golden Bough. The scene, suffused with the golden glow of imagination in which the divine mind of Turner steeped and transfigured even the fairest natural landscape, is a dream-like vision of the little woodland lake of Nemi— "Diana's Mirror," as it was called by the ancients. No one who has seen that calm water, lapped in a green hollow of the Alban hills, can ever forget it. The two characteristic Italian villages which slumber on its banks, and the equally Italian palace whose terraced gardens descend steeply to the lake, hardly break the stillness and even the solitariness of the scene. Diana herself might still linger by this lonely shore, still haunt these woodlands wild.

In antiquity this sylvan landscape was the scene of a strange and recurring tragedy. On the northern shore of the lake, right under the precipitous cliff on which the modern village of Nemi is perched, stood the sacred grove and sanctuary of Diana Nemorensis, or Diana of the Wood. The lake and the grove were sometimes known as the lake and grove of Aricia. But the town of Aricia (the modern Ariccia) was situated about three miles off, at the foot of the Alban Mount, and separated by a steep descent from the lake, which lies in a small crater-like hollow on the mountain side.

In this sacred grove there grew a certain tree round which at any time of the day, and probably far into the night, a grim figure might be seen to prowl. In his hand

Above: *The Greek goddess Artemis, depicted as mistress of the animals, shown with wings and accompanied by lions. In Roman times, she became known as Diana. She symbolized the moon and her brother Apollo, the sun. Detail of a gold necklace plaque from Rhodes, seventh century B.C. British Museum, London.*

Opposite: *Joseph Mallord Turner first exhibited* The Golden Bough *in 1834. This detail shows the sibyl of Cumae holding aloft the golden bough, which would give Aeneas entry into the world of souls. In the background are the lake and grove of Nemi. Tate Gallery, London.*

Above: *Jupiter, stern god of lightning and thunder, with one of his mortal mistresses, Thetis, the mother of Achilles. The Olympian deities were thought to have been immense compared to nymphs and mortals.* Jean Baptiste Dominique Ingres. Musée Granet, Aix-en-Provence.

Opposite: *Diana, the fearless virgin huntress, roamed the forests with bow in hand and accompanied by swift hunting dogs. She hunted down deer, fiercer beasts, and mortals who offended her.* Sixteenth-century painting of the Fontainbleu school. The Louvre, Paris.

dreams than his. For year in, year out, in summer and winter, in fair weather and in foul, he had to keep his lonely watch, and whenever he snatched a troubled slumber it was at the peril of his life. The least relaxation of his vigilance, the smallest abatement of his strength of limb or skill of fence, put him in jeopardy; grey hairs might seal his death-warrant. To gentle and pious pilgrims at the shrine the sight of him might well seem to darken the fair landscape, as when a cloud suddenly blots out the sun on a bright day. The dreamy blue of Italian skies, the dappled shade of summer woods, and the sparkle of waves in the sun, can have accorded but ill with that stern and sinister figure. Rather we picture to ourselves the scene as it may have been witnessed by a belated wayfarer on one of the those wild autumn nights when the dead leaves are falling thick, and the winds seem to sing the dirge of the dying year.

The strange rule of this priesthood has no parallel in classical antiquity, and cannot be explained from it. In order to form some understanding of this extraordinary tradition, I will first set forth the few facts and legends which have come down to us on the subject. We shall then return to the myth of Balder and see the strong connection between the two traditions, which are in fact two aspects of a common heritage. At the heart of it all is the nature of *the golden bough.*

But first the stories preserved by ancient authors concerning the origins of the strange practices at Nemi: According to one story the worship of Diana at Nemi was instituted by Orestes, who, after killing Thoas, King of the Tauric Chersonese (now called the Crimea), fled with his sister to Italy, bringing with him the image of the Tauric Diana hidden in a faggot of sticks. After his death his bones were transported from Aricia to Rome and buried in front of the temple of Saturn, on the Capitoline slope, beside the temple of Concord.

The bloody ritual which legend ascribed to the Tauric Diana said that every stranger who landed on the shore was sacrificed on her altar. The historian Diodorus Siculus records many examples of how strangers sailing into the Black Sea were seized when they landed to find drinking water and executed for religious purposes. In

he carried a drawn sword, and he kept peering warily about him as if at every instant he expected to be set upon by an enemy. He was a priest and a murderer; and the man for whom he looked was sooner or later to murder him and hold the priesthood in his stead. Such was the rule of sanctuary. A candidate for the priesthood could only succeed to office by slaying the priest, and having slain him, he retained office till he was himself slain by a stronger or a craftier.

The post which he held by this precarious tenure carried with it the title of king; but surely no crowned head ever lay uneasier, or was visited by more evil

Above: *Orestes at Delphi, with a sleeping Erinyes, a statue of Apollo and the prophesying Sibyl's tripod. His flight to Nemi from the Crimea with an image of the goddess Diana was reputed to be the source of her worship in Aricia.* Roman marble relief, first century B.C., from Herculaneum. National Museum of Archaeology, Naples.

Opposite (above): *The death of Hippolytus. According to legend, Hippolytus was Virbius, the archetype of the line of Diana's priests known as Kings of the Wood.* Painting by Peter Paul Rubens, 1611. Fitzwilliam Museum, Cambridge, England.

antiquity the Black Sea was well known as a sea which one entered at one's peril.

However, when the rite was transported to Italy it assumed a milder and less violent form. Within the sanctuary at Nemi grew a certain tree of which no branch might be broken. Only a runaway slave was allowed to break off, if he could, one of its boughs. Success in the attempt entitled him to fight the priest in single combat, and if he slew him he reigned in his stead with the title of King of the Wood (Rex Nemorensis). According to the public opinion of the ancients, the fateful branch was the Golden Bough which, at the

Sibyl's bidding, Aeneas plucked before he essayed the perilous journey to the world of the dead.

The flight of the slave represented, it was said, the flight of Orestes; his combat with the priest was a reminiscence of the human sacrifices once offered to the Tauric Diana. This rule of succession by the sword was observed down to imperial times; for amongst his other freaks Caligula, thinking that the priest of Nemi had held office too long, hired a more stalwart ruffian to slay him; and a Greek traveller, who visited Italy in the age of the Antonines, remarks that down to his time the priesthood was still the prize of victory in a single combat.

Of the worship of Diana at Nemi some leading features can still be made out. From the votive offerings which have been found on the site, it appears that she was conceived of especially as a huntress, and further as blessing men and women with offspring, and granting expectant mothers an easy delivery. Again, fire seems to have played a foremost part in her ritual. For during her annual festival, held on the thirteenth of August, at the hottest time of the year, her grove shone with a multitude of torches, whose ruddy glare was reflected by the lake; and throughout the length and breath of Italy the day was kept with holy rites at every domestic hearth.

Bronze statuettes found in her precinct represent the goddess herself holding a torch in her raised right hand; and women whose prayers had been heard by her came crowned with wreaths and bearing lighted torches to the sanctuary in fulfilment of their vows. Someone unknown dedicated a perpetually burning lamp in a little shrine at Nemi for the safety of the Emperor Claudius and his family. The terracotta lamps which have been discovered in the grove may perhaps have served a like purpose for humbler persons. If so, the analogy of the custom to the Catholic practice of dedicating holy candles in churches would be obvious. Further, the title of Vesta borne by Diana at Nemi points clearly to the maintenance of a perpetual holy fire in her sanctuary. A large circular basement at the northeast corner of the temple, raised on three steps and bearing traces of a mosaic pavement, probably supported a round temple of Diana in her character of Vesta, like the round temple

of Vesta in the Roman Forum. Here the sacred fire would seem to have been tended by Vestal Virgins, for the head of a Vestal in terracotta was found on the spot, and the worship of a perpetual fire, cared for by holy maidens, appears to have been common in Latium from the earliest to the latest times. Further, at the annual festival of the goddess, hunting dogs were crowned and wild beasts were not molested; young people went through a purificatory ceremony in her honour; wine was brought forth, and the feast consisted of a kid, cakes served piping hot on plates of leaves, and apples still hanging in clusters on the boughs.

But Diana did not reign alone in her grove at Nemi. Two lesser divinities shared her forest sanctuary. One was Egeria, the nymph of the clear water which, bubbling from the basaltic rocks, used to fall in graceful cascades into the lake at the place called Le Mole, because here were established the mills of the modern village of Nemi. The purling of the stream as it ran over the pebbles is mentioned by Ovid, who tells us that he had often drunk of its water. Women with child used to sac-

Below: *Mistletoe (*Viscum album*), the "golden bough" of legend, with yew and moss.* A nineteenth-century color engraving.

Above: *Roman head of the Greek mother-goddess Cybele, vengeful lover of the mortal Attis, who suspected him of infidelity and drove him mad. Her worship was imported to Rome from Phrygia in Asia Minor in the second century B.C.* Museo Nazionale Romano, Rome.

rifice to Egeria, because she was believed, like Diana, to be able to grant them an easy delivery. Tradition ran that the nymph had been the wife or mistress of the wise king Numa, that he had consorted with her in the secrecy of the sacred grove, and that the laws which he gave the Romans had been inspired by communion with her divinity. Plutarch compares the legend with other tales of the loves of goddesses for mortal men, such as the love of Cybele and the Moon for the fair youths Attis and Endymion.

According to some, the trysting-place of the lovers was not in the woods of Nemi but in a grove outside the dripping Porta Capena at Rome, where another sacred spring of Egeria gushed from a dark cavern. Every day the Roman Vestals fetched water from this spring to wash the temple of Vesta, carrying it in earthenware pitchers on their heads. In Juvenal's time the natural rock had been encased in marble, and the hallowed spot was profaned by gangs of poor Jews, who were suffered to squat, like gypsies, in the grove. We may suppose that the spring which fell into the lake of Nemi was the true original Egeria, and that when the first settlers moved down from the Alban hills to the banks of the Tiber they brought the nymph with them and found a new home for her in a grove outside the gates. The remains of baths which have been discovered within the sacred precinct, together with many terracotta models of various parts of the human body, suggest that the waters of Egeria were used to heal the sick, who may have signified their hopes or testified their gratitude by dedicating likenesses of the diseased members to the goddess, in accordance with a custom which is still observed in many parts of Europe. To this day it would seem that the spring retains medicinal virtues.

The other of the minor deities at Nemi was Virbius. Legend had it that Virbius was the young Greek hero Hippolytus, chaste and fair, who learned the art of venery from the centaur Chiron, and spent all his days in the greenwood chasing wild beasts with the virgin huntress Artemis (the Greek counterpart of Diana) for his only comrade. Proud of her divine society, he spurned the love of women, and this proved his bane. For Aphrodite, stung by his scorn, inspired his stepmother Phaedra with love of him; and when he disdained her wicked advances she falsely accused him to his father Theseus. The slander was believed, and Theseus prayed to his sire Poseidon to avenge the imagined wrong. So while Hippolytus drove in a chariot by the shore of the Saronic Gulf, the sea-god sent a fierce bull forth from the waves. The terrified horses bolted, threw Hippolytus from the chariot, and dragged him at their hoofs to death. But Diana, for the love she bore Hippolytus, persuaded the physician Aesculapius to bring her fair young hunter back to life by his medical skill with herbs. Jupiter, indignant that a mortal man should return from the gates of death, thrust down the meddling physician himself to Hades. But Diana hid her favourite from the angry god in a thick cloud, disguised his features by adding years to his life, and then bore him far away to the dells of Nemi, where she entrusted him to the nymph Egeria, to live there, unknown and solitary, under the name of Virbius, in the depth of the Italian forest. There he reigned a king, and there he dedicated a precinct to Diana. He had a comely son, Virbius, who, undaunted by his father's fate, drove a team of fiery steeds to join the Latins in the war against Aeneas and the Trojans. Virbius was worshipped as a god not only at Nemi but elsewhere; for in Campania we hear of a special priest devoted to his service.

Horses were excluded from the Arician grove and sanctuary because horses had killed Hippolytus. It was unlawful to touch his image. Some thought that he was the sun. "But the truth is," says Servius, "that he is a deity associated with Diana, as Attis is associated with the Mother of the Gods, and Erichthonius with Minerva, and Adonis with Venus." What the nature of that association was we shall enquire presently. Here it is worth observing that in his long and chequered career this mythical personage has displayed a remarkable tenacity of life. For we can hardly doubt that the Saint Hippolytus of the Roman Calendar, who was dragged by horses to death on the thirteenth of August, Diana's own day, is no other than the Greek hero of the same name, who, after dying twice over as a heathen sinner, has been happily resuscitated as a Christian saint.

It needs no elaborate demonstration to convince us that the stories told to account for Diana's worship at Nemi are unhistorical. Clearly they belong to that large class of myths which are made up to explain the origin of a religious ritual and have no other foundation than the resemblance, real or imaginary, which may be traced between it and some foreign ritual. The incongruity of these Nemi myths is indeed transparent, since the foundation of the worship is traced now to Orestes and now to Hippolytus, according as this or that feature of the ritual has to be accounted for. The real value of such

tales is that they serve to illustrate the nature of the worship by providing a standard with which to compare it; and further, that they bear witness indirectly to its venerable age by showing that the true origin was lost in the mists of a fabulous antiquity. In the latter respect these Nemi legends are probably more to be trusted than the apparently historical tradition, vouched for by Cato the Elder, that the sacred grove was dedicated to Diana by a certain Egerius Baebius or Laevius of Tusculum, a Latin dictator, on behalf of the peoples of Tusculum, Aricia, Lanuvium, Laurentum, Cora, Tibur, Pometia, and Ardea. This tradition indeed speaks for the great age of the sanctuary, since it seems to date its foundation sometime before 495 B.C., the year in which Pometia was sacked by the Romans and disappears from history. But we cannot suppose that so barbarous a rule as that of the Arician priesthood was deliberately instituted by a league of civilised communities, such as the Latin cities undoubtedly were. It must have been handed down from a time beyond the memory of man, when Italy was still in a far ruder state than any known to us in the historical period.

The credit of the tradition is rather shaken than confirmed by another story which ascribes the foundation of the sanctuary to a certain Manius Egerius, who gave rise to the saying, "There are many Manii at Aricia." This proverb some explained by alleging that Manius Egerius was the ancestor of a long and distinguished line, whereas others thought it meant that there were many ugly and deformed people at Aricia, and they derived the name Manius from Mania, a bogey or bugbear to frighten children. A Roman satirist uses the name Manius as typical of the beggars who lay in wait for pilgrims on the Arician slopes. These differences of opinion, together with the discrepancy between Manius Egerius of Aricia and Egerius Laevius of Tusculum, as well as the resemblance of both names to the mythical Egeria, excite our suspicion. Yet the tradition recorded by Cato seems too circumstantial, and its sponsor too respectable, to allow us to dismiss it as an idle fiction. Rather we may suppose that it refers to some ancient restoration or reconstruction of the sanctuary, which was actually carried out by the confederate states. At any rate it testifies to a belief that the grove had been from early times a common place of worship for many of the oldest cities of the country, if not for the whole Latin confederacy.

The Arician legends of Orestes and Hippolytus, though worthless as history, have a certain value in so far as they may help us to understand the worship at Nemi better by comparing it with the ritual and myths of other sanctuaries. We must ask ourselves, Why did the author of these legends pitch upon Orestes and Hippolytus in order to explain Virbius and the King of the Wood? In regard to Orestes, the answer is obvious. He and the image of the Tauric Diana, which could only be appeased with human blood, were dragged in to render intelligible the murderous rule of succession to the Arician priesthood. In regard to Hippolytus the case is not so plain. The manner of his death suggests readily enough a reason for the exclusion of horses from the grove; but this by itself seems hardly enough to account for the identification. We must try to probe deeper by examining the worship as well as the legend or myth of Hippolytus.

He had a famous sanctuary at his ancestral home of Troezen, situated on that beautiful, almost landlocked bay, where groves of oranges and lemons, with tall cypresses soaring like dark spires above the garden of Hesperides, now clothe the strip of fertile shore at the foot of the rugged mountains. Across the blue water of the tranquil bay, which it shelters from the open sea, rises Poseidon's sacred island, its peaks veiled in the sombre green of the pines. On this fair coast Hippolytus was worshipped. Within his sanctuary stood a temple with an ancient image. His service was performed by a priest who held office for life; every year a sacrificial festival was held in his honour; and his untimely fate was yearly mourned, with weeping and doleful chants, by unwedded maids. Youths and maidens dedicated locks of their hair in his temple before marriage. His grave existed at Troezen, though the people would not show it. It has been suggested, with great plausibility, that in the handsome Hippolytus, beloved of Artemis, cut off in his youthful prime, and yearly mourned by damsels, we have one of those mortal lovers of a goddess who appear so often in ancient religion, and of whom Adonis is the most familiar type. The rivalry of Artemis and Phaedra for the affection of Hippolytus reproduces, it is said, under different names, the rivalry of Aphrodite and Proserpine for the love of Adonis, for Phaedra is merely a double of Aphrodite. The theory probably does no injustice either to Hippolytus or to Artemis. For Artemis was originally a great goddess of fertility, and, on the principles of early religion, she who fertilises nature must herself be fertile, and to be that she must necessarily have a male consort. On this view, Hippolytus was the consort of Artemis at Troezen, and the shorn tresses offered to him by the Troezenian youths and maidens before marriage were designed to strengthen his union with the goddess, and so to promote the fruitfulness of the earth, of cattle, and of mankind.

It is some confirmation of this view that within the precinct of Hippolytus at Troezen there were worshipped two female powers named Damia and Auxesia, whose connexion with the fertility of the ground is unquestionable. When Epidaurus suffered from a dearth, the people, in obedience to an oracle, carved images of Damia and Auxesia out of sacred olive wood, and no sooner had they done so and set them up than the earth bore fruit again. Moreover, at Troezen itself, and apparently within the precinct of Hippolytus, a curious festival of stone-throwing was held in honour of these maidens, as the Troezenians called them; and it is easy to show that similar customs have been practiced in many lands for the express purpose of ensuring good crops.

Above: *Diana was a fierce protectress of young women and their virginity, and the penalties for offending the modesty of her followers were severe. This detail shows Diana and her nymphs surprised by Acteon.* Painting by Titian, 1556-59. National Gallery of Scotland.

Opposite: *Ceres (known in Greek mythology as Demeter) presided over crops and the harvest. Her daughter Persephone was carried off to the underworld by Hades but, permitted to return to earth each year from spring to autumn, was a symbol of renewal and rebirth.* Seventeenth-century painting by Pietro Bianchi.

In the story of the tragic death of the youthful Hippolytus we may discern an analogy with similar tales of other fair but mortal youths who paid with their lives for the brief rapture of the love of an immortal goddess. These hapless lovers were probably not always mere myths, and the legends which traced their split blood in the purple bloom of the violet, the scarlet stain of the anemone, or the crimson flush of the rose were no idle poetic emblems of youth and beauty fleeting as the summer flowers. Such fables contain a deeper philosophy of the relation of the life of man to the life of nature—a sad philosophy which gave birth to a tragic practice of human sacrifice.

We can now perhaps understand why the ancients identified Hippolytus, the consort of Artemis, with Virbius, who, according to Servius, stood to Diana as Adonis to Venus, or Attis to the Mother of the Gods. For Diana, like Artemis, was a goddess of fertility in general, and of childbirth in particular. As such she, like her Greek counterpart, needed a male partner. That partner,

if Servius is right, was Virbius. In his character of the founder of the sacred grove and first king of Nemi, Virbius is clearly the mythical predecessor or archetype of the line of priests who served Diana under the title of Kings of the Wood, and who came, like him, one after the other, to a violent end. It is natural, therefore, to conjecture that they stood to the goddess of the grove in the same relation in which Virbius stood to her; in short, that the mortal King of the Wood had for his queen the woodland Diana herself. If the sacred tree which he guarded with his life was supposed, as seems probable, to be her special embodiment, her priest may not only have worshipped it as his goddess but embraced it as his wife. There is at least nothing absurd in the supposition, since even in the time of Pliny a noble Roman used thus to treat a beautiful beech tree in another sacred grove of Diana on the Alban hills. He embraced it, he kissed it, he lay under its shadow, he poured wine on its trunk. Apparently he took the tree for the goddess. The custom of physically marrying men and women to trees is still practiced in India and other parts of the East. Why should it not have obtained in ancient Latium?

Reviewing the evidence as a whole, we may conclude that the worship of Diana in her sacred grove at Nemi was of great importance and immemorial antiquity; that she was revered as the goddess of woodlands and of wild creatures, probably also of domestic cattle and of the fruits of the earth; that she was believed to bless men and women with offspring and to aid mothers in childbed; that her holy fire, tended by chaste virgins, burned perpetually in a round temple within the precinct; that associated with her was a water-nymph Egeria who discharged one of Diana's own functions by succouring women in travail, and who was popularly supposed to have mated with an old Roman king in the sacred grove; further, that Diana of the Wood herself had a male companion Virbius by name, who was to her what Adonis was to Venus, or Attis to Cybele; and, lastly, that this mythical Virbius was represented in historical times by a line of priests known as Kings of the Wood, who regularly perished by the swords of their successors, and whose lives were in a manner bound up with a certain tree in the grove, because so long as that tree was uninjured they were safe from attack.

Clearly these conclusions do not of themselves suffice to explain the peculiar rule of succession to the priesthood. But perhaps the survey of a wider field may lead us to think that they contain in germ the solution to the problem. To that wider survey we must now address ourselves. It will be long, but may possess something of the interest and charm of a voyage of discovery, in which we shall visit many strange foreign lands, with strange foreign peoples and still stranger customs. The wind is in the shrouds: we shake our sails to it, and leave the coast of Italy behind us for a time.

Opposite: *A monumental Greek statue of the Great Artemis of Ephesus, circa A.D. 150. In Turkey, Artemis was worshipped as a fertility goddess. She is depicted here with many breasts and wears a cloak decked with animal skins. Ephesus Archaeological Museum, Turkey.*

Below: *The legendary voyage of the Greek hero Odysseus (also known as Ulysses) took him to many strange lands. Fresco by Alessandro Allori Bronzino, 1580. Palazzo Salviati, Florence.*

Chapter Two

SYMPATHETIC MAGIC

I F WE ANALYSE the principles of thought on which
magic is based, they will probably be found to
resolve themselves into two: first, that like produces
like, or that an effect resembles its cause; and, second,
that things which have once been in contact with each
other continue to act on each other at a distance after
the physical contact has been severed. The former principle may be called the Law of Similarity, the latter the
Law of Contact or Contagion. From the first of these
principles, namely the Law of Similarity, the magician
infers that he can produce any effect he desires merely
by imitating it: from the second he infers that whatever
he does to a material object will affect equally the person with whom the object was once in contact, whether
it formed part of his body or not.

Magic is a spurious system of natural law as well as a
fallacious guide of conduct; it is a false science as well as
an abortive art. Regarded as a system of natural law, that
is, as a statement of the rules which determine the
sequence of events throughout the world, it may be
called theoretical magic; regarded as a set of precepts
which human beings observe in order to compass their
ends, it may be called practical magic. At the same time
it is to be borne in mind that the primitive magician
knows magic only on its practical side; he never analy-
ses the mental processes on which his practice is based,
never reflects on the abstract principles involved in his
actions. With him, as with the vast majority of men,
logic is implicit, not explicit: he reasons just as he

Above: *Science and magic combined in the medieval study of
alchemy. This painting shows the mysterious laboratory of an
alchemist. Giovanni Stradano, 1570. Palazzo Vecchio, Florence.*

Opposite: *A Binzar witch-doctor of the Dinka tribe in
southern Sudan.*

digests his food in complete ignorance of the intellectual and physiological processes which are essential to the one operation and to the other. In short, to him magic is always an art, never a science; the very idea of science is lacking in his undeveloped mind. It is for the philosophic student to trace the train of thought which underlies the magician's practice; to draw out the few simple threads of which the tangled skein is composed; to disengage the abstract principles from their concrete applications; in short, to discern the spurious science behind the bastard art.

If my analysis of the magician's logic is correct, its two great principles turn out to be merely two different misapplications of the association of ideas. The first is the association of ideas by similarity. The second is the association of ideas by contiguity. The former commits the mistake of assuming that things which resemble each other are the same, whereas the latter commits the mistake of assuming that things which have once been in contact with each other are always in contact. Both trains of thought are in fact extremely simple and elementary. It could hardly be otherwise, since they are familiar in the concrete, though certainly not in the abstract, to the crude intelligence not only of the savage, but of ignorant and dull-witted people everywhere. Both branches of magic assume that things act on each other at a distance through a secret sympathy, the impulse being transmitted from one to the other by means of what we may conceive as a kind of invisible ether, not unlike that which is postulated by modern science for a precisely similar purpose, namely, to explain how things can physically affect each other through a space which appears to be empty.

Perhaps the most familiar application of the principle that like produces like is the attempt which has been made by many peoples in many ages to injure or destroy an enemy by injuring or destroying an image of him, in the belief that, just as the image suffers, so does the man, and that when it perishes he must die. Thus the North American Indians, we are told, believe that by drawing the figure of a person in sand, ashes, or clay, or by considering any object as his body, and then pricking

it with a sharp stick or doing it any other injury, they inflict a corresponding injury on the person represented. For example, when an Ojebway Indian desires to work evil on any one, he makes a little wooden image of his enemy and runs a needle into its head or heart, or he shoots an arrow into it, believing that wherever the needle pierces or the arrow strikes the image, his foe will the same instant be seized with a sharp pain in the corresponding part of his body; but if he intends to kill the person outright, he burns or buries the puppet, uttering certain magic words as he does so. The Peruvian Indians moulded images of fat mixed with grain to imitate the persons whom they disliked or feared, and then burned the effigy on the road where the intended victim was to pass. This they called burning his soul.

If imitative magic, working by means of images, has commonly been practised for the spiteful purpose of putting obnoxious people out of the world, it has also, though far more rarely, been employed with the benevolent intention of helping others into it. In other words,

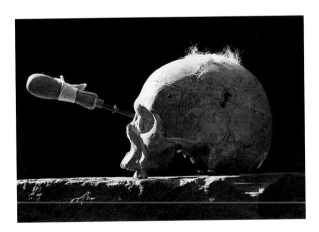

Above: *In black magic a human being could be cursed to death by spearing a skull with a metal point bearing the name of the intended victim.*

Opposite: *Drawings on a Torne-Lapp drum. The Finno-Ugric people, particularly the Lapps, were renowned for shamanism and magic. The sacred drum was a powerful part of the shaman's equipment and they were still in use at the end of the nineteenth century. From The Mythology of the Races, vol. IV, London 1925.*

it has been used to facilitate childbirth and to procure offspring for barren women. Thus among the Bataks of Sumatra a barren woman, who would become a mother, will make a wooden image of a child and hold it in her lap, believing that this will lead to the fulfilment of her wish. In the Babar Archipelago, when a woman desires to have a child, she invites a man who is himself the father of a large family to pray on her behalf to Upulero, the spirit of the sun. A doll is made of red cotton, which the woman clasps in her arms, as if she would suckle it. Then the father of many children takes a fowl and holds it by the legs to the woman's head, saying, "O Upulero, make use of the fowl; let fall, let descend a child, I beseech you, I entreat you, let a child fall and descend into my hands and on my lap." Then he asks the woman, "Has the child come?" and she answers, "Yes, it is sucking already." After that the man holds the fowl on the husband's head, and mumbles some form of words. Lastly, the bird is killed and laid, together with some betel, on the domestic place of sacrifice. When the ceremony is over, word goes about in the village that the woman has been brought to bed, and her friends come and congratulate her. Here the pretence that a child has been born is a purely magical rite designed to secure, by means of imitation or mimicry, that a child really shall be born; but an attempt is made to add to the efficacy of the rite by means of prayer and sacrifice. To put it otherwise, magic is here blent with and reinforced by religion.

Opposite: *A diviner of the Dogon tribe of Mali, West Africa, drawing his divination table in the sand. At night the fox will come and tread across the various boxes, leaving his footprints, and their positions will reveal the future.*

Below: *This prehistoric cave painting of a bison, dated 15,000 B.C., from the Altamira caves in Spain, is an example of sympathetic hunting magic.*

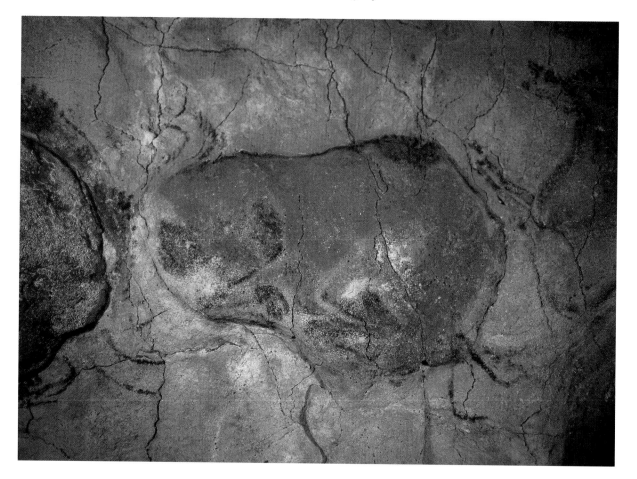

The same principle of make-believe, so dear to children, has led other peoples to employ a simulation of birth as a form of adoption, and even as a mode of restoring a supposed dead person to life. If you pretend to give birth to a boy, or even to a great bearded man who has not a drop of your blood in his veins, then, in the eyes of primitive law and philosophy, that boy or man is really your son to all intents and purposes. Thus Diodorus tells us that when Zeus persuaded his jealous wife Hera to adopt Hercules, the goddess got into bed, and clasping the burly hero to her bosom, pushed him through her robes and let him fall to the ground in imitation of a real birth; and the historian adds that in his own day the same mode of adopting children was practised by the barbarians. At the present time it is said to be still in use in Bulgaria and among the Bosnian Turks. A woman will take a boy whom she intends to adopt and push or pull him through her clothes; ever afterwards he is regarded as her very son, and inherits the whole property of his adoptive parents.

Sympathetic magic plays a great part in the measures taken by the rude hunter or fisherman to secure an abundant supply of food. On the principle that like produces like, many things are done by him and his friends in deliberate imitation of the result which he seeks to attain; and, on the other hand, many things are scrupulously avoided because they bear some more or less fanciful resemblance to others which would really be disastrous.

The Indians of British Columbia live largely upon the fish which abound in their seas and rivers. If the fish do not come in due season, and the Indians are hungry, a Nootka wizard will make an image of a swimming fish and put it into the water in the direction from which the fish generally appear. This ceremony, accompanied by a prayer to the fish to come, will cause them to arrive at once. The islanders of Torres Straits use models of dugong and turtles to charm dugong and turtle to their destruction. The Toradjas of Central Celebes believe that things of the same sort attract each other by means of their indwelling spirits of vital ether. Hence they hang

up the jawbones of deer and wild pigs in their houses, in order that the spirits which animate these bones may draw the living creatures of the same kind into the path of the hunter. In the island of Nias, when a wild pig has fallen into the pit prepared for it, the animal is taken out and its back is rubbed with nine fallen leaves, in the belief that this will make nine more wild pigs fall into the pit, just as the nine leaves fell from the tree.

The system of sympathetic magic is not merely composed of positive precepts; it comprises a very large number of negative precepts, that is, prohibitions. It tells you not merely what to do, but also what to leave undone. The positive precepts are charms: the negative precepts are taboos. In fact the whole doctrine of taboo, or at all events a large part of it, would seem to be only a special application of sympathetic magic, with its two great laws of similarity and contact.

Thus taboo is so far a negative application of practical magic. Positive magic or sorcery says, "Do this in order that so and so may happen." Negative magic or taboo says, "Do not do this, lest so and so should happen." The aim of positive magic or sorcery is to produce a desired event; the aim of negative magic or taboo is to avoid an undesirable one. But both consequences, the desirable and the undesirable, are supposed to be brought about in accordance with the laws of similarity and contact.

If the supposed evil necessarily followed a breach of taboo, the taboo would not be a taboo but a precept of morality or common sense. It is not a taboo to say, "Do not put your hand in the fire"; it is a rule of common sense, because the forbidden action entails a real, not an imaginary evil. In short, those negative precepts which we call taboo are just as vain and futile as those positive precepts which we call sorcery. The two things are merely opposite sides or poles of one great disastrous fallacy, a mistaken conception of the association of ideas. Of that fallacy, sorcery is the positive, and taboo the negative pole. If we give the general name of magic to the whole erroneous system, both theoretical and practical, then taboo may be defined as the negative side of practical magic. To put this in tabular form:

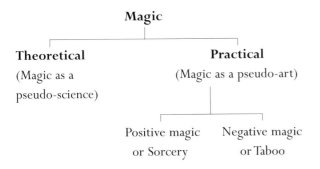

Magic

Theoretical
(Magic as a pseudo-science)

Practical
(Magic as a pseudo-art)

Positive magic
or Sorcery

Negative magic
or Taboo

I have made these remarks on taboo and its relations to magic because I am about to give some instances of taboos observed by hunters, fishermen, and others, and I wished to show that they fall under the head of sympathetic magic, being only particular applications of that general theory. Thus, among the Esquimaux boys are forbidden to play cat's cradle, because if they did so their fingers might in later life become entangled in the harpoon-line. Here the taboo is obviously an application of the law of similarity, which is a basis of magic: as the child's fingers are entangled by the string in playing cat's cradle, so they will be entangled by the harpoon-line when he is a man and hunts whales. Again, among the Huzuls of the Carpathian Mountains the wife of a hunter may not spin while her husband is eating, or the game will turn and wind like the spindle, and the hunter will be unable to hit it. Here again the taboo is clearly derived from the law of similarity.

Among the taboos observed by savages none perhaps are more numerous or important than the prohibitions to eat certain foods, and of such prohibitions many are demonstrably derived from the law of similarity and are accordingly examples of negative magic. Just as the savage eats many animals or plants in order to acquire certain desirable qualities with which he believes them to be endowed, so he avoids eating many other animals and plants lest he should acquire certain undesirable qualities with which he believes them to be infected. In eat-

ing the former he practises positive magic; in abstaining from the latter he practises negative magic. Many examples of such positive magic will meet us later on; here I will give a few instances of such negative magic or taboo. For example, in Madagascar soldiers are forbidden to eat a number of foods lest on the principle of magical similarity they should be tainted by certain dangerous or undesirable properties which are supposed to inhere in these particular viands. Thus they may not

Opposite: *Detail of the "war shirt" of an unidentified plains Native American, circa 1830. The flying figures on the shirt front represent bullets and are meant to confer protection against them upon the owner, who did not have to wear the shirt into battle in order to enjoy this protection. As bullet holes are missing from the shirt, perhaps the owner was lucky.*

Below: *An ivory bracket of the Inuit (Eskimo) people of northwest Alaska. This would have been lashed near the bow of a boat of eight whalehunters, to hold the harpoon steady. It is carved with a magical whale effigy to bring good luck in hunting.* Musuem of Mankind, London.

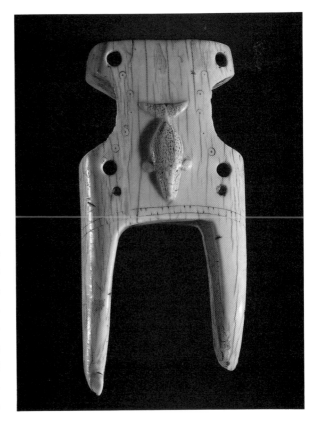

Above: *Bear claw medicine. This token was worn attached to the scalplock by a Crow warrior. With face and body paint and a medicine song, it ensured the close presence of a supernatural "sacred helper."* Plains Indian Museum, Cody, Wyoming.

Opposite: *Animal spirits are a central part of Native American mythology. These dancers at Santa Clara imitate the actions of the eagle.*

taste hedgehog, "as it is feared that this animal, from its propensity of coiling up into a ball when alarmed, will impart a timid shrinking disposition to those who partake of it." Again, no soldier should eat an ox's knee, lest like an ox he should become weak in the knees and unable to march. Further, the warrior should be careful to avoid partaking of a cock that has died fighting or anything that has been speared to death; and no male animal may on any account be killed in his house while he is away at the wars. For it seems obvious that if he were to eat a cock that had died fighting, he would himself be slain on the field of battle; if he were to partake

of an animal that had been speared, he would be speared himself; if a male animal were killed in his house during his absence, he would himself be killed in like manner and perhaps at the same instant. Further, the Malagasy soldier must eschew kidneys, because in the Malagasy language the word for kidney is the same as that for "shot," so shot he would certainly be if he ate a kidney.

The reader may have observed that in some of the foregoing examples of taboos the magical influence is supposed to operate at considerable distances; thus among the Blackfeet Indians the wives and children of an eagle hunter were forbidden to use an awl during his absence, lest the eagles should scratch the distant husband and father; and again no male animal may be killed in the house of a Malagasy soldier while he is away at the wars, lest the killing of the animal should entail the killing of the man.

This belief in the sympathetic influence exerted on each other by persons or things at a distance is of the essence of magic. Whatever doubts science may entertain as to the possibility of action at a distance, magic has none; faith in telepathy is one of its first principles. A modern advocate of the influence of mind upon mind at a distance would have no difficulty in convincing a savage; the savage believed in it long ago, and what is more, he acted on his belief with a logical consistency such as his civilised brother in the faith has not yet, so far as I am aware, exhibited in his conduct. For the savage is convinced not only that magical ceremonies affect persons and things afar off, but that the simplest acts of daily life may do so too. Hence on important occasions the behaviour of friends and relations at a distance is often regulated by a more or less elaborate code of rules, the neglect of which by the one set of persons would, it is supposed, entail misfortune or even death on the absent ones. In particular when a party of men are out hunting or fighting, their kinsfolk at home are often expected to do certain things or to abstain from doing certain others, for the sake of ensuring the safety and success of the distant hunters or warriors.

Many of the indigenous tribes of Sarawak are firmly persuaded that were the wives to commit adultery while

their husbands are searching for camphor in the jungle, the camphor obtained by the men would evaporate. Husbands can discover, by certain knots in the tree, when the wives are unfaithful; and it is said that in former days many women were killed by jealous husbands on no better evidence than that of these knots. Further, the wives dare not touch a comb while their husbands are away collecting the camphor; for if they did so, the interstices between the fibres of the tree, instead of being filled with the precious crystals, would be empty like the spaces between the teeth of a comb.

The notion that a person can influence a plant magically by his act or condition comes out clearly in a remark made by a Malay woman. Being asked why she stripped the upper part of her body naked in reaping the rice, she explained that she did it to make the rice-husks thinner, as she was tired of pounding thick-husked rice. Clearly, she thought that the less clothing she wore the less husk there would be on the rice.

Animals are often conceived to possess qualities or properties which might be useful to man, and imitative magic seeks to communicate these properties to human

Left: *An Incan effigy of a maize plant made of silver, from Peru, 1430-1532. Sacred beer made from maize was drunk at religious festivals. This is a rare example of the fabled Incan treasure, which may have included silver and gold fruit, trees, and plants hidden in caves from the Conquistadores and never recovered.* Museum vör Völkerkunde, Berlin.

Opposite (left): *A twentieth-century image of the influence of mind at a distance: supposed psychic phenomena in the form of glowing emanations round the head of William Hope.* Photo, 1923, London.

Opposite (right): *The spirit enters a priest at the Festival of Ogen, celebrated by the Yoruba tribe, Nigeria.*

own intrinsic nature and the skill of the wizard to tap or dam, as the case may be, the stream of weal or woe.

The common custom of swearing upon a stone may be based partly on a belief that the strength and stability of the stone lend confirmation to an oath. Thus the old Danish historian Saxo Grammaticus tells us that "the ancients, when they were to choose a king, were wont to stand on stones planted in the ground, and to proclaim their votes, in order to foreshadow from the steadfastness of the stones that the deed would be lasting."

But while a general magical efficacy may be suposed to reside in all stones by reason of their common properties of weight and solidity, special magical virtues are attributed to particular stones, or kinds of stone, in accordance with their individual or specific qualities of shape and colour. For example, the Indians of Peru employed certain stones for the increase of maize, others for the increase of potatoes, and others again for the increase of cattle. The stones used to make maize grow were fashioned in the likeness of cobs of maize, and the stones destined to multiply cattle had the shape of sheep.

The ancients set great store on the magical qualities of precious stones. The wine-coloured amethyst received its name, which means "not drunken," because it was supposed to keep the wearer of it sober; and two brothers who desired to live at unity were advised to carry magnets about with them, which, by drawing the twain together, would clearly prevent them from falling out.

beings in various ways. Thus some Bechuanas wear a ferret as a charm, because, being very tenacious of life, it will make them difficult to kill.

Again, it seems plain that a South African warrior who twists tufts of rat's hair among his own curly black locks will have just as many chances of avoiding the enemy's spear as the nimble rat has of avoiding things thrown at it; hence in these regions rat's hair is in great demand when war is expected.

Inanimate things, as well as plants and animals, may diffuse blessing or bane around them, according to their

Another application of the maxim that like produces like is seen in the Chinese belief that the fortunes of a town are deeply affected by its shape, and that they must vary according to the character of the thing which that shape most nearly resembles. Thus it is related that long ago the town of Tsuen-cheu-fu, the outlines of which are like those of a carp, frequently fell a prey to the depredations of the neighbouring city of Yung-chun, which is shaped like a fishing-net, until the inhabitants of the former town conceived the plan of erecting two tall pagodas in their midst. These pagodas, which still tower above the city of Tsuen-cheu-fu, have ever since exercised the happiest influence over its destiny by intercepting the imaginary net before it could descend and entangle in its meshes the imaginary carp.

Some forty years ago the wise men of Shanghai were much exercised to discover the cause of a local rebellion. On careful enquiry they ascertained that the rebellion was due to the shape of a large new temple which had most unfortunately been built in the shape of a tortoise, an animal of the very worst character. The difficulty was serious, the danger was pressing; for to pull down the temple would have been impious, and to let it stand as it was would be to court a succession of similar or worse disasters. However, the genius of the local professors of geomancy, rising to the occasion, triumphantly surmounted the difficulty and obviated the danger. By filling up two wells, which represented the eyes of the tortoise, they at once blinded that disreputable animal and rendered him incapable of doing further mischief.

Chapter Three

WEATHER MAGIC

TWO TYPES OF human gods may conveniently be distinguished: the religious and the magical man-god. In the former, a being of an order different from and superior to man is supposed to become incarnate, for a longer or a shorter time, in a human body, manifesting his super-human power and knowledge by miracles wrought and prophecies uttered through the medium of the fleshy tabernacle in which he has deigned to take up his abode. This may also appropriately be called the inspired or incarnate type of man-god. In it the human body is merely a frail earthly vessel filled with a divine and immortal spirit. On the other hand, a man-god of the magical sort is nothing but a man who possesses in an unusually high degree powers which most of his fellows arrogate to themselves on a smaller scale; for in rude society there is hardly a person who does not dabble in magic. Thus, whereas a man-god of the former or inspired type derives his divinity from a deity who has stooped to hide his heavenly radiance behind a dull mask of earthly mould, a man-god of the latter type draws his extraordinary power from a certain physical sympathy with nature. He is not merely the receptacle of a divine spirit. His whole being, body and soul, is so delicately attuned to the harmony of the world that a touch of his hand or a turn of his head may send a thrill vibrating through the universal framework of things; and conversely his divine organism is acutely sensitive to such slight changes of environment as would leave ordinary mortals wholly unaffected. But

Opposite: *A gigantic Toltec statue, weighing nearly 60 tons, of the goddess Chalchiutlicue, who presided over fresh water.* National Anthropological Museum, Mexico City.

Above: *The so-called Pyramid of the Magician, at the Mayan site of Uxmal on the Yucatan Peninsula, dating from between A.D. 1000 and 1500. Weather gods feature prominently in Mayan mythology.*

33

Above: *Detail of a carved wooden figure of the Sea Mother, thought to be the work of the Kwakiutl tribe, northwest coast of the United States.*

Below: *The celebration of the Sea Festival on the island of Okinawa, Japan.*

Among the objects of public utility which magic may be employed to secure, the most essential is an adequate supply of food. The purveyors of food—the hunter, the fisher, the farmer—all resort to magical practices in the pursuit of their various callings; but they do so as private individuals for the benefit of themselves and their families, rather than as public functionaries acting in the interest of the whole people. It is otherwise when the rites are performed, not by the hunters, the fishers, the farmers themselves, but by professional magicians on their behalf. In primitive society, where uniformity of occupation is the rule, and the distribution of the community into various classes of workers has hardly begun, every man is more or less his own magician; he practises charms and incantations for his own good and the injury of his enemies. But a great step in advance has been taken when a special class of magicians has been instituted; when, in other words, a number of men have been set apart for the express purpose of benefiting the whole community by their skill, whether that skill be directed to the healing of diseases, the forecasting of the future, the regulation of the weather, or any other object of general utility. The impotence of the means adopted by most of these practitioners to accomplish their ends ought not to blind us to the immense importance of the institution itself. Here is a body of men relieved, at least in the higher stages of savagery, from the need of earning their livelihood by hard manual toil, and allowed, nay, expected and encouraged, to prosecute researches into the secret ways of nature. It was at once their duty and their interest to know more than their fellows, to acquaint themselves with everything that could aid man in his arduous struggle with nature, everything that could mitigate his sufferings and prolong his life. The properties of drugs and minerals, the causes of rain and drought, of thunder and lightning, the changes of the seasons, the phases of the moon, the daily and yearly journeys of the sun, the motions of the stars, the mystery of life, and the mystery of death, all these things must have excited the wonder of these early philosophers, and stimulated them to find solutions of problems that were doubtless often thrust on their

the line between these two types of man-god, however sharply we may draw it in theory, is seldom to be traced with precision in practice, and in what follows I shall not insist on it.

In practice the magic art may be employed for the benefit either of individuals or of the whole community, and according as it is directed to one or other of these two objects it may be called private or public magic. Further, I would stress that the public magician occupies a position of great influence, from which, if he is a prudent and able man, he may advance step by step to the rank of a chief or king. Thus an examination of public magic conduces to an understanding of the early kingship, since in savage and barbarous society many chiefs and kings appear to owe their authority in great measure to their reputation as magicians.

attention in the most practical form by the importunate demands of their clients, who expected them not merely to understand but to regulate the great processes of nature for the good of man. That their first shots fell very far wide of the mark could hardly be helped. The slow, the never-ending approach to truth consists in perpetually forming and testing hypotheses, accepting those which at the time seem to fit the facts and rejecting the others. The views of natural causation embraced by the savage magician no doubt appear to us manifestly false and absurd; yet in their day they were legitimate hypotheses, though they have not stood the test of experience. Ridicule and blame are the just meed, not of those who devised these crude theories, but of those who obstinately adhered to them after better had been propounded. Certainly no men ever had stronger incentives in the pursuit of truth than these savage sorcerers. To maintain at least a show of knowledge was absolute-

ly necessary; a single mistake detected might cost them their life. This no doubt led them to practise imposture for the purpose of concealing their ignorance; but it also supplied them with the most powerful motive for substituting a real for a sham knowledge, since, if you would appear to know anything, by far the best way is actually to know it. Thus, however justly we may reject the extravagant pretensions of magicians and condemn the deceptions which they have practised on mankind, the original institution of this class of men has, take it all in all, been productive of incalculable good to humanity. They were the direct predecessors, not merely of our physicians and surgeons, but of our investigators and discoverers in every branch of natural science. They began the work which has since been carried to such glorious and beneficent issues by their successors in after ages; and if the beginning was poor and feeble, this is to be imputed to the inevitable difficulties which beset

the path of knowledge rather than to the natural incapacity or willful fraud of the men themselves.

Of the things which the public magician sets himself to do for the good of the tribe, one of the chief is to control the weather and especially to ensure an adequate fall of rain. Water is an essential of life, and in most countries the supply of it depends upon showers. Without rain vegetation withers, animals and men languish and die. Hence in savage communities the rain-maker is a very important personage; and often a special class of magicians exists for the purpose of regulating the heavenly water-supply. The methods by which they attempt to discharge the duties of their office are commonly, though not always, based on the principle of imitative magic. If they wish to make rain they simulate it by sprinkling water or mimicking clouds: if their object is to stop rain and cause drought, they avoid water and resort to warmth and fire for the sake of drying up the too abundant moisture. Such attempts are by

no means confined, as the cultivated reader might imagine, to the naked inhabitants of those sultry lands like Central Australia and some parts of eastern and southern Africa, where often for months together the pitiless sun beats down out of a blue and cloudless sky on the parched and gaping earth. They are, or used to be, common enough among outwardly civilised folk in the moister climate of Europe. I will now illustrate them by instances drawn from the practice both of public and private magic.

Thus, for example, in a village near Dorpat, in Russia, when rain was much wanted, three men used to climb up the fir trees of an old sacred grove. One of them drummed with a hammer on a kettle or small cask to imitate thunder; the second knocked two fire-brands together and made the sparks fly, to imitate lightning; and the third, who was called "the rain-maker," had a bunch of twigs with which he sprinkled water from a vessel on all sides. To put an end to drought and bring down rain, women and girls of the village of Ploska are wont to go naked by night to the boundaries of the village and there pour water on the ground. In Halmahera, or Gilolo, a large island to the west of New Guinea, a wizard makes rain by dipping a branch of a particular kind of tree in water and then scattering the moisture from the dripping bough over the ground. In New Britain the rain-maker wraps some leaves of a red and green striped creeper in a banana-leaf, moistens the bundle with water, and buries it in the ground; then he imitates with his mouth the plashing of rain. Amongst the Omaha Indians of North America, when the corn is withering for want of rain, the members of the sacred Buffalo Society fill a large vessel with water and dance four times round it. One of them drinks some of the water and spirts it into the air, making

Opposite: The splendid dragon-head prow of a boat in the annual Dragon Boat race in Hong Kong, held to appease the water gods.

Below: *A man performs a Do Not Rain Dance in Nigeria.*

a fine spray in imitation of a mist or drizzling rain. Then he upsets the vessel, spilling the water on the ground; whereupon the dancers fall down and drink up the water, getting mud all over their faces. Lastly, they squirt the water into the air, making a fine mist. This saves the corn. In spring-time the Natchez of North America used to club together to purchase favourable weather for their crops from the wizards. If rain was needed, the wizards fasted and danced with pipes full of water in their mouths. The pipes were perforated like the nozzle of a watering-can, and through the holes the rain-maker blew the water towards that part of the sky where the clouds hung heaviest. But if fine weather was wanted, he mounted the roof of his hut, and with extended arms, blowing with all his might, he beckoned to the clouds to pass by. When the rains do not come in due season the people of Central Angoniland repair to what is called the rain-temple. Here they clear away the grass, and the leader pours beer into a pot which is buried in the ground, while he says, "Master Chauta, you have hardened your heart

Above: *Twin ibeji figures of the Yoruba tribe of Nigeria (twentieth-century wooden beads). If a twin died, the diviner would order the carving of such figures; they would be fed and cared for, to placate the powerful spirit of the dead child.* P. Goldman Collection, London.

towards us, what would you have us do? We must perish indeed. Give your children the rains, there is the beer we have given you." Then they all partake of the beer that is left over, even the children being made to sip it. Next they take branches of trees and dance and sing for rain. When they return to the village they find a vessel of water set at the doorway by an old woman; so they dip their branches in it and wave them aloft, so as to scatter the drops. After that the rain is sure to come driving up in heavy clouds. In these practices we see a combination of religion with magic; for while the scattering of the water-drops by means of branches is a purely magical cere-mony, the prayer for rain and the offering of beer are purely religious rites. In the Mara tribe of northern Australia the rain-maker goes to a pool and sings over it his magic song. Then he takes some of the water in his hands, drinks it, and spits it out in various directions. After that he throws water all over himself, scatters it about, and returns quietly to the camp. Rain is supposed to follow.

The Arab historian Makrizi describes a method of stopping rain which is said to have been resorted to by a tribe of nomads called Alqamar in Hadramaut. They cut a branch from a certain tree in the desert, set it on fire, and then sprinkled the burning brand with water. After that the vehemence of the rain abated, just as the water vanished when it fell on the glowing brand. Some of the eastern Angamis of Manipur are said to perform a some-what similar ceremony for the opposite purpose, in order, namely, to produce rain. The head of the village puts a burning brand on the grave of a man who has died of burns, and quenches the brand with water, while he prays that rain may fall. Here the putting out the fire with water, which is an imitation of rain, is reinforced by the influence of the dead man, who, having been burnt to death, will naturally be anxious for the descent of rain to cool his scorched body and assuage his pangs.

Other people besides the Arabs have used fire as a means of stopping rain. Thus the Sulka of New Britain heat stones red hot in the fire and then put them out in the rain, or they throw hot ashes in the air. They think that the rain will soon cease to fall, for it does not like to be burned by the hot stones or ashes. The Telugus send a little girl out naked into the rain with a burning piece of wood in her hand, which she has to show to the rain. That is supposed to stop the downpour. At Port Stevens in New South Wales the medicine-men used to drive away rain by throwing fire-sticks into the air, while at the same time they puffed and shouted. Any man of the Anula tribe in northern Australia can stop rain by simply warming a green stick in the fire, and then striking it against the wind.

In time of severe drought the Dieri of Central Australia, loudly lamenting the impoverished state of the country and their own half-starved condition, call upon the spirits of their remote predecessors, whom they call Mura-muras, to grant them power to make a heavy rainfall. For they believe that the clouds are bodies in which rain is generated by their own ceremonies or those of neighbouring tribes, through the influence of the Mura-muras. The way in which they set about drawing rain from the clouds is this. A hole is dug about twelve feet long and eight or ten broad, and over this hole a conical hut of logs and branches is made. Two wizards, supposed to have received a special inspiration from the Mura-muras, are bled by an old and influential man with a sharp flint; and the blood, drawn from their arms below the elbow, is made to flow on the other men of the tribe, who sit huddled together in the hut. At the same time the two bleeding men throw handfuls of down about, some of which adheres to the blood-stained bodies of their comrades, while the rest floats in the air. The blood is thought to represent the rain, and the down the clouds. During the ceremony two large stones are placed in the middle of the hut; they stand for gathering clouds and presage rain. Then the wizards who were bled carry away the two stones for about ten or fifteen miles, and place them as high as they can in the tallest tree. Meanwhile the other men gather gypsum, pound it fine, and throw it into a water-hole. This the Mura-muras see, and at once they cause clouds to appear in the sky. Lastly, the men, young and old, surround the hut, and, stooping down, butt at it with their heads, like so many rams. Thus they force their way through it and reappear on the other side, repeating the process till the hut is wrecked. In doing this they are forbidden to use their hands or arms; but when the

heavy logs alone remain, they are allowed to pull them out with their hands. "The piercing of the hut with their heads symbolises the piercing of the clouds; the fall of the hut, the fall of the rain." Obviously, too, the act of placing high up in trees the two stones, which stand for clouds, is a way of making the real clouds to mount up in the sky. The Dieri also imagine that the foreskins taken from lads at circumcision have a great power of producing rain. Hence the Great Council of the tribe always keeps a small stock of foreskins ready for use. They are carefully concealed, being wrapt up in feathers with the fat of the wild dog and of the carpet snake. A woman may not see such a parcel opened on any account. When the ceremony is over, the foreskin is buried, its virtue being exhausted. After the rains have fallen, some of the tribe always undergo a surgical operation, which consists in cutting the skin of their chest and arms with a sharp flint. The wound is then tapped with a flat stick to increase the flow of blood, and red ochre is rubbed into it. Raised scars are thus produced. The reason alleged by the natives for this practice is that they are pleased with the rain, and that there is a connexion between the rain and the scars. Apparently the operation is not very painful, for the patient laughs and jokes while it is going on. Indeed, little children have been seen to crowd round the operator and patiently take their turn; then after being operated on, they ran away, expanding their little chests and singing for the rain to beat upon them. However, they were not so well pleased next day, when they felt their wounds stiff and sore. In Java, when rain is wanted, two men will sometimes thrash each other with supple rods till the blood flows down their backs; the streaming blood represents the rain, and no doubt is supposed to make it fall on the ground. The people of Egghiou, a district of Abyssinia, used to engage in sanguinary conflicts with each other, village against village, for a week together every January for the purpose of procuring rain. Some years ago the emperor Menelik forbade the custom. However, the following year the rain was deficient, and the popular outcry so great that the emperor yielded to it, and allowed the murderous fights to be resumed, but for two days a year only. The writer who mentions the custom regards the blood shed on these occasions as a propitiatory sacrifice offered to spirits who control the showers; but perhaps, as in the Australian and Javanese ceremonies, it is an imitation of rain. The prophets of Baal, who sought to procure rain by cutting themselves with knives till the blood gushed out, may have acted on the same principle.

There is a widespread belief that twin children possess magical powers over nature, especially over rain and the weather. This curious superstition prevails among some of the Indian tribes of British Columbia, and has led them often to impose certain singular restrictions or taboos on the parents of twins, though the exact meaning of these restrictions is generally obscure. Thus the Tsimshian Indians of British Columbia believe that twins control the weather; therefore they pray to wind and rain, "Calm down, breath of the twins." Further, they think that the wishes of twins are always fulfilled; hence twins are feared, because they can harm the man they hate. They can also call the salmon and the

olachen or candle-fish, and so they are known by a name which means "making plentiful." In the opinion of the Kwakiutl Indians of British Columbia twins are transformed salmon; hence they may not go near water, lest they should be changed back again into the fish. In their childhood they can summon any wind by motions of their hands, and they can make fair or foul weather, and also cure diseases by swinging a large wooden rattle. The Nootka Indians of British Columbia also believe that twins are somehow related to salmon. Hence among them twins may not catch salmon, and they may not eat or even handle the fresh fish. They can make fair or foul weather, and can cause rain to fall by painting their faces black and then washing them, which may represent the rain dripping from the dark clouds. The Shuswap Indians, like the Thompson Indians, associate twins with the grizzly bear, for they call them "young grizzly bears." According to them, twins remain throughout life endowed with supernatural powers. In particular they can make good or bad weather. They produce rain by

spilling water from a basket in the air; they make fine weather by shaking a small flat piece of wood attached to a stick by a string; they raise storms by strewing down the ends of spruce branches.

The same power of influencing the weather is attributed to twins by the Baronga, a tribe of Bantu Negroes who inhabit the shores of Delagoa Bay in southeastern Africa. They bestow the name of Tilo—that is, the sky—on a woman who has given birth to twins, and the infants themselves are called children of the sky. Now when the storms which generally burst in the months of September and October have been looked for in vain, when a drought with its prospect of famine is threatening, and all nature, scorched and burnt up by a sun that has shone for six months from a cloudless sky, is panting for the beneficent showers of the south African spring, the women perform ceremonies to bring down the longed-for rain on the parched earth. Stripping themselves of all their garments, they assume in their stead girdles and headdresses of grass, or short petticoats made of the leaves of a particular sort of creeper. Thus attired, uttering peculiar cries and singing ribald songs, they go about from well to well, cleansing them of the mud and impurities which have accumulated in them. The wells, it may be said, are merely holes in the sand where a little turbid unwholesome water stagnates. Further, the women must repair to the house of one of their gossips who has given birth to twins, and must drench her with water, which they carry in little pitchers. Having done so they go on their way, shrieking out their loose songs and dancing immodest dances. No man may see these leaf-clad women going their rounds. If they meet a man, they maul him and thrust him aside. When they have cleansed the wells, they must go and pour water on the graves of their ancestors in the sacred grove. It often happens, too, that at the bidding of the wizard they go and pour water on the graves of twins. For they think that the grave of a twin ought always to be moist, for which reason twins are regularly buried near a lake. If all their efforts to procure rain prove abortive, they will remember that such and such a twin was buried in a dry place on the side of a hill. "No won-

Above: *This image cut out of buffalo hide was attached to the top of a pole during the annual Sun Dance Ceremony of the Oglala Sioux tribe. The Sun Dance gave thanks to the sun and requested renewed protection.* Collected in 1880. Peabody Museum, Harvard.

Opposite: *The Corroboree Dance of the Australian aborigines, from Mornington Island in the Gulf of Carpentaria.*

der," says the wizard in such a case, "that the sky is fiery. Take up his body and dig him a grave on the shore of the lake." His orders are at once obeyed, for this is supposed to be the only means of bringing down the rain.

It is interesting to observe that where an opposite result is desired, primitive logic enjoins the weather-doctor to observe precisely opposite rules of conduct. In the tropical island of Java, where the rich vegetation attests the abundance of the rainfall, ceremonies for the making of rain are rare, but ceremonies for the prevention of it are not uncommon. When a man is about to give a great feast in the rainy season and has invited many people, he goes to a weather-doctor and asks him to "prop up the clouds that may be lowering." If the doc-

Above: *Sumerian or Akkadian cylinder seal, circa 2300 B.C. It shows the sun god, Shamash, rising between two mountain peaks and Enki, god of fresh water.* British Museum, London.

tor consents to exert his professional powers, he begins to regulate his behaviour by certain rules as soon as his customer has departed. He must observe a fast, and may neither drink nor bathe; what little he eats must be eaten dry, and in no case may he touch water. The host, on his side, and his servants, both male and female, must neither wash clothes nor bathe so long as the feast lasts, and they have all during its continuance to observe strict chastity. The doctor seats himself on a new mat in his bedroom, and before a small oil-lamp he murmurs, shortly before the feast takes place, the following prayer or incantation: "Grandfather and Grandmother Sroekoel" (the name seems to be taken at random; others are sometimes used), "return to your country. Akkemat is your country. Put down your water-cask, close it properly, that not a drop may fall out." While he utters this prayer the sorcerer looks upwards, burning incense the while. So among the Toradjas the rain-doctor, whose special business it is to drive away rain, takes care not to touch water before, during, or after the discharge of his professional duties. He does not bathe, he eats with unwashed hands, he drinks nothing but palm wine, and if he has to cross a stream he is careful not to step in the water. Having thus prepared himself for his

task he has a small hut built for himself outside of the village in a rice-field, and in this hut he keeps up a little fire, which on no account may be suffered to go out. In the fire he burns various kinds of wood, which are supposed to possess the property of driving off rain; and he puffs in the direction from which the rain threatens to come, holding in his hand a packet of leaves and bark which derive a similar cloud-compelling virtue, not from their chemical composition, but from their names, which happen to signify something dry or volatile. If clouds should appear in the sky while he is at work, he takes lime in the hollow of his hand and blows it towards them. The lime, being so very dry, is obviously well adapted to disperse the damp clouds. Should rain afterwards be wanted, he has only to pour water on his fire, and immediately the rain will descend in sheets.

Among the Greeks of Thessaly and Macedonia, when a drought has lasted a long time, it is customary to send a procession of children round to all the wells and springs of the neighbourhood. At the head of the procession walks a girl adorned with flowers, whom her companions drench with water at every halting-place, while they sing an invocation, of which the following is part:

Perperia all fresh bedewed,
Freshen all the neighbourhood;
By the woods, on the highway,
As thou goest, to God now pray:
O my God, upon the plain,
Send thou us a still, small rain;
That the fields may fruitful be,
And the vines in blossom we may see;
That the grain be full and sound,
And wealthy grow the folks around

In time of drought the Serbians strip a girl to her skin and clothe her from head to foot in grass, herbs, and flowers, even her face being hidden behind a veil of living green. Thus disguised she is called the Dodola, and goes through the village with a troop of girls. They stop before every house; the Dodola keeps turning herself round and dancing, while the other girls form a ring about her singing one of the Dodola songs, and the housewife pours a pail of water over her. One of the songs they sing runs thus:

We go through the village;
The clouds go in the sky;
We go faster,
Faster go the clouds;
They have overtaken us,
And wetted the corn and the vine.

At Poona in India, when rain is needed, the boys dress up one of their number in nothing but leaves and call him King of Rain. Then they go round to every house in the village, where the householder or his wife sprinkles the Rain King with water, and gives the party food of various kinds. When they have thus visited all the houses, they strip the Rain King of his leafy robes and feast upon what they have gathered.

Bathing is practised as a rain-charm in some parts of southern and western Russia. Sometimes after service in church the priest in his robes has been thrown down on the ground and drenched with water by his parishioners. Sometimes it is the women who, without stripping off their clothes, bathe in crowds on the day of St. John the Baptist, while they dip in the water a figure made of branches, grass, and herbs, which is supposed to represent the saint. In Kursk, a province of southern Russia, when rain is much wanted, the women seize a passing stranger and throw him into the river, or souse him from head to foot. Later on we shall see that a passing stranger is often taken for a deity or the personification of some natural power. It is recorded in official documents that during a drought in 1790 the peasants of Scheroutz and Werboutz collected all the women and compelled them to bathe, in order that rain might fall. An Armenian rain-charm is to throw the wife of a priest into the water and drench her. The Arabs of North Africa fling a holy man, willy-nilly, into a spring as a remedy for drought. In Minahassa, a province of North Celebes, the priest bathes as a rain-charm. In Central Celebes when there has been no rain for a long time and the rice-stalks begin to shrivel up, many of the villagers, especially the young folk, go to a neighbouring brook and splash each other with water, shouting noisily, or squirt water on one another through bamboo tubes. Sometimes they imitate the plump of rain by smacking the surface of the water with their hands, or by placing an inverted gourd on it and drumming on the gourd with their fingers.

Sometimes the rain-charm operates through the dead. Thus in New Caledonia the rain-makers blackened themselves all over, dug up a dead body, took the bones to a cave, jointed them, and hung the skeleton over some taro leaves. Water was poured over the skeleton to run down on the leaves. They believed that the soul of the deceased took up the water, converted it into rain, and showered it down again. In Russia, if common report may be believed, it is not long since the peasants of any district that chanced to be afflicted with drought used to dig up the corpse of someone who had drunk

himself to death and sink it in the nearest swamp or lake, fully persuaded that this would ensure the fall of the needed rain. In 1868 the prospect of a bad harvest, caused by a prolonged drought, induced the inhabitants of a village in the Tarashchansk district to dig up the body of a Raskolnik, or Dissenter, who had died in the preceding December. Some of the party beat the corpse, or what was left of it, about the head, exclaiming, "Give us rain!" while others poured water on it through a sieve. Here the pouring of water through a sieve seems plainly an imitation of a shower, and reminds us of the manner in which Strepsiades in Aristophanes imagined that rain was made by Zeus.

Sometimes, in order to procure rain, the Toradjas make an appeal to the pity of the dead. Thus, in the village of Kalingooa, there is the grave of a famous chief, the grandfather of the present ruler. When the land suffers from unseasonable drought, the people go to this grave, pour water on it, and say, "O grandfather, have pity on us; if it is your will that this year we should eat, then give rain." After that they hang a bamboo full of water over the grave; there is a small hole in the lower end of the bamboo, so that the water drips from it continually. The bamboo is always refilled with water until rain drenches the ground. Here, as in New Caledonia, we find religion blent with magic, for the prayer to the dead chief, which is purely religious, is eked out with a magical imitation of rain at his grave. We have seen that the Baronga of Delagoa Bay drench the tombs of their ancestors, especially the tombs of twins, as a rain-charm. Among some of the Indian tribes in the region of the Orinoco it was customary for the relations of a deceased person to disinter his bones a year after burial, burn them, and scatter the ashes to the winds, because they believed that the ashes were changed into rain, which the dead man sent in return for his obsequies.

The Chinese are convinced that when human bodies remain unburied, the souls of their late owners feel the discomfort of rain, just as living men would do if they were exposed without shelter to the inclemency of the weather. These wretched souls, therefore, do all in their power to prevent the rain from falling, and often their efforts are only too successful. Then drought ensues, the most dreaded of all calamities in China, because bad harvests, dearth, and famine follow in its train. Hence it has been a common practice of the Chinese authorities in time of drought to inter the dry bones of the unburied dead for the purpose of putting an end to the scourge and conjuring down the rain.

The intimate association of frogs and toads with water has earned for these creatures a widespread reputation as custodians of rain; and hence they often play a part in charms designed to draw needed showers from the sky. Some of the Indians of the Orinoco held the toad to be the god or lord of the waters, and for that reason feared to kill the creature. They have been known to keep frogs under a pot and to beat them with rods when there was a drought. It is said that the Aymara Indians often make little images of frogs and other aquatic animals and place them on the tops of the hills as a means of bringing down rain. The Thompson Indians of British Columbia and some people in Europe think that to kill a frog will cause rain to fall. In order to procure rain people of low caste in the Central Provinces of India will tie a frog to a rod covered with green leaves and branches of the nim tree (*Azadirachta indica*) and carry it from door to door singing:

Send soon, O frog, the jewel of water!
And ripen the wheat and millet in the field.

The Kapus or Reddis are a large caste of cultivators and landowners in the Madras Presidency. When rain falls, women of the caste will catch a frog and tie it alive to a new winnowing fan made of bamboo. On this fan they spread a few margosa leaves and go from door to door singing, "Lady frog must have her bath. Oh! rain-god, give a little water for her at least." While the Kapu women sing this song, the woman of the house pours water over the frog and gives an alms, convinced that by so doing she will soon bring rain down in torrents.

Sometimes, when a drought has lasted a long time, people drop the usual hocus-pocus of imitative magic altogether, and being far too angry to waste their breath in prayer they seek by threats and curses or even down-right physical force to extort the waters of heaven from the supernatural being who has, so to say, cut them off at the main. In a Japanese village, when the guardian divinity had long been deaf to the peasants' prayers for rain, they at last threw down his image and, with curses loud and long, hurled it head foremost into a stinking rice-field. "There," they said, "you may stay yourself for a while, to see how you will feel after a few days' scorching in this broiling sun that is burning the life from our cracking fields." In the like circumstances the Feloupes of Senegambia cast down their fetishes and drag them about the fields, cursing them till rain falls.

The Chinese are adepts in the art of taking the kingdom of heaven by storm. Thus, when rain is wanted they make a huge dragon of paper or wood to represent the rain-god, and carry it about in procession; but if no rain follows, the mock-dragon is execrated and torn to pieces. At other times they threaten and beat the god if he does not give rain; sometimes they publicly depose him from the rank of deity. On the other hand, if the wished-for rain falls, the god is promoted to a higher rank by an imperial decree. In April 1888 the mandarins of Canton prayed to the god Lung-wong to stop the incessant downpour of rain; and when he turned a deaf ear to their petitions they put him in a lock-up for five days. This had a salutary effect. The rain ceased and the god was restored to liberty. Some years before, in time of drought, the same deity had been chained and exposed to the sun for days in the courtyard of his temple in order that he might feel for himself the urgent need of rain. So when the

Left: *A wooden staff used by devotees of Shango, a deity of thunder and lightning, and carried in dances when possessed by the deity.* Yoruba tribe, Nigeria, probably nineteenth century. Private collection.

The reader may smile at the meterology of the Far East; but precisely similar modes of procuring rain have been resorted to in Christian Europe within our own lifetime. By the end of April 1893 there was great distress in Sicily for lack of water. The drought had lasted six months. Every day the sun rose and set in a sky of cloudless blue. The gardens of the Conca d'Oro, which surround Palermo with a magnificent belt of verdure, were withering. Food was becoming scarce. The people were in great alarm. All the most approved methods of procuring rain had been tried without effect. Processions had traversed the streets and the fields. Men, women, and children, telling their beads, had lain whole nights before the holy images. Consecrated candles had burned day and night in the churches. Palm branches, blessed on Palm Sunday, had been hung on the trees. At Solaparuta, in accordance with a very old custom, the dust swept from the churches on Palm Sunday had been spread on the fields. In ordinary years these holy sweepings preserve the crops; but that year, if you will believe me, they had no effect whatever. At Nicosia the inhabitants, bare-headed and bare-foot, carried the crucifixes through all the wards of the town and scourged each other with iron whips. It was all in vain. Even the great St. Francis of Paolo himself, who annually performs the miracle of rain and is carried every spring through the market-gardens, either could not or would not help. Masses, vespers, concerts, illuminations, fire-works—nothing could move him. At last the peasants began to lose patience. Most of the saints were banished. At Palermo they dumped St. Joseph in a garden to see the state of things for himself, and they swore to leave him there in the sun till rain fell. Other saints were turned, like naughty children, with their faces to the wall. Others again, stripped of their beautiful robes, were exiled far from their parishes, threatened, grossly insulted, ducked in horse-ponds. At Caltanisetta the golden wings of St. Michael the Archangel were torn

Siamese need rain, they set out their idols in the blazing sun; but if they want dry weather, they unroof the temples and let the rain pour down on the idols. They think that the inconvenience to which the gods are thus subjected will induce them to grant the wishes of their worshippers.

Above: *A scene showing the paradise of the rain god, Tlaloc, where the souls who have pleased him are in bliss.* Wall painting of the Teotihuacan culture at Tepantitla, Mexico.

Opposite:. *The storm god, Adad, with his arm raised to hold a spear of lightning.* Bronze and gold statuette, 1400-1200 B.C. Found at the Ugaritic site of Ras Shamra, in Syria.

from his shoulders and replaced with wings of pasteboard; his purple mantle was taken away and a cloud wrapt about him instead. At Licata the patron saint, St. Angelo, fared even worse, for he was left without any garments at all; he was reviled, he was put in irons, he was threatened with drowning or hanging. "Rain or the rope!" roared the angry people at him, as they shook their fists in his face.

Sometimes an appeal is made to the pity of the gods. When their corn is being burnt up by the sun, the Zulus look out for a "heaven bird," kill it, and throw it into a pool. Then the heaven melts with tenderness for the death of the bird; "it wails for it by raining, wailing a funeral wail." In Zululand women sometimes bury their children up to the neck in the ground, and then retiring to a distance keep up a dismal howl for a long time. The sky is supposed to melt with pity at the sight. Then the women dig the children out and feel sure that rain will soon follow. They say that they call to "the lord above" and ask him to send rain. If it comes they declare that "Usondo rains." In times of drought the Guanches of

Teneriffe led their sheep to sacred ground, and there they separated the lambs from their dams, that their plaintive bleating might touch the heart of the god. In Kumaon a way of stopping rain is to pour hot oil in the left ear of a dog. The animal howls with pain, his howls are heard by Indra, and out of pity for the beast's sufferings the god stops the rain. Sometimes the Toradjas attempt to procure rain as follows. They place the stalks of certain plants in water, saying, "Go and ask for rain, and so long as no rain falls I will not plant you again, but there shall you die." Also they string some fresh-water snails on a cord, and hang the cord on a tree, and say to the snails, "Go and ask for rain, and so long as no rain comes, I will not take you back to the water." Then the snails go and weep, and the gods take pity and send rain. However, the foregoing ceremonies are religious rather than magical, since they involve an appeal to the compassion of higher powers.

Stones are often supposed to possess the property of bringing on rain, provided they be dipped in water or sprinkled with it, or treated in some other appropriate manner. In a Samoan village a certain stone was carefully housed as the representative of the rain-making god, and in time of drought his priests carried the stone in procession and dipped it in a stream. Among the Ta-ta-thi tribe of New South Wales, the rain-maker breaks off a piece of quartz-crystal and spits it towards the sky; the rest of the crystal he wraps in emu feathers, soaks both crystal and feathers in water, and carefully hides them. In the Keramin tribe of New South Wales the wizard retires to the bed of a creek, drops water on a round flat stone, then covers up and conceals it. Among some tribes of northwestern Australia the rain-maker repairs to a piece of ground which is set apart for the purpose of rain-making. There he builds a heap of stones or sand, places on the top of it his magic stone, and walks or dances round the pile chanting his incantations for hours, till sheer exhaustion obliges him to desist, when his place is taken by his assistant. Water is sprinkled on the stone and huge fires are kindled. No layman may approach the sacred spot while the mystic ceremony is being performed. When the Sulka of New Britain wish

Above: *"How Vivien tricks the magician Merlin to his underground death."* Illustration by Ford, Andrew Lang's *Book of Romance*, 1902.

to procure rain they blacken stones with the ashes of certain fruits and set them out, along with certain other plants and buds, in the sun. Then a handful of twigs is dipped in water and weighted with stones, while a spell is chanted. After that rain should follow. In Manipur, on a lofty hill to the east of the capital, there is a stone which the popular imagination likens to an umbrella. When rain is wanted, the rajah fetches water from a spring below and sprinkles it on the stone. At Sagami in Japan there is a stone which draws down rain whenever water is poured on it. When the Wakondyo, a tribe of Central Africa, desire rain, they send to the Wawamba, who dwell at the foot of snowy mountains, and are the happy possessors of a "rain-stone." In consideration of a proper payment, the Wawamba wash the precious stone,

anoint it with oil, and put it in a pot full of water. After that the rain cannot fail to come. In the arid wastes of Arizona and New Mexico the Apaches sought to make rain by carrying water from a certain spring and throwing it on a particular point high up on a rock; after that they imagined that the clouds would soon gather, and that rain would begin to fall.

But customs of this sort are not confined to the wilds of Africa and Asia or the torrid deserts of Australia and the New World. They have been practised in the cool air and under the grey skies of Europe. There is a fountain called Barenton, of romantic fame, in those "wild woods of Broceliande," where, if legend be true, the wizard Merlin still sleeps his magic slumber in the hawthorn shade. Thither the Breton peasants used to resort when they needed rain. They caught some of the water in a tankard and threw it on a slab near the spring. On Snowdon there is a lonely tarn called Dulyn, or the Black Lake, lying "in a dismal dingle surrounded by high and dangerous rocks." A row of stepping-stones runs out into the lake, and if any one steps on the stones and throws water so as to wet the farthest stone, which is called the Red Altar, "it is but a chance that you do not get rain before night, even when it is hot weather." In these cases it appears probable that, as in Samoa, the stone is regarded as more or less divine. This appears from the custom sometimes observed of dipping a cross in the Fountain of Barenton to procure rain, for this is plainly a Christian substitute for the old pagan way of throwing water on the stone. At various places in France it is, or used till lately to be, the practice to dip the image of a saint in water as a means of procuring rain. Thus, beside the old priory of Commagny, there is a spring of St. Gervais, whither the inhabitants go in procession to obtain rain or fine weather according to the needs of the crops. In times of great drought they throw into the basin of the fountain an ancient stone image of the saint that stands in a sort of niche from which the-fountain flows. At Collobrieres and Carpentras a similar practice was observed with the images of St. Pons and St. Gens respectively. In several villages of Navarre prayers for rain used to be offered to St. Peter, and by

way of enforcing them the villagers carried the image of the saint in procession to the river, where they thrice invited him to reconsider his resolution and to grant their prayers; then, if he was still obstinate, they plunged him in the water, despite the remonstrances of the clergy, who pleaded with as much truth as piety that a simple caution or admonition administered to the image would produce an equally good effect. After this the rain was sure to fall within twenty-four hours. Catholic countries do not enjoy a monopoly of making rain by ducking holy images in water. In Mingrelia, when the crops are suffering from want of rain, they take a particularly holy image and dip it in water every day till a shower falls; and in the Far East the Shans drench the images of Buddha with water when the rice is perishing of drought. In all such cases the practice is probably at bottom a sympathetic charm, however it may be disguised under the appearance of a punishment or a threat.

Like other peoples, the Greeks and Romans sought to obtain rain by magic, when prayers and processions had proved ineffectual. For example, in Arcadia, when the corn and trees were parched with drought, the priest of Zeus dipped an oak branch into a certain spring on Mount Lycaeus. Thus troubled, the water sent up a misty cloud, from which rain soon fell upon the land. A similar mode of making rain is still practised in Halmahera near New Guinea. The people of Crannon in Thessaly had a bronze chariot which they kept in a temple. When they desired a shower they

shook the chariot and the shower fell. Probably the rattling of the chariot was meant to imitate thunder; we have already seen that mock thunder and lightning form part of a rain-charm in Russia and Japan. The legendary Salmoneus, King of Elis, made mock thunder by dragging bronze kettles behind his chariot, or by driving over a bronze bridge, while he hurled blazing torches in imitation of lightning. It was his impious wish to mimic the thundering car of Zeus as it rolled across the vault of heaven. Indeed he declared that he was actually Zeus, and caused sacrifices to be offered to himself as such. Near a temple of Mars, outside the walls of Rome, there was kept a certain stone known as the lapis manalis. In time of drought the stone was dragged into Rome, and this was supposed to bring down rain immediately.

Above: *Mount Snowdon in North Wales is traditionally considered a mystical site. In its Black Lake lie stepping stones leading to the Red Altar which could bring rain before nightfall when water was thrown upon it.*

Below: *A matrix for a sixth-century Viking helmet plaque illustrating a scene from the Norse creation myth, in which cataclysmic events followed the death of the god Balder and the earth was reborn.* Statens Historiska Museum, Stockholm.

Chapter Four

THE SOVEREIGN MAGICIAN

WHAT HAS ALREADY been said may satisfy us that in many lands and many races magic has claimed to control the great forces of nature for the good of man. If that has been so, the practitioners of the art must necessarily be personages of importance and influence in any society which puts faith in their extravagant pretensions, and it would be no matter for surprise if, by virtue of the reputation which they enjoy and of the awe which they inspire, some of them should attain to the highest position of authority over their credulous fellows. In point of fact magicians appear to have developed often into chiefs and kings.

Let us begin by looking at the aborigines of Australia. They are ruled neither by chiefs nor kings. So far as their tribes can be said to have a political constitution, it is a democracy or rather an oligarchy of old and influential men, who meet in council and decide on all measures of importance to the practical exclusion of the younger men. Their deliberative assembly answers to the senate of later times: if we had to coin a word for such a government of elders we might call it a gerontocracy. The elders who in aboriginal Australia thus meet and direct the affairs of their tribe appear to be for the most part the head-men of their respective totem

Above (top): *Aboriginal art featuring fish motifs, probably connected with hunting magic, from the Obiri Rock in Australia.*

Above (bottom): *Traditional song and dance festival of the Mangai of Papua New Guinea, Bismarck Archipelago, New Ireland.*

Opposite: *A man from the Aranda tribe of Australian aborigines, who live near Alice Springs. The principal functions of headmen in Central Australia were generally sacred or magical.*

clans. Now in Central Australia, where the desert nature of the country and the almost complete isolation from foreign influences have retarded progress and preserved the natives on the whole in their most primitive state, the headmen of the various totem clans are charged with the important task of performing magical ceremonies for the multiplication of the totems, and as the great majority of the totems are edible animals or plants, it follows that these men are commonly expected to provide the people with food by means of magic. Others have to make the rain to fall or to render other services to the community. In short, among the tribes of Central Australia the headmen are public magicians. Further, their most important function is to take charge of the sacred storehouse, usually a cleft in the rocks or a hole in the ground, where are kept the holy stones and sticks (churinga) with which the souls of all the people, both living and dead, are apparently supposed to be in a manner bound up. Thus while the headmen have cer-

tainly to perform what we should call civil duties, such as to inflict punishment for breaches of tribal custom, their principal functions are sacred or magical.

When we pass from Australia to New Guinea we find that, though the natives stand at a far higher level of culture than the Australian aborigines, the constitution of society among them is still essentially democratic or oligarchic, and chieftainship exists only in embryo. Thus Sir William MacGregor tells us that in British New Guinea no one has ever arisen wise enough, bold enough, and strong enough to become the despot even of a single district. "The nearest approach to this has been the very distant one of some person becoming a renowned wizard; but that has only resulted in levying a certain amount of blackmail."

According to a native account, the origin of the power of Melanesian chiefs lies entirely in the belief that they have communication with mighty ghosts, and wield that supernatural power whereby they can bring the influence of the ghosts to bear. If a chief imposed a fine, it was paid because the people universally dreaded his ghostly power, and firmly believed that he could inflict calamity and sickness upon such as resisted him. As soon as any considerable number of his people began to disbelieve in his influence with the ghosts, his power to levy fines was shaken. Again, Dr. George Brown tells us that in New Britain "a ruling chief was always supposed to exercise priestly functions, that is, he professed to be in constant communication with the tebarans (spirits), and through their influence he was enabled to bring rain or sunshine, fair winds or foul ones, sickness or health, success or disaster in war, and generally to procure any blessing or curse for which the applicant was willing to pay a sufficient price."

Still rising in the scale of culture we come to Africa, where both the chieftainship and the kingship are fully developed; and here the evidence for the evolution of the chief out of the magician, and especially out of the rain-maker, is comparatively plentiful. Thus among the Wambugwe, a Bantu people of East Africa, the original form of government was a family republic, but the enormous power of the sorcerers, transmitted by inheri-

Above: *Rock crystals were believed by the tribes of the Upper Nile to have rain-making properties. This globe, probably used originally as a magnifier, was later set in silver and used as a magical charm to cure cattle of warts in Scotland.*

Opposite: *Hands of conjuration. These wood-carvings of magical gestures were supposed to give protection from evil.*

tance, soon raised them to the rank of petty lords or chiefs. Of the three chiefs living in the country in 1894 two were much dreaded as magicians, and the wealth of cattle they possessed came to them almost wholly in the shape of presents bestowed for their services in that capacity. Their principal art was that of rain-making. The chiefs of the Wataturu, another people of East Africa, are said to be nothing but sorcerers destitute of any direct political influence. Again, among the Wagogo of East Africa the main power of the chiefs, we are told, is derived from their art of rain-making. If a chief cannot make rain himself, he must procure it from some one who can.

Again, among the tribes of the Upper Nile the medicine-men are generally the chiefs. Their authority rests above all upon their supposed power of making rain, for "rain is the one thing which matters to the people in those districts, as if it does not come down at the right time it means untold hardships for the community. It is therefore small wonder that men more cunning than their fellows should arrogate to themselves the power of producing it, or that having gained such a reputation, they should trade on the credulity of their simpler neighbours." Hence "most of the chiefs of these tribes are rain-makers, and enjoy a popularity in proportion to their powers to give rain to their people at the proper season . . . Rain-making chiefs always build their villages on the slopes of a fairly high hill, as they no doubt know

that the hills attract the clouds, and that they are, therefore, fairly safe in their weather forecasts." Each of these rain-makers has a number of rain-stones, such as rock-crystal, aventurine, and amethyst, which he keeps in a pot. When he wishes to produce rain he plunges the stones in water, and taking in his hand a peeled cane, which is split at the top, he beckons with it to the clouds to come or waves them away in the way they should go, muttering an incantation the while. Or he pours water and the entrails of a sheep or goat into a hollow in a stone and then sprinkles the water towards the sky. Though the chief acquires wealth by the exercise of his supposed magical powers, he often, perhaps generally, comes to a violent end; for in time of drought the angry people assemble and kill him, believing that it is he who prevents the rain from falling. Yet the office is usually hereditary and passes from father to son. Among the tribes which cherish these beliefs and observe these customs are the Latuka, Bari, Laluba, and Lokoiya.

In Central Africa, again, the Lendu tribe, to the west of Lake Albert, firmly believe that certain people possess the power of making rain. Among them the rain-maker either is a chief or almost invariably becomes one. The Banyoro also have a great respect for the dispensers of rain, whom they load with a profusion of gifts. The great dispenser, he who has absolute and uncontrollable power over the rain, is the king; but he

exerts tremendous control over the people, and so it would be most important to keep this function connected with royalty. Tradition always places the power of making rain as the fundamental glory of ancient chiefs and heroes, and it seems probable that it may have been the origin of chieftainship. The man who made the rain would naturally become the chief. In the same way Chaka [the famous Zulu despot] used to declare that he was the only diviner in the country, for if he allowed rivals his life would be insecure." Similarly speaking of the South African tribes in general, Dr. Moffat says that "the rain-maker is in the estimation of the people no mean personage, possessing an influence over the minds of the people superior even to that of the king, who is likewise compelled to yield to the dictates of this arch-official."

The foregoing evidence renders it probable that in Africa the king has often been developed out of the public magician, and especially out of the rain-maker. The unbounded fear which the magician inspires and the wealth which he amasses in the exercise of his profession may both be supposed to have contributed to his promotion. But if the career of a magician and especially of a rain-maker offers great rewards to the successful practitioner of the art, it is beset with many pitfalls into which the unskillful or unlucky artist may fall. The position of the public sorcerer is indeed a very precarious one; for where the people firmly believe that he has it in his power to make the rain to fall, the sun to shine, and the fruits of the earth to grow, they naturally impute drought and dearth to his culpable negligence or willful obstinacy, and they punish him accordingly. Hence in Africa the chief who fails to procure rain is often exiled or killed. Thus, in some parts of West Africa, when prayers and offerings presented to the king have failed to procure rain, his subjects bind him with ropes and take him by force to the grave of his forefathers that he may obtain from them the needed rain. The Banjars in West Africa ascribe to their king the power of causing rain or fine weather. So long as the weather is fine they load him with presents of grain and cattle. But if long drought or rain threatens to spoil the crops, they insult and beat him till the weather changes. When the harvest

can depute his power to other persons, so that the benefit may be distributed and the heavenly water laid on over the various parts of the kingdom.

In western as well as in eastern and central Africa we meet with the same union of chiefly with magical functions. Thus in the Fan tribe the strict distinction between chief and medicine-man does not exist. The chief is also a medicine-man and a smith to boot; for the Fans esteem the smith's craft sacred, and none but chiefs may meddle with it.

As to the relation between the offices of chief and rain-maker in south Africa a well-informed writer observes: "In very old days the chief was the great rain-maker of the tribe. Some chiefs allowed no one else to compete with them, lest a successful rain-maker should be chosen as chief. There was also another reason: the rain-maker was sure to become a rich man if he gained a great reputation, and it would manifestly never do for the chief to allow any one to be too rich. The rain-maker fails or the surf on the coast is too heavy to allow of fishing, the people of Loango accuse their king of a "bad heart" and depose him. On the Grain Coast the high priest or fetish king, who bears the title of Bodio, is responsible for the health of the community, the fertility of the earth, and the abundance of fish in the sea and rivers; and if the country suffers in any of these respects the Bodio is deposed from his office. In Ussukuma, a great district on the southern bank of the Victoria Nyanza, "the rain and locust question is part and parcel of the Sultan's government. He, too, must know how to make rain and drive away the locusts. If he and his medicine-men are unable to accomplish this, his whole existence is at stake in times of distress. On a certain occasion, when the rain so greatly desired by the people did not come, the Sultan was simply driven out (in Ututwa, near Nassa). The people, in fact, hold that rulers must have power over Nature and her phenomena." Again, we are told of the natives of the Nyanza region generally that "they are persuaded that rain only falls as a result of magic, and the important duty of causing it to descend devolves on the chief of the tribe. If rain does not come at the proper time, everybody complains. More than one petty king has been banished from his country because of drought." Among the Latuka of the Upper Nile, when the crops are withering, and all the efforts of the chief to draw down rain have proved fruitless, the people commonly attack him by night, rob him of all he possesses, and drive him away. But often they kill him.

In many other parts of the world kings have been expected to regulate the course of nature for the good of their people and have been punished if they failed to do so. It appears that the Scythians, when food was scarce, used to put their king in bonds. In ancient Egypt the sacred kings were blamed for the failure of the crops, but the sacred beasts were also held responsible for the course of nature. When pestilence and other calamities had fallen on the land, in consequence of a long and severe drought, the priests took the animals by night and threatened them, but if the evil did not abate they slew the beasts. On the coral island of Niue or Savage Island, in the South Pacific, there formerly reigned a line of kings. But as the kings were also high priests, and were supposed to make the food grow, the people became angry with them in times of scarcity and killed them; till at last, as one after another was killed, no one would be king, and the monarchy came to an end. Ancient Chinese writers inform us that in Korea the blame was laid on the king whenever too much or too little rain fell and the crops did not ripen. Some said that he must be deposed, others that he must be slain.

Among the American Indians the furthest advance towards civilisation was made under the monarchical and theocratic governments of Mexico and Peru; but we know too little of the early history of these countries to

Below: *A portrait of See-non-ty-a, a medicine man of the Iowa tribe in the United States.* Painted from life by George Catlin, about 1845.

Opposite: *Montezuma II, last emperor of the Aztecs, who was worshipped as a god by his people and died in 1520. Mexican kings were believed to have control of the heavens and earth.* Detail of a sixteenth-century portrait by an unknown Spanish artist. Pitti Palace, Florence.

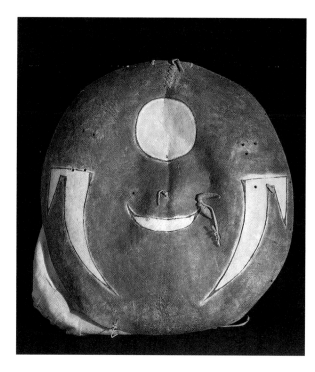

Above: *A shield from the Native American Cree tribe of the North American plains. The magical figures in the center are thought to represent the sun and the moon. Such war designs were communicated in dreams and trance visions.* British Museum, London.

Opposite: *In Egypt sacred kings were blamed for the failure of crops. Joseph enabled Egypt to avoid years of want by interpreting pharoah's dream and predicting years of good and bad harvests.* From *The Nuremberg Bible*, 1483. Victoria and Albert Museum, London.

greatest respect is paid to them by the whole community; not only for their skill in their materia medica, but more especially for their tact in magic and mysteries, in which they all deal to a very great extent . . . In all tribes their doctors are conjurers—are magicians—are sooth-sayers, and I had like to have said high-priests, inasmuch as they superintend and conduct all their religious ceremonies; they are looked upon by all as oracles of the nation. In all councils of war and peace, they have a seat with the chiefs, are regularly consulted before any public step is taken, and the greatest deference and respect is paid to their opinions." Similarly in California "the shaman was, and still is, perhaps the most important individual among the Maidu. In the absence of any definite system of government, the word of a shaman has great weight: as a class they are regarded with much awe, and as a rule are obeyed much more than the chief."

In South America also the magicians or medicine-men seem to have been on the highroad to chieftainship or kingship. One of the earliest settlers on the coast of Brazil, the Frenchman Thevet, reports that the Indians "hold these pages (or medicine-men) in such honour and reverence that they adore, or rather idolise them. You may see the common folk go to meet them, prostrate themselves, and pray to them, saying, 'Grant that I be not ill, that I do not die, neither I nor my children,' or some such request. And he answers, 'You shall not die, you shall not be ill,' and such like replies. But sometimes if it happens that these pages do not tell the truth, and things turn out otherwise than they predicted, the people make no scruple of killing them as unworthy of the title and dignity of pages." Among the Lengua Indians of the Gran Chaco every clan has its cazique or chief, but he possesses little authority. In virtue of his office he has to make many presents, so he seldom grows rich and is generally more shabbily clad than any of his subjects. "As a matter of fact the magician is the man who has most power in his hands, and he is accustomed to receive presents instead of to give them." It is the magician's duty to bring down misfortune and plagues on the enemies of his tribe, and to guard his

say whether the predecessors of their deified kings were medicine-men or not. Perhaps a trace of such a succession may be detected in the oath which the Mexican kings, when they mounted the throne, swore that they would make the sun to shine, the clouds to give rain, the rivers to flow, and the earth to bring forth fruits in abundance. Certainly, in aboriginal America the sorcerer or medicine-man, surrounded by a halo of mystery and an atmosphere of awe, was a personage of great influence and importance, and he may well have developed into a chief or king in many tribes, though positive evidence of such a development appears to be lacking. Thus Catlin tells us that in North America the medicine-men "are valued as dignitaries in the tribe, and the

own people against hostile magic. For these services he is well paid, and by them he acquires a position of great influence and authority.

Throughout the Malay region the rajah or king is commonly regarded with superstitious veneration as the possessor of supernatural powers, and there are grounds for thinking that he too, like apparently so many African chiefs, has been developed out of a simple magician. At the present day the Malays firmly believe that the king possesses a personal influence over the works of nature, such as the growth of the crops and the bearing of fruit-trees. The same prolific virtue is supposed to reside, though in a lesser degree, in his delegates, and even in the persons of Europeans who chance to have charge of districts. Thus in Selangor, one of the native states of the Malay Peninsula, the success or failure of the rice-crops is often attributed to a change of district officers. The Toorateyas of Southern Celebes hold that the prosperity of the rice depends on the behaviour of their princes, and that bad government, by which they mean a government which does

not conform to ancient custom, will result in a failure of the crops.

The Dyaks of Sarawak believed that their famous English ruler, Rajah Brooke, was endowed with a certain magical virtue which, if properly applied, could render the rice-crops abundant. Hence when he visited a tribe, they used to bring him the seed which they intended to sow next year, and he fertilised it by shaking over it the women's necklaces, which had been previously dipped in a special mixture. And when he entered a village, the women would wash and bathe his feet, first with water, and then with the milk of a young cocoanut, and lastly with water again, and all this water which had touched his person they preserved for the purpose of distributing it on their farms, believing that it ensured an abundant harvest. Tribes which were too far off for him to visit used to send him a small piece of white cloth and a little gold or silver, and when these things had been impregnated by his generative virtue they buried them in their fields, and confidently expected a heavy crop. Once when a European remarked that the rice-crops of

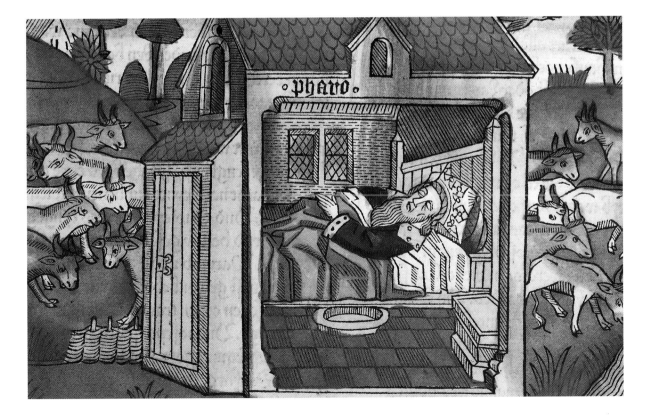

Opposite: *Palawan Islanders of the Philippines preparing for a Lambay ritual, a thanksgiving ceremony for the spirits of honey and rice.*

Below: *Roman relief showing the god Mithras slaying the bull, symbolically the first of all living creatures, from whose blood corn and all other forms of life arose.* Museo Nazionale Romano, Rome.

the Samban tribe were thin, the chief immediately replied that they could not be otherwise, since Rajah Brooke had never visited them, and he begged that Mr. Brooke might be induced to visit his tribe and remove the sterility of their land.

The belief that kings possess magical or supernatural powers by virtue of which they can fertilise the earth and confer other benefits on their subjects would seem to have been shared by the ancestors of all the Aryan races from India to Ireland, and it has left clear traces of itself in our own country down to modern times. Thus the ancient Hindoo law-book called The Laws of Manu describes as follows the effects of a good king's reign: "In that country where the king avoids taking the property

of mortal sinners, men are born in due time and are long-lived. And the crops of the husbandmen spring up, each as it was sown, and the children die not, and no misshaped offspring is born." In Homeric Greece kings and chiefs were spoken of as sacred or divine; their houses, too, were divine and their chariots sacred; and it was thought that the reign of a good king caused the black earth to bring forth wheat and barley, the trees to be loaded with fruit, the flocks to multiply, and the sea to yield fish. In the Middle Ages, when Waldemar I, King of Denmark, travelled in Germany, mothers brought their infants and husbandmen their seed for him to lay his hands on, thinking that children would both thrive the better for the royal touch, and for a like reason farmers asked him to throw the seed for them. It was the belief of the ancient Irish that when their kings observed the customs of their ancestors, the seasons were mild, the crops plentiful, the cattle fruitful, the waters abounded with fish, and the fruit trees had to be propped up on account of the weight of their produce. A canon attributed to St. Patrick enumerates among the

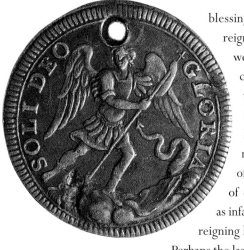

blessings that attend the reign of a just king "fine weather, calm seas, crops abundant, and trees laden with fruit." On the other hand, dearth, dryness of cows, blight of fruit, and scarcity of corn were regarded as infallible proofs that the reigning king was bad.

Perhaps the last relic of such superstitions which lingered about our English kings was the notion that they could heal scrofula by their touch. The disease was accordingly known as the King's Evil. Queen Elizabeth often exercised this miraculous gift of healing. On Midsummer Day 1633, Charles I cured a hundred patients at one swoop in the chapel royal at Holyrood. But it was under his son Charles II that the practice seems to have attained its highest vogue. It is said that in the course of his reign Charles II touched near a hundred thousand persons for scrofula. The press to get near him was sometimes terrific. On one occasion six or seven of those who came to be healed were trampled to death. The cool-headed William III contemptuously refused to lend himself to the hocus-pocus; and when his palace was besieged by the usual unsavoury crowd, he ordered them to be turned away with a dole. On the only occasion when he was importuned into laying his hand on a patient, he said to him, "God give you better health and more sense." However, the practice was continued, as might have been expected, by the dull bigot James II who preceded William and thus by his dull daughter Queen Anne.

The kings of France also claimed to possess the same gift of healing by touch, which they are said to have derived from Clovis or from St. Louis, while our English kings inherited it from Edward the Confessor. Similarly the savage chiefs of Tonga were believed to heal scrofula and cases of indurated liver by the touch of their feet; and the cure was strictly magical, for the disease as well as the cure was thought to be caused by contact with the royal person or with anything that belonged to it.

On the whole, then, we seem to be justified in inferring that in many parts of the world the king is the lineal successor of the old magician or medicine-man. When once a special class of sorcerers has been segregated from the community and entrusted by it with the discharge of duties on which the public safety and welfare are believed to depend, these men gradually rise to wealth and power, till their leaders blossom out into sacred kings. But the great social revolution which thus begins with democracy and ends in despotism is attended by an intellectual revolution which affects both the conception and the functions of royalty. For as time goes on, the fallacy of magic becomes more and more apparent to the acuter minds and is slowly displaced by religion; in other words, the magician gives way to the priest, who, renouncing the attempt to control directly the processes of nature for the good of man, seeks to attain the same end indirectly by appealing to the gods to do for him what he no longer fancies he can do for himself. Hence the king, starting as a magician, tends gradually to exchange the practice of magic for the priestly functions of prayer and sacrifice. And while the distinction between the human and the divine is still imperfectly drawn, it is often imagined that men may themselves attain to godhead, not merely after their death, but in their lifetime, through the temporary or permanent possession of their whole nature by a great and powerful spirit. No class of the community has benefited so much as kings by this belief in the possible incarnation of a god in human form. The doctrine of that incarnation, and with it the theory of the divinity of kings in the strict sense of the word, will form the subject of the following chapter.

Opposite: *Charles II of England is reputed to have touched as many as a hundred thousand persons to cure the "the King's Evil," a name given to scrofula.* Engraving by George Vertue.

Above: *A silver touchpiece of George III of England, presented to persons he touched for scrofula.* British Museum, London.

Chapter Five

GODS AS MORTALS

THE INSTANCES WHICH in the preceding
chapters I have drawn from the beliefs and
practices of rude peoples all over the world,
may suffice to prove that the savage fails to recognise
those limitations to his power over nature which seem
so obvious to us. In a society where every man is supposed to be endowed more or less with powers which
we should call supernatural, it is plain that the distinction between gods and men is somewhat blurred, or
rather has scarcely emerged. The conception of gods as
superhuman beings endowed with powers to which man
possesses nothing comparable in degree and hardly even
in kind, has been slowly evolved in the course of history. By primitive peoples the supernatural agents are not
regarded as greatly, if at all, superior to man; for they
may be frightened and coerced by him into doing his
will. At this stage of thought the world is viewed as a
great democracy; all beings in it, whether natural or
supernatural, are supposed to stand on a footing of tol-
erable equality. But with the growth of his knowledge
man learns to realise more clearly the vastness of nature
and his own littleness and feebleness in the presence of
it. The recognition of his helplessness does not, however, carry with it a corresponding belief in the impotence
of those supernatural beings with which his imagination
peoples the universe. On the contrary, it enhances his
conception of their power. For the idea of the world as
a system of impersonal forces acting in accordance with
fixed and invariable laws has not yet fully dawned or

Above: *An Aztec statue of the deified spirit of a woman who died in
childbirth.* National Anthropological Museum, Mexico City.

Opposite: *Head of a Yoruba king from Ife, Nigeria (fourteenth or
fifteenth century).* British Museum, London.

darkened upon him. The germ of the idea he certainly has, and he acts upon it, not only in magic art, but in much of the business of daily life. But the idea remains undeveloped, and so far as he attempts to explain the world he lives in, he pictures it as the manifestation of conscious will and personal agency. If then he feels himself to be so frail and slight, how vast and powerful must he deem the beings who control the gigantic machinery of nature! Thus as his old sense of equality with the gods slowly vanishes, he resigns at the same time the hope of directing the course of nature by his own unaided resources, that is, by magic, and looks more and more to the gods as the sole repositories of those supernatural powers which he once claimed to share with them. With the advance of knowledge, therefore, prayer and sacrifice assume the leading place in religious ritual; and magic, which once ranked with them as a legitimate equal, is gradually relegated to the background and sinks to the level of a black art. It is now regarded as an encroachment, at once vain and impious, on the domain of the gods, and as such encounters the steady opposition of the priests, whose reputation and influence rise or fall with those of their gods. Hence, when at a late period the distinction between religion and superstition has emerged, we find that sacrifice and prayer are the resource of the pious and enlightened portion of the community, while magic is the refuge of the superstitious and ignorant. But when, still later, the conception of the elemental forces as personal agents is giving way to the recognition of natural law; then magic, based as it implicitly is on the idea of a necessary and invariable sequence of cause and effect, independent of personal will, reappears from the obscurity and discredit into which it had fallen, and by investigating the causal sequences in nature, directly prepares the way for science. Alchemy leads up to chemistry.

The notion of a man-god, or of a human being endowed with divine or supernatural powers, belongs essentially to that earlier period of religious history in which gods and men are still viewed as beings of much the same order, and before they are divided by the impassable gulf which, to later thought, opens out between them. Strange, therefore, as may seem to us the idea of a god incarnate in human form, it has nothing very startling for early man, who sees in a man-god or a god-man only a higher degree of the same supernatural powers which he arrogates in perfect good faith to himself. Nor does he draw any very sharp distinction between a god and a powerful sorcerer. His gods are often merely invisible magicians who behind the veil of nature work the same sort of charms and incantations which the human magician works in a visible and bodily form among his fellows. And as the gods are commonly believed to exhibit themselves in the likeness of men to their worshippers, it is easy for the magician, with his supposed miraculous powers, to acquire the reputation of being an incarnate deity. Thus beginning as little more than a simple conjurer, the medicine-man or magician tends to blossom out into a full-blown god and king in one. Only in speaking of him as a god we must beware of importing into the savage conception of deity those very abstract and complex ideas which we attach to the term. Our ideas on this profound subject are the fruit of a long intellectual and moral evolution, and they are so far from being shared by the savage that he cannot even understand them when they are explained to him. Much of the controversy which has raged as to the religion of the lower races has sprung merely from a mutual misunderstanding. The savage does not understand the thoughts of the civilised man, and few civilised men understand the thoughts of the savage. When the savage uses his word for god, he has in his mind a being of a certain sort: when the civilised man uses his word for god, he has in his mind a being of a very different sort;

and if, as commonly happens, the two men are equally unable to place themselves at the other's point of view, nothing but confusion and mistakes can result from their discussions. If we civilised men insist on limiting the name of God to that particular conception of the divine nature which we ourselves have formed, then we must confess that the savage has no god at all. But we shall adhere more closely to the facts of history if we allow most of the higher savages at least to possess a rudimentary notion of certain supernatural beings who may fittingly be called gods, though not in the full sense in which we use the word. That rudimentary notion represents in all probability the germ out of which the civilised peoples have gradually evolved their own high conceptions of deity; and if we could trace the whole course of religious development, we might find that the chain which links our idea of the Godhead with that of the savage is one and unbroken.

With these explanations and cautions I will now adduce some examples of gods who have been believed by their worshippers to be incarnate in living human beings, whether men or women. The persons in whom a deity is thought to reveal himself are by no means always kings or descendants of kings; the supposed incarnation may take place even in men of the humblest rank. In India, for example, one human god started in life as a cotton-bleacher and another as the son of a carpenter. I shall therefore not draw my examples exclusively from royal personages, as I wish to illustrate the general principle of the deification of living men, in other words, the incarnation of a deity in human form. Such incarnate gods are common in rude society. The incarnation may be temporary or permanent. In the former case, the incarnation—commonly known as inspiration or possession—reveals itself in supernatural knowledge rather than in supernatural power. In other words, its usual manifestations are divination and prophecy rather than miracles. On the other hand, when the incarnation is not merely temporary, when the divine spirit has permanently taken up its abode in a human body, the god-man is usually expected to vindicate his character by working miracles. Only we have to

Above: *A traditional Nigerian witchdoctor in a state of trance.*

Opposite: *Gold coin bearing a portrait of Caligula, Roman emperor between A.D. 37 and 41. This despotic ruler demanded to be worshipped as a god.* Private collection.

remember that by men at this stage of thought miracles are not considered as breaches of natural law. Not conceiving the existence of natural law, primitive man cannot conceive a breach of it. A miracle is to him merely an unusually striking manifestation of a common power.

The belief in temporary incarnation or inspiration is world-wide. Certain persons are supposed to be possessed from time to time by a spirit or deity. While the possession lasts, their own personality lies in abeyance, the presence of the spirit is revealed by convulsive shiverings and shakings of the man's whole body, by wild gestures and excited looks, all of which are referred, not to the man himself, but to the spirit which has entered into him; and in this abnormal state all his utterances are

accepted as the voice of the god or spirit dwelling in him and speaking through him. Thus, for example, in the Sandwich Islands, the king, personating the god, uttered the responses of the oracle from his conceal-ment in a frame of wicker-work. But in the southern islands of the Pacific the god "frequently entered the priest, who, inflated as it were with the divinity, ceased to act or speak as a voluntary agent, but moved and spoke as entirely under supernatural influence. In this respect there was a striking resemblance between the rude oracles of the Polynesians, and those of the celebrated nations of ancient Greece. As soon as the god was supposed to have entered the priest, the lat-ter became violently agitated, and worked himself up to the highest pitch of apparent frenzy, the muscles of the limbs seemed convulsed, the body swelled, the countenance became terrific, the features distorted, and the eyes wild and strained. In this state he often rolled on the earth, foaming at the mouth, as if labouring under the influence of the divinity by whom he was possessed, and, in shrill cries, and violent and often indistinct sounds, revealed the will of the god. The priests, who were attending, and versed in the mysteries, received, and reported to the people, the declarations which had been thus received. When the priest had uttered the response of the oracle, the vio-lent paroxysm gradually subsided, and comparative composure ensued. The god did not, however, always leave him as soon as the communication had been made. Sometimes the same taura, or priest, continued for two or three days possessed by the spirit or deity; a piece of a native cloth, of a peculiar kind, worn round one arm, was an indication of inspiration, or of the indwelling of the god with the individual who wore it. The acts of the man during this period were considered as those of the god, and hence the greatest attention was paid to his expressions, and the whole of his deportment . . . When uruhia (under the inspira-tion of the spirit), the priest was always considered as sacred as the god, and was called, during this period, atua, god, though at other times only denominated taura or priest."

But examples of such temporary inspiration are so common in every part of the world and are now so familiar through books on ethnology that it is needless to multiply illustrations of the general principle. It may be well, however, to refer to two particular modes of producing temporary inspiration, because they are per-haps less known than some others. One of these modes of producing inspiration is by sucking the fresh blood of a sacrificed victim. In the temple of Apollo Diradiotes at Argos, a lamb was sacrificed by night once a month; a woman, who had to observe a rule of chastity, tasted the blood of the lamb, and thus being inspired by the god she prophesied or divined. At Aegira in Achaia the priestess of Earth drank the fresh blood of a bull before she descended into the cave to prophesy. Similarly among the Kuruvikkarans, a class of bird-catchers and beggars in southern India, the goddess Kali is believed to descend upon the priest, and he gives oracular replies after sucking the blood which streams from the cut throat of a goat. At a festival of the Alfoors of Minahassa, in northern Celebes, after a pig has been killed, the priest rushes furiously at it, thrusts his head into the car-case, and drinks of the blood. Then he is dragged away from it by force and set on a chair, whereupon he begins

Above: *Consultation of the ancient Greek oracle of Delphi. The proph-esying sibyl is seated on her tripod holding a laurel branch.* Painting by J.H. Vaida, 1914. From *The History of the Nations.*

Opposite: *The Hindu goddess Kali, who with her lolling tongue drinks blood out of a human skull.* Victoria and Albert Museum, London.

to prophesy how the rice-crop will turn out that year. A second time he runs at the carcase and drinks of the blood; a second time he is forced into the chair and continues his predictions. It is thought that there is a spirit in him which possesses the power of prophecy.

The other mode of producing temporary inspiration, to which I shall here refer, consists in the use of a sacred tree or plant. Thus in the Hindoo Koosh a fire is kindled with twigs of the sacred cedar; and the Dainyal or sibyl, with a cloth over her head inhales the thick pungent smoke till she is seized with convulsions and falls senseless to the ground. Soon she rises and raises a shrill chant, which is caught up and loudly repeated by her audience. So Apollo's prophetess ate the sacred laurel and was fumigated with it before she prophesied. The Bacchanals ate ivy, and their inspired fury was by some believed to be due to the exciting and intoxicating properties of the plant. In Uganda the priest, in order to be inspired by his god, smokes a pipe of tobacco fiercely till he works himself into a frenzy; the loud excited tones in which he then talks are recognised as the voice of the god speaking through him. In Madura, an island off the north coast of Java, each spirit has its regular medium, who is oftener a woman than a man. To prepare herself for the reception of the spirit she inhales the fumes of incense, sitting with her head over a smoking censer. Gradually she falls into a sort of trance accompanied by shrieks, grimaces, and violent spasms. The spirit is now supposed to have entered into her, and when she grows calmer her words are regarded as oracular, being the utterances of the indwelling spirit, while her own soul is temporarily absent.

The person temporarily inspired is believed to acquire, not merely divine knowledge, but also, at least occasionally, divine power. In Cambodia, when an epidemic breaks out, the inhabitants of several villages unite and go with a band of music at their head to look for the man whom the local god is supposed to have chosen for his temporary incarnation. When found, the man is conducted to the altar of the god, where the mystery of incarnation takes place. Then the man becomes an object of veneration to his fellows, who implore him to protect the village against the plague. A certain image of Apollo, which stood in a sacred cave at Hylae near Magnesia, was thought to impart superhuman strength. Sacred men, inspired by it, leaped down precipices, tore up huge trees by the roots, and carried them on their backs along the narrowest defiles. The feats performed by inspired dervishes belong to the same class.

Thus far we have seen that the savage, failing to discern the limits of his ability to control nature, ascribes to himself and to all men certain powers which we should now call supernatural. Further, we have seen that, over and above this general supernaturalism, some persons are supposed to be inspired for short periods by a divine spirit, and thus temporarily to enjoy the knowledge and power of the indwelling deity. From beliefs like these it is an easy step to the conviction that certain men are permanently possessed by a deity, or in some other undefined way are imbued with so high a degree of supernatural power as to be ranked as gods and to receive the homage of prayer and sacrifice. Sometimes these human gods are restricted to purely supernatural or spiritual functions. Sometimes they exercise supreme political power in addition. In the latter case they are kings as well as gods, and the government is a theocracy. Thus in the Marquesas or Washington Islands there was a class of men who were deified in their lifetime. They were supposed to wield a supernatural power over the elements: they could give abundant harvests or smite the ground with barrenness; and they could inflict disease or death. Human sacrifices were offered to them to avert their wrath. There were not many of them, at the most one or two in each island. They lived in mystic seclusion. Their powers were sometimes, but not always, hereditary. A missionary has described one of these human gods from personal observation. The god was a very old man who lived in a large house within an enclosure. In the house was a kind of altar, and on the beams of the house and on the trees round it were hung human skeletons, head down. No one entered the enclosure except the persons dedicated to the service of the god; only on days when human victims were sacrificed might ordinary people penetrate into the precinct.

Above: *Human sacrifices were made to appease the gods. This terracotta sculpture from Ife in Nigeria is thought to depict a gagged sacrificial victim.* Circa thirteenth century. Museum vör Völkerkunde, Berlin.

This human god received more sacrifices than all the other gods; often he would sit on a sort of scaffold in front of his house and call for two or three human victims at a time. They were always brought, for the terror he inspired was extreme. He was invoked all over the island, and offerings were sent to him from every side. Again, on the South Sea Islands in general we are told that each island had a man who represented or personified the divinity. Such men were called gods, and their substance was confounded with that of the deity. The man-god was sometimes the king himself; oftener he was a priest or subordinate chief.

The ancient Egyptians, far from restricting their adoration to cats and dogs and such small beer, very liberally extended it to men. One of these human deities resided at the village of Anabis, and burnt sacrifices were offered to him on the altars; after which, says Porphyry, he would eat his dinner just as if he were an ordinary mortal. In classical antiquity the Sicilian philosopher Empedocles gave himself out to be not merely a wizard but a god. Addressing his fellow-citizens in verse he said:

> O friends, in this great city that climbs the yellow slope
> Of Agrigentum's citadel, who make good works your scope,
> Who offer to the stranger a haven quiet and fair,
> All hail! Among you honoured I walk with lofty air.
> With garlands, blooming garlands you crown my
>   noble brow,
> A mortal man no longer, a deathless godhead now.
> Where e'er I go, the people crowd round and worship pay,
> And thousands follow seeking to learn the better way.
> Some crave prophetic visions, some smit with anguish sore
> Would fain hear words of comfort and suffer pain
>   no more.

He asserted that he could teach his disciples how to make the wind to blow or be still, the rain to fall and the sun to shine, how to banish sickness and old age and to raise the dead. When Demetrius Poliorcetes restored the Athenian democracy in 307 B.C., the Athenians decreed divine honours to him and his father Antigonus, both of them being then alive, under the title of the Saviour Gods. Altars were set up to the Saviours, and a priest appointed to attend to their worship. The people went forth to meet their deliverer with hymns and dances, with garlands and incense and libations; they lined the streets and sang that he was the only true god, for the other gods slept, or dwelt far away, or were not. In the words of a contemporary poet, which were chanted in public and sung in private:

> Of all the gods the greatest and the dearest
> To the city are come.
> For Demeter and Demetrius
> Together time has brought.
> She comes to hold the Maiden's awful rites,
> And he joyous and fair and laughing,
> As befits a god.
> A glorious sight, with all his friends about him,

Above (left): *Entrance to the palace of the oba, or king, of Benin, Nigeria. A turret features a python, king of snakes and messenger of the god Oluku, ruler of the seas.* Museum vör Völkerkunde, Berlin.

Above (right): *Sopono worshippers from Africa, who have been hypnotized by their witchdoctor and are being carried to the house for safety.*

Opposite: *The right to wear coral beads was restricted to senior chiefs in Benin, Nigeria.*

> *He in their midst,*
> *They like to stars, and he the sun.*
> *Son of Poseidon the mighty, Aphrodite's son,*
> *All hail!*
> *The other gods dwell far away,*
> *Or have no ears,*
> *Or are not, or pay us no heed.*
> *But thee we present see*
> *No god of wood or stone, but godhead true.*
> *Therefore to thee we pray.*

The ancient Germans believed that there was something holy in women, and accordingly consulted them as oracles. Their sacred women, we are told, looked on the eddying rivers and listened to the murmur or the roar of the water, and from the sight and sound foretold what would come to pass. But often the veneration of the men went further, and they worshipped women as true and living goddesses. For example, in the reign of Vespasian a certain Veleda, of the tribe of the Bructeri, was commonly held to be a deity, and in that character reigned over her people, her sway being acknowledged far and wide. She lived in a tower on the river Lippe, a tributary of the Rhine. When the people of Cologne sent to make a treaty with her, the ambassadors were not admitted to her presence; the negotiations were conducted through a minister, who acted as the mouthpiece of her divinity and reported her oracular utterances. The example shows how easily among our rude forefathers the ideas of divinity and royalty coalesced. It is said that among the Getae down to the beginning of our era there was always a man who personified a god and was called God by the people. He dwelt on a sacred mountain and acted as adviser to the king,

According to the early Portuguese historian, Dos Santos, the Zimbas, or Muzimbas, a people of southeastern Africa, "do not adore idols or recognize any god, they venerate and honour their king, whom they regard as a divinity, and they say he is the greatest and best in the world. And the said king says of himself that he alone is god of the earth, for which reason if it rains when he does not wish it to do so, or is too hot, he shoots arrows at the sky for not obeying him." The Mashona of southern Africa informed their bishop that they had once had a god, but that the Matabeles had driven him away. "This last was in reference to a curious custom in some villages of keeping a man they called their god. He seemed

Above: *The water-faeries or undines as Rhine-Maidens.* Arthur Rackham illustration for *The Rhine and the Valkyrie*, 1910.

Opposite: *Whirling dervishes of the Middle East. These Islamic mystics performed ecstatic dances.* From *Picart's Religious Ceremonies*, 1731.

which testified to the strength and elasticity of his divine legs.

The Baganda of Central Africa believed in a god of Lake Nyanza, who sometimes took up his abode in a man or woman. The incarnate god was much feared by all the people, including the king and the chiefs. When the mystery of incarnation had taken place, the man, or rather the god, removed about a mile and a half from the margin of the lake, and there awaited the appearance of the new moon before he engaged in his sacred duties. From the moment that the crescent moon appeared faintly in the sky, the king and all his subjects were at the command of the divine man, or Lubare (god), as he was called, who reigned supreme not only in matters of faith and ritual, but also in questions of war and state policy. He was consulted as an oracle; by his word he could inflict or heal sickness, withhold rain, and cause famine. Large presents were made him when his advice was sought. The chief of Urua, a large region to the west of Lake Tanganyika, "arrogates to himself divine honours and power and pretends to abstain from food for days without feeling its necessity; and, indeed, declares that as a god he is altogether above requiring food and only eats, drinks, and smokes for the pleasure it affords him." Among the Gallas, when a woman grows tired of the cares of housekeeping, she begins to talk incoherently and to demean herself extravagantly. This is a sign of the descent of the holy spirit Callo upon her. Immediately her husband prostrates himself and adores her; she ceases to bear the humble title of wife and is called "Lord;" domestic duties have no further claim on her, and her will is a divine law.

The king of Loango is honoured by his people "as though he were a god, and he is called Sambee and Pango, which mean god. They believe that he can let them have rain when he likes; and once a year, in December, which is the time they want rain, the people come to beg of him to grant it to them." On this occasion the king, standing on his throne, shoots an arrow into the air, which is supposed to bring on rain. Much the same is said of the king of Mombasa. Down to a few years ago, when his spiritual reign on earth was brought to an abrupt end by the car-

to be consulted by the people and had presents given to him. There was one at a village belonging to a chief Magondi, in the old days. We were asked not to fire off any guns near the village, or we should frighten him away." This Mashona god was formerly bound to render an annual tribute to the king of the Matabeles in the shape of four black oxen and one dance. A missionary has seen and described the deity discharging the latter part of his duty in front of the royal hut. For three mortal hours, without a break, to the banging of a tambourine, the click of castanettes, and the drone of a monotonous song, the swarthy god engaged in a frenzied dance, crouching on his hams like a tailor, sweating like a pig, and bounding about with an agility

nal weapons of English marines and bluejackets, the king of Benin was the chief object of worship in his dominions. "He occupies a higher post here than the Pope does in Catholic Europe; for he is not only God's vicegerent upon earth, but a god himself, whose subjects both obey and adore him as such, although I believe their adoration to arise rather from fear than love." The king of Iddah told the English officers of the Niger Expedition, "God made me after his own image; I am all the same as God; and he appointed me a king."

A peculiarly bloodthirsty monarch of Burma, by name Badonsachen, whose very countenance reflected the inbred ferocity of his nature, and under whose reign more victims perished by the executioner than by the common enemy, conceived the notion that he was something more than mortal, and that this high distinc-

tion had been granted him as a reward for his numerous good works. Accordingly he laid aside the title of king and aimed at making himself a god. With this view, and in imitation of Buddha, who, before being advanced to the rank of a divinity, had quitted his royal palace and seraglio and retired from the world, Badonsachen withdrew from his palace to an immense pagoda, the largest in the empire, which he had been engaged in constructing for many years. Here he held conferences with the most learned monks, in which he sought to persuade them that the five thousand years assigned for the observance of the law of Buddha were now elapsed, and that he himself was the god who was destined to appear after that period, and to abolish the old law by substituting his own. But to his great mortification many of the monks undertook to demonstrate the contrary; and this disap-

Above: *An Indian painting of the Hindu god Krishna.*

Opposite: *A priest of the Todas, a small tribe in the Nilghiri Hills of southern India, which has its own gods and survives from a pre-Hindu Indian culture. The priest stands beside a sacred buffalo and wears a patterned robe.*

pointment, combined with his love of power and his impatience under the restraints of an ascetic life, quickly disabused him of his imaginary godhead, and drove him back to his palace and his harem. The king of Siam "is venerated equally with a divinity. His subjects ought not to look him in the face; they prostrate themselves before him when he passes, and appear before him on their knees, their elbows resting on the ground." There is a special language devoted to his sacred person and attributes, and it must be used by all who speak to or of him. Even the natives have difficulty in mastering this

peculiar vocabulary. The hairs of the monarch's head, the soles of his feet, the breath of his body, indeed every single detail of his person, both outward and inward, have particular names. When he eats or drinks, sleeps or walks, a special word indicates that these acts are being performed by the sovereign, and such words cannot possibly be applied to the acts of any other person whatever. There is no word in the Siamese language by which any creature of higher rank or greater dignity than a monarch can be described; and the missionaries, when they speak of God, are forced to use the native word for king.

But perhaps no country in the world has been so prolific of human gods as India; nowhere has the divine grace been poured out in a more liberal measure on all classes of society from kings down to milkmen. Thus amongst the Todas, a pastoral people of the Nilghiri Hills of southern India, the dairy is a sanctuary, and the milkman who attends to it has been described as a god. On being asked whether the Todas salute the sun, one of these divine milkmen replied, "Those poor fellows do so, but I," tapping his chest, "I, a god! why should I salute the sun?" Everyone, even his own father, prostrates himself before the milkman, and no one would dare to refuse him anything. No human being, except another milkman, may touch him; and he gives oracles to all who consult him, speaking with the voice of a god.

Further, in India "every king is regarded as little short of a present god." The Hindoo law-book of Manu goes farther and says that "even an infant king must not be despised from an idea that he is a mere mortal; for he is a great deity in human form." There is said to have been a sect in Orissa some years ago who worshipped the late Queen Victoria in her lifetime as their chief divinity. And to this day in India all living persons remarkable for great strength or valour or for supposed miraculous powers run the risk of being worshipped as gods. Thus, a sect in the Punjab worshipped a deity whom they called Nikkal Sen. This Nikkal Sen was no other than the redoubted General Nicholson, and nothing that the general could do or say damped the ardour of his adorers. The more he punished them, the greater grew the religious awe with which they worshipped

him. At Benares not many years ago a celebrated deity was incarnate in the person of a Hindoo gentleman who rejoiced in the euphonious name of Swami Bhaskaranandaji Saraswati, and looked uncommonly like the late Cardinal Manning, only more ingenuous. His eyes beamed with kindly human interest, and he took what is described as an innocent pleasure in the divine honours paid him by his confiding worshippers.

At Chinchvad, a small town about ten miles from Poona in western India, there lives a family of whom one in each generation is believed by a large proportion of the Mahrattas to be an incarnation of the elephant-headed god Gunputty. That celebrated deity was first made flesh about the year 1640 in the person of a Brahman of Poona, by name Mooraba Gosseyn, who sought to work out his salvation by abstinence, mortification, and prayer. His piety had its reward. The god himself appeared to him in a vision of the night and promised that a portion of his, that is, of Gunputty's holy spirit should abide with him and with his seed after him even to the seventh generation. The divine promise was fulfilled. Seven successive incarnations, transmitted from father to son, manifested the light of Gunputty to a dark world. The last of the direct line, a heavy-looking god with very weak eyes, died in the year 1810. But the cause of truth was too sacred, and the value of the church property too considerable, to allow the Brahmans to contemplate with equanimity the unspeakable loss that would be sustained by a world which knew not Gunputty. Accordingly they sought and found a holy vessel in whom the divine spirit of the master had revealed itself anew, and the revelation has been happily continued in an unbroken succession of vessels from that time to this. But a mysterious law of spiritual economy, whose operation in the history of religion we may deplore though we cannot alter, has decreed that the miracles wrought by the god-man in these degenerate days cannot compare with those which were wrought by his predecessors in days gone by: and it is even reported that the only sign vouchsafed by him to the present generation of worshippers is the miracle of feeding the multitude whom he annually entertains to dinner at Chinchvad.

Above: *Queen Victoria was among a number of individuals said to have been worshipped by Indian sects.* Jubilee portrait by the nineteenth-century painter, Henry Campotosto.

Opposite: *The disciples of St. Columba (A.D. 421-597) worshipped him as an embodiment of Christ.* Illustration from Stephen Reid's *The Mighty Army*, London, 1912.

A Hindoo sect, which has many representatives in Bombay and central India, holds that its spiritual chiefs or Maharajas, as they are called, are representatives or even actual incarnations on earth of the god Krishna. And as Krishna looks down from heaven with most favour on such as minister to the wants of his successors and vicars on earth, a peculiar rite called self-devotion has been instituted, whereby his faithful worshippers make over their bodies, their souls, and, what is perhaps still more important, their worldly substance to his adorable incarnations; and women are taught to believe that the highest bliss for themselves and their families is to be attained by yielding themselves to the embraces of those beings in whom the divine nature mysteriously coexists with the form and even the appetites of true humanity.

Christianity itself has not uniformly escaped the taint of these unhappy delusions; indeed it has often been sullied by the extravagances of vain pretenders to a divinity equal to or even surpassing that of its great Founder. In the second century Montanus the Phrygian claimed to be the incarnate Trinity, uniting in his single person God the Father, God the Son, and God the Holy Ghost. Nor is this an isolated case, the exorbitant pretension of a single ill-balanced mind. From the earliest times down to the present day many sects have believed that Christ, nay God himself, is incarnate in every fully initiated Christian, and they have carried this belief to its logical conclusion by adoring each other. Tertullian records that this was done by his fellow-Christians at Carthage in the second century; the disciples of St. Columba worshipped him as an embodiment of Christ; and in the eighth century Elipandus of Toledo spoke of Christ as "a god among gods," meaning that all believers were gods just as truly as Jesus himself. The adoration of each other was customary among the Albigenses, and is noticed hundreds of times in the records of the Inquisition at Toulouse in the early part of the fourteenth century.

In the thirteenth century there arose a sect called the Brethren and Sisters of the Free Spirit, who held that by long and assiduous contemplation any man might be united to the deity in an inevitable manner and become one with the source and parent of all things, and that he who had thus ascended to God and been absorbed in his beatific essence, actually formed part of the godhead, was the Son of God in the same sense and manner with Christ himself, and enjoyed thereby a glorious immunity from the trammels of all laws human and divine. Inwardly transported by this blissful persuasion, though outwardly presenting in their aspect and manners a shocking air of lunacy and distraction, the sectaries roamed from place to place, attired in the most fantastic apparel and begging their bread with wild shouts and clamour, spurning indignantly every kind of honest labour and industry as an obstacle to divine contemplation and to the ascent of the soul towards the Father of spirits. In all their excursions they were followed by women with whom they lived on terms of the closest familiarity. Those of them who conceived they had made the greatest proficiency in the higher spiritual life dispensed with the use of clothes altogether in their assemblies, looking upon decency and modesty as marks of inward corruption, characteristics of a soul that still grovelled under the dominion of the flesh and had not yet been elevated into communion with the divine spirit, its centre and source. Sometimes their progress towards this mystic communion was accelerated by the Inquisition, and they expired in the flames, not merely with unclouded serenity, but with the most triumphant feelings of cheerfulness and joy.

Opposite: *Many Christian sects have believed that Christ is incarnate in every Christian. Christ on a Floral Cross by Harry Clarke.*

Below: *Tibetan Buddhist monks in the Labrung Monastery, China. The Dalai Lama of Lhasa is regarded as a living god, who on his death is reincarnated in a child.*

About the year 1830 there appeared, in one of the States of the American Union bordering on Kentucky, an imposter who declared that he was the Son of God, the Saviour of mankind, and that he had reappeared on earth to recall the impious, the unbelieving, and sinners to their duty. He protested that if they did not mend their ways within a certain time, he would give the signal, and in a moment the world would crumble to ruins. These extravagant pretensions were received with favour even by persons of wealth and position in society. At last a German humbly besought the new Messiah to announce the dreadful catastrophe to his fellow-countrymen in the German language, as they did not understand English, and it seemed a pity that they should be damned merely on that account. The would-be Saviour in reply confessed with great candour that he did not know German. "What!" retorted the German, "you the Son of God, and don't speak all languages, and don't even know German? Come, come, you are a knave, a hypocrite, and a mad-man. Bedlam is the place for you." The spectators laughed, and went away ashamed of their credulity.

Sometimes, at the death of the human incarnation, the divine spirit transmigrates into another man. The Buddhist Tartars believe in a great number of living Buddhas, who officiate as Grand Lamas at the head of the most important monasteries. When one of these Grand Lamas dies his disciples do not sorrow, for they know that he will soon reappear, being born in the form of an infant. Their only anxiety is to discover the place of his birth. If at this time they see a rainbow they take it as a sign sent them by the departed Lama to guide them to his cradle. Sometimes the divine infant himself reveals his identity. "I am the Grand Lama," he says, "the living Buddha of such and such a temple. Take me to my old monastery. I am its immortal head." In whatever way the birthplace of the Buddha is revealed, whether by the Buddha's own avowal or by the sign in the sky, tents are struck, and the joyful pilgrims, often headed by the king or one of the most illustrious of the royal family, set forth to find and bring home the infant god. Generally he is born in Tibet, the holy land, and to reach him the caravan has often to traverse the most frightful deserts. When at last they find the child they fall down and worship him. Before, however, he is acknowledged as the Grand Lama whom they seek he must satisfy them of his identity. He is asked the name of the monastery of which he claims to be the head , how far off it is, and how many monks live in it; he must also describe the habits of the deceased Grand Lama and the manner of his death. Then various articles, as prayer-books, tea-pots, and cups, are placed before him, and he has to point out those used by himself in his previous life. If he does so without a mistake his claims are admitted, and he is conducted in triumph to the monastery. At the head of all the Lamas is the Dalai Lama of Lhasa, the Rome of Tibet. He is regarded as a living god, and at death his divine and immortal spirit is born again in a child. According to some accounts the mode of discovering the Dalai Lama is similar to the method, already described, of discovering an ordinary Grand Lama. Other accounts speak of an election by drawing lots from a golden jar. Wherever he is born, the trees and plants put forth green leaves; at his bid-

Opposite: *The kings of Egypt were deified during their lifetimes and were given splendid burials to prepare them for the afterlife. This gold funerary mask of the Pharaoh Psusennes I is inlaid with lapis lazuli and black and white glass.* Egyptian National Museum, Cairo.

Above: *Ram caught in a thicket. An offering stand made of gold and precious stones which may have been a fertility symbol.* From the Royal Cemetery at Ur, Iraq, circa 2600 B.C. British Museum, London.

Above: *The site of the former Incan city of Macchu Pichu in the Peruvian Andes. The Incas believed they were descendants of the sun, which was the focus of their worship.*

Opposite: *Celebrants at the Sun Festival of the Quechua Indians of the Peruvian Andes.*

ding flowers bloom and springs of water rise; and his presence diffuses heavenly blessings.

But he is by no means the only man who poses as a god in these regions. A register of all the incarnate gods in the Chinese empire is kept in the Li fan yu an or Colonial Office at Peking. The number of gods who have thus taken out a license is 160. Tibet is blessed with thirty of them, northern Mongolia rejoices in nineteen, and southern Mongolia basks in the sunshine of no less than fifty-seven. The Chinese government, with a paternal solicitude for the welfare of its subjects, forbids the gods on the register to be reborn anywhere but in Tibet. They fear lest the birth of a god in Mongolia should have serious political consequences by stirring the dormant patriotism and warlike spirit of the Mongols, who might rally round an ambitious native deity of royal lineage and seek to win for him, at the point of the sword, a temporal as well as a spiritual kingdom. But besides these public or licensed gods there are a great many little private gods, or unlicensed practitioners of divinity, who work miracles and bless their people in holes and corners; and of late years the Chinese government has winked at the rebirth of these pettifogging deities outside of Tibet. However, once

they are born, the government keeps its eye on them as well as on the regular practitioners, and if any of them misbehaves he is promptly degraded, banished to a distant monastery, and strictly forbidden ever to be born again in the flesh.

From our survey of the religious position occupied by the king in rude societies we may infer that the claim to divine and supernatural powers put forward by the monarchs of great historical empires, like those of Egypt, Mexico, and Peru, was not the simple outcome of inflated vanity or the empty expression of a grovelling adulation; it was merely a survival and extension of the old savage apotheosis of living kings. Thus, for example, as children of the Sun the Incas of Peru were revered like gods; they could do no wrong, and no one dreamed of offending against the person, honour, or property of the monarch or of any of the royal race. Hence, too, the Incas did not, like most people, look on sickness as an evil. They considered it as a messenger sent from their father the Sun to call them to come and rest with him in heaven. Therefore the usual words in which an Inca announced his approaching end were these: "My father calls me to come and rest with him." They would not oppose their father's will by offering sacrifice for recovery, but openly declared that he had called them to his rest. Issuing from the sultry valleys upon the lofty tableland of the Colombian Andes, the Spanish conquerors were astonished to find, in contrast to the savage hordes they had left in the sweltering jungles below, a people enjoying a fair degree of civilisation, practising agriculture, and living under a government which Humboldt has compared to the theocracies of Tibet and Japan. These were the Chibchas, Muyscas, or Mozcas, divided into two kingdoms, with capitals at Bogota and Tunja, but united apparently in spiritual allegiance to the high pontiff of Sogapozo or Iraca. By a long and ascetic novitiate, this ghostly ruler was reputed to have acquired such sanctity that the waters and the rain obeyed him, and the weather depended on his will. The Mexican kings at their accession took an oath that they would make the sun to shine, the clouds to give rain, the rivers to flow, and the earth to bring forth fruits in

celebrated in special temples and by special priests. Indeed the worship of the kings sometimes cast that of the gods into the shade. Thus in the reign of Merenra a high official declared that he had built many holy places in order that the spirits of the king, the ever-living Merenra, might be invoked "more than all the gods." "It has never been doubted that the king claimed actual divinity; he was the 'great god,' the 'golden Horus,' and son of Ra. He claimed authority not only over Egypt, but over 'all lands and nations,' 'the whole world in its length and its breadth, the east and the west,' 'the entire compass of the great circuit of the sun,' 'the sky and what is in it, the earth and all that is upon it,' 'every creature that walks upon two or upon four legs, all that fly or flutter, the whole world offers her productions to him.' Whatever in fact might be asserted of the Sun-god, was dogmatically predicable of the king of Egypt. His titles were directly derived from those of the Sun-god." "In the course of his existence," we are told, "the king of Egypt exhausted all the possible conceptions of divinity which the Egyptians had framed for themselves. A superhuman god by his birth and by his royal office, he became the deified man after his death. Thus all that was known of the divine was summed up in him."

abundance. We are told that Montezuma, the last king of Mexico, was worshipped by his people as a god.

The early Babylonian kings, from the time of Sargon I till the fourth dynasty of Ur or later, claimed to be gods in their lifetime. The monarchs of the fourth dynasty of Ur in particular had temples built in their honour; they set up statues in various sanctuaries and commanded the people to sacrifice to them; the eighth month was especially dedicated to the kings, and sacrifices were offered to them at the new moon and on the fifteenth of each month. Again, the Parthian monarchs of the Arsacid house styled themselves brothers of the sun and moon and were worshipped as deities. It was esteemed sacrilege to strike even a private member of the Arsacid family in a brawl.

The kings of Egypt were deified in their lifetime, sacrifices were offered to them, and their worship was

We have now completed our sketch, for it is no more than a sketch, of the evolution of that sacred kingship which attained its highest form, its most absolute expression, in the monarchies of Peru and Egypt. Historically, the institution appears to have originated in the order of public magicians or medicine-men; logically it rests on a mistaken deduction from the association of ideas. Men mistook the order of their ideas for the order of nature, and hence imagined that the control which they have, or seem to have, over their thoughts, permitted them to exercise a corresponding control over things. The men who for one reason or another, because of the strength or the weakness of their natural parts, were supposed to possess these magical powers in the highest degree, were gradually marked off from their fellows and became a separate class, who were destined to exercise a most far-reaching influence on the political, religious, and intellectual evolution of mankind. Social progress, as we know, consists mainly in a successive differentiation of functions, or, in simpler language, a division of labour. The work which in primitive society is done by all alike and by all equally ill, or nearly so, is gradually distributed among different classes of workers and executed more and more perfectly; and so far as the products, material or immaterial, of this specialised labour are shared by all, the whole community benefits by the increasing specialisation. Now magicians or medicine-men appear to constitute the oldest artificial or professional class in the evolution of society. For sorcerers are found in every savage tribe known to us; and among the simplest peoples, such as the Australian aborigines, they are the only professional class that exists. As time goes on, and the process of differentiation continues, the order of medicine-men is itself subdivided into such classes as the healers of disease, the makers of rain, and so forth; while the most powerful member of the order wins for himself a position as chief and gradually develops into a sacred king, his old magical functions falling more and more into the background and being exchanged for priestly or even divine duties, in proportion as magic is slowly ousted by religion. Still later, a partition is effected between the civil and the religious aspect of the kingship, the temporal power being committed to one man and the spiritual to another. Meanwhile the magicians, who may be repressed but cannot be extirpated by the predominance of religion, still addict themselves to their old occult arts in preference to the newer ritual of sacrifice and prayer; and in time the more sagacious of their number perceive the fallacy of magic and hit upon a more effectual mode of manipulating the forces of nature for the good of man; in short, they abandon sorcery for science. I am far from affirming that the course of development has everywhere rigidly followed these lines: it has doubtless varied greatly in different societies. I merely mean to indicate in the broadest outline what I can see to have been its general trend. Regarded from the industrial point of view the evolution has been from uniformity to diver-

sity of function; regarded from the political point of view, it has been from democracy to despotism. With the later history of monarchy, especially with the decay of despotism and its displacement by forms of government better adapted to the higher needs of humanity, we are not concerned in this enquiry: our theme is the growth, not the decay, of a great and, in its time, beneficent institution.

Opposite: *A seventeenth-century magician, possibly portraying Faust, with a magic mirror.* Etching by Rembrandt, c. 1650. British Museum, London.

Below: *"Feeding the sacred ibises in the Halls of Karnak."* Engraving by Joubert, 1874, of a painting by E.J. Poynter.

Chapter Six

TREE WORSHIP

IN THE RELIGIOUS history of the Aryan race in Europe the worship of trees has played an important part. Nothing could be more natural. For at the dawn of history Europe was covered with immense primaeval forests, in which the scattered clearings must have appeared like islets in an ocean of green. Down to the first century before our era the Hercynian forest stretched eastward from the Rhine for a distance at once vast and unknown; Germans whom Caesar questioned had travelled for two months through it without reaching the end. Four centuries later it was visited by the Emperor Julian, and the solitude, the gloom, the silence of the forest appear to have made a deep impression on his sensitive nature. He declared that he knew nothing like it in the Roman empire. In our own country the wealds of Kent, Surrey, and Sussex are remnants of the great forest of Anderida, which once clothed the whole of the south-eastern portion of the island. Westward it seems to have stretched till it joined another forest that extended from Hampshire to Devon. In the reign of Henry II the citizens of London still hunted the wild bull and the boar in the woods of Hampstead, now firmly a part of London. Even under the later Plantagenets the royal forests were sixty-eight in number. In the forest of Arden it was said that down to modern times a squirrel might leap from tree to tree for nearly the whole length of Warwickshire. The excavation of ancient pile-villages in the valley of the Po has shown that long before the rise and probably the foun-

dation of Rome the north of Italy was covered with dense woods of elms, chestnuts, and especially of oaks. Archaeology is here confirmed by history; for classical writers contain many references to Italian forests which have now disappeared. As late as the fourth century before our era Rome was divided from central Etruria by the dreaded Ciminian forest, which Livy compares to the woods of Germany. No merchant, if we may trust the Roman historian, had ever penetrated its pathless solitudes; and it was deemed a most daring feat when a Roman general, after sending two scouts to

Above: *A Druid priestess with the sacred mistletoe.* Engraving from *Harper's Monthly Magazine* in 1885.

Opposite: *Daphne and Apollo, showing the nymph at the moment of her metamorphosis into a tree, which was to bear her name.* Painting by Antonio Pollaiuolo, 1470-80. National Gallery, London.

explore its intricacies, led his army into the forest and, making his way to a ridge of the wooded mountains, looked down on the rich Etrurian fields spread out below. In Greece beautiful woods of pine, oak, and other trees still linger on the slopes of the high Arcadian mountains, still adorn with their verdure the deep gorge through which the Ladon hurries to join the sacred Alpheus, and were still, down to a few years ago, mirrored in the dark blue waters of the lonely lake of Pheneus; but they are mere fragments of the forests which clothed great tracts in antiquity, and which at a

Above: *The sacred tree Irmensul of Teutonic mythology, represented as here as a man, but often taking the form of a tree-trunk. From P. Lacroix's* Manners, Customs and Dress in the Middle Ages, *1876.*

Opposite: *A deer eating from the World-Tree of Viking mythology. Carving on the side of the stave church at Urnes in Norway.*

more remote epoch may have spanned the Greek peninsula from sea to sea.

From an examination of the Teutonic words for "temple" Grimm has made it probable that amongst the Germans the oldest sanctuaries were natural woods. However that may be, tree-worship is well attested for all the great European families of the Aryan stock. Amongst the Celts the oak-worship of the Druids is familiar to every one, and their old word for sanctuary seems to be identical in origin and meaning with the Latin nemus, a grove or woodland glade, which still survives in the name of Nemi, in Italy. Sacred groves were common among the ancient Germans, and tree-worship is hardly extinct amongst their descendants at the present day. How serious that worship was in former times may be gathered from the ferocious penalty appointed by the old German laws for such as dared to peel the bark of a standing tree. The culprit's navel was to be cut out and nailed to the part of the tree which he had peeled, and he was to be driven round and round the tree till all his guts were wound about its trunk. The intention of the punishment clearly was to replace the dead bark by a living substitute taken from the culprit; it was a life for a life, the life of a man for the life of a tree. At Upsala, the old religious capital of Sweden, there was a sacred grove in which every tree was regarded as divine. The heathen Slavs worshipped trees and groves. The Lithuanians were not converted to Christianity till towards the close of the fourteenth century, and amongst them at the date of their conversion the worship of trees was prominent. Some of them revered remarkable oaks and other great shady trees, from which they received oracular responses. Some maintained holy groves about their villages or houses, where even to break a twig would have been a sin. They thought that he who cut a bough in such a grove either died suddenly or was crippled on one of his limbs. Proofs of the prevalence of tree-worship in ancient Greece and Italy are abundant. In the sanctuary of Aesculapius at Cos, for example, it was forbidden to cut down the cypress-trees under a penalty of a thousand drachms. But nowhere, perhaps, in the ancient world was this antique form of religion better preserved than in the heart of the great metropolis itself. In the Forum, the busy centre of Roman life, the sacred fig-tree of Romulus was worshipped down to the days of the empire, and the withering of its trunk was enough to spread consternation through the city. Again, on the slope of the Palatine Hill grew a cornel-tree which was esteemed one of the most sacred objects in Rome. Whenever the tree appeared to a passer-by to be drooping, he set up a hue and cry which was echoed by the people in the street, and soon a crowd might be seen running helter-skelter from all sides with buckets of water, as if (says Plutarch) they were hastening to put out a fire.

Among the tribes of the Finnish-Ugrian stock in Europe the heathen worship was performed for the most part in sacred groves, which were always enclosed with a fence. Such a grove often consisted merely of a glade or clearing with a few trees dotted about, upon which in former times the skins of the sacrificial victims were hung. The central point of the grove, at least among the tribes of the Volga, was the sacred tree, beside which everything else sank into insignificance. Before it the worshippers assembled and the priest offered his prayers, at its roots the victim was sacrificed, and its boughs sometimes served as a pulpit. No wood might be hewn and no branch broken in the grove, and women were generally forbidden to enter it.

But it is necessary to examine in some detail the notions on which the worship of trees and plants is based. To the savage the world in general is animate, and trees and plants are no exception to the rule. He thinks that they have souls like his own, and he treats them accordingly. "They say," writes the ancient vegetarian Porphyry, "that primitive men led an unhappy life, for their superstition did not stop at animals but extended even to plants. For why should the slaughter of an ox or a sheep be a greater wrong than the felling of a fir or an oak, seeing that a soul is implanted in these trees also?" Similarly, the Hidatsa Indians of North America believe that every natural object has its spirit, or to speak more properly, its shade. To these shades some consideration

or respect is due, but not equally to all. For example, the shade of the cottonwood, the greatest tree in the valley of the Upper Missouri, is supposed to possess an intelligence which, if properly approached, may help the Indians in certain undertakings; but the shades of shrubs and grasses are of little account. When the Missouri, swollen by a freshet in spring, carries away part of its banks and sweeps some tall tree into its current, it is said that the spirit of the tree cries, while the roots still cling to the land and until the trunk falls with a splash into the stream. Formerly the Indians considered it wrong to fell one of these giants, and when large logs were needed they made use only of trees which had fallen of themselves. Till lately some of the more credulous old men declared that many of the misfortunes of their people were caused by this modern disregard for the rights of the living cottonwood. The Iroquois believed that each species of tree, shrub, plant, and herb had its own spirit, and to these spirits it was their custom to return thanks. The Wanika of Eastern Africa fancy that every tree, and especially every cocoanut

Above: *This shrine in Ghana is that of the Omanhe of Anomabu, of the Fanti tribe, and his household. On the death of the king, his personal stool is returned to the root of the tree, its place of origin and source of spiritual power.*

Opposite: *An elder of the Kayopo tribe of the Brazilian Amazon. To appease the tree spirits. he paints his face before going into the forest.*

tree, has its spirit; "the destruction of a cocoanut tree is regarded as equivalent to matricide, because that tree gives them life and nourishment, as a mother does her child." Siamese monks, believing that there are souls everywhere, and that to destroy anything whatever is forcibly to dispossess a soul, will not break a branch of a tree, "as they will not break the arm of an innocent person." These monks, of course, are Buddhists. But Buddhist animism is not a philosophical theory. It is simply a common savage dogma incorporated in the system of an historical religion. To suppose, with Benfey and others, that the theories of animism and transmigration current among rude peoples of Asia are derived from Buddhism, is to reverse the facts.

Sometimes it is only particular sorts of trees that are supposed to be tenanted by spirits. At Grbalj in Dalmatia it is said that among great beeches, oaks, and other trees there are some that are endowed with shades or souls, and whoever fells one of them must die on the spot, or at least live an invalid for the rest of his days. If a woodman fears that a tree which he has felled is one of this sort, he must cut off the head of a live hen on the stump of the tree with the very same axe with which he cut down the tree. This will protect him from all harm, even if the tree be one of the animated kind. The silk-cotton trees, which rear their enormous trunks to a stupendous height, far out-topping all the other trees of the forest, are regarded with reverence throughout West Africa, from the Senegal to the Niger, and are believed to be the abode of a god or spirit. Among the Ewe-speaking peoples of the Slave Coast the indwelling god of this giant of the forest goes by the name of Huntin. Trees in which he specially dwells—for it is not every silk-cotton tree that he thus honours—are surrounded by a girdle of palm-leaves; and sacrifices of fowls, and occasionally of human beings, are fastened to the trunk or laid against the foot of the tree. A tree distinguished by a girdle of palm-leaves may not be cut down or injured in any way; and even silk-cotton trees which are not supposed to be animated by Huntin may not be felled unless the woodman first offers a sacrifice of fowls and palm-oil to purge himself of the proposed sacrilege. To omit the sacrifice is an offence which may be punished with death. Among the Kangra mountains of the Punjaub a girl used to be annually sacrificed to an old cedar-tree, the families of the village taking it in turn to supply the victim. The tree was cut down not very many years ago.

If trees are animate, they are necessarily sensitive and the cutting of them down becomes a delicate surgical operation, which must be performed with as tender a regard as possible for the feelings of the sufferers, who otherwise may turn and rend the careless or bungling operator. When an oak is being felled "it gives a kind of shriekes or groanes, that may be heard a mile off, as if it were the genius of the oake lamenting. E. Wyld, Esq., hath heard it severall times."

The Ojebways "very seldom cut down green or living trees, from the idea that it puts them to pain, and some of their medicine-men profess to have heard the wailing of the trees under the axe." Trees that bleed and utter cries of pain or indignation when they are hacked or burned occur very often in Chinese books, even in standard histories. Old peasants in some parts of Austria still believe that forest-trees are animate, and will not allow an incision to be made in the bark without special cause; they have heard from their fathers that the tree feels the cut not less than a wounded man his hurt. In felling a tree they beg its pardon. It is said that in the Upper Palatinate of Germany also old woodmen still secretly ask a fine, sound tree to forgive them before they cut it down. So in Jarkino the woodman craves pardon of the tree he fells. Before the Ilocanes of Luzon cut down trees in the virgin forest or on the mountains, they recite some verses to the following effect: "Be not uneasy, my friend, though we fell what we have been ordered to fell." This they do in order not to draw down on themselves the hatred of the spirits who live in the trees, and who are apt to avenge themselves by visiting with grievous sickness those who injure them wantonly. The Basoga of Central Africa think that, when a tree is cut down, the angry spirit which inhabits it may cause the death of the chief and his family. To prevent this dis-

aster they consult a medicine-man before they fell a tree. If the man of skill gives leave to proceed, the woodman first offers a fowl and a goat to the tree; then as soon as he has given the first blow with the axe, he applies his mouth to the cut and sucks some of the sap. In this way he forms a brotherhood with the tree, just as two men become blood-brothers by sucking each other's blood. After that he can cut down his tree-brother with impunity.

But the spirits of vegetation are not always treated with deference and respect. If fair words and kind treatment do not move them, stronger measures are sometimes resorted to. The durian-tree of the East Indies, whose smooth stem often shoots up to a height of eighty or ninety feet without sending out a branch, bears a fruit of the most delicious flavour and the most disgusting stench. The Malays cultivate the tree for the sake of its fruit, and have been known to resort to a peculiar ceremony for the purpose of stimulating its fertility. Near Jugra in Selangor there is a small grove of durian-trees, and on a specially chosen day the villagers used to assemble in it. Thereupon one of the local sorcerers would take a hatchet and deliver several shrewd blows on the trunk of the most barren of the trees, saying, "Will you now bear fruit or not? If you do not, I shall fell you." To this the tree replied through the mouth of another man who had climbed a mangostin-tree hard by (the durian-tree being unclimbable), "Yes, I will now bear fruit; I beg of you not to fell me." Similarly, in Japan to make trees bear fruit two men go into an orchard. One of them climbs up a tree and the other stands at the foot with an axe. The man with the axe asks the tree whether it will yield a good crop next year and threatens to cut it down if it does not. To this the man among the branches replies on behalf of the tree that it will bear abundantly. Odd as this mode of horticulture may seem to us, it has its exact parallels in Europe. On Christmas Eve many a South Slavonian and Bulgarian peasant swings an axe threateningly against a barren fruit-tree, while another man standing by intercedes for the menaced tree, saying, "Do not cut it down; it will soon bear fruit." Thrice the axe is swung, and thrice the

Above: *In China, trees are planted on graves to strengthen the souls of the deceased. A traditional graveyard in the province of Yunnan.*

Opposite: *The Assyrian King Ashurnasirpal II standing before the Tree of Life, which is surmounted by the symbol of the god Ashur. Relief from Nimrud in Iraq, 883-859 B.C. British Museum, London.*

impending blow is arrested at the entreaty of the intercessor. After that the frightened tree will certainly bear fruit next year.

The conception of trees and plants as animated beings naturally results in treating them as male and female, who can be married to each other in a real, and not merely a figurative or poetical, sense of the word. The notion is not purely fanciful, for plants like animals have their sexes and reproduce their kind by the union of the male and female elements. But whereas in all the higher animals the organs of the two sexes are regularly separated between different individuals, in most plants they exist together in every individual of the species. This rule, however, is by no means universal, and in

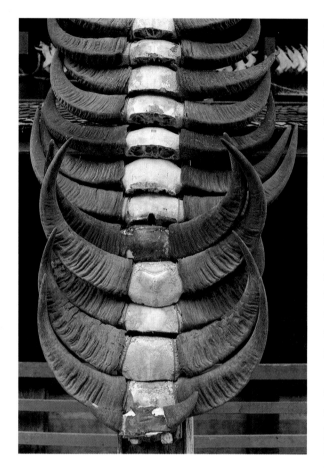

Above: *The Toradja people of Sulawesi kill a buffalo, pig or goat when a new house is built. The main pillar in this house is garnished with sets of buffalo horns.*

Opposite: *The Tree of Life is a potent symbol in many cultures. Nineteenth-century Persian carpet design.*

many species the male plant is distinct from the female. The distinction appears to have been observed by some savages, for we are told that the Maoris "are acquainted with the sex of trees, etc., and have distinct names for the male and female of some trees." The ancients knew the difference between the male and the female date-palm, and fertilised them artificially by shaking the pollen of the male tree over the flowers of the female. The fertilisation took place in spring. Among the heathen of Harran the month during which the palms were fertilised bore the name of the Date Month, and at this time they celebrated the marriage festival of all the gods and goddesses. Different from this true and fruitful marriage of the palm are the false and barren marriages of plants which play a part in Hindoo superstition. For example, if a Hindoo has planted a grove of mangos, neither he nor his wife may taste of the fruit until he has formally married one of the trees, as a bridegroom, to a tree of a different sort, commonly a tamarind-tree, which grows near it in the grove. If there is no tamarind to act as bride, a jasmine will serve the turn. The expenses of such a marriage are often considerable, for the more Brahmans are feasted at it, the greater the glory of the owner of the grove. A family has been known to sell its golden and silver trinkets, and to borrow all the money they could in order to marry a mango-tree to a jasmine with due pomp and ceremony. On Christmas Eve German peasants used to tie fruit-trees together with straw ropes to make them bear fruit, saying that the trees were thus married.

In the Moluccas, when the clove-trees are in blossom, they are treated like pregnant women. No noise may be made near them; no light or fire may be carried past them at night; no one may approach them with his hat on, all must uncover in their presence. These precautions are observed lest the tree should be alarmed and bear no fruit, or should drop its fruit too soon, like the untimely delivery of a woman who has been frightened in her pregnancy. So in the East the growing rice-crop is often treated with the same considerate regard as a breeding woman. Thus in Amboyna, when the rice is in bloom, the people say that it is pregnant and fire no guns and make no other noises near the field, for fear lest, if the rice were thus disturbed, it would miscarry, and the crop would be all straw and no grain.

Sometimes it is the souls of the dead which are believed to animate trees. The Dieri tribe of Central Australia regard as very sacred certain trees which are supposed to be their fathers transformed; hence they speak with reverence of these trees, and are careful that they shall not be cut down or burned. If the settlers require them to hew down the trees, they earnestly protest against it, asserting that were they to do so they would have no luck, and might be punished for not pro-

tecting their ancestors. Some of the Philippine Islanders believe that the souls of their ancestors are in certain trees, which they therefore spare. If they are obliged to fell one of these trees, they excuse themselves to it by saying that it was the priest who made them do it. The spirits take up their abode, by preference, in tall and stately trees with great spreading branches. When the wind rustles the leaves, the natives fancy it is the voice of the spirit; and they never pass near one of these trees without bowing respectfully, and asking pardon of the spirit for disturbing his repose. Among the Igorrotes, every village has its sacred tree, in which the souls of the dead forefathers of the hamlet reside. Offerings are made to the tree, and any injury done to it is believed to entail some misfortune on the village. Were the tree cut down, the village and all its inhabitants would inevitably perish.

In Korea the souls of people who die of the plague or by the road-side, and of women who expire in childbirth, invariably take up their abode in trees. To such spirits offerings of cake, wine, and pork are made on heaps of stones piled under the trees. In China it has been customary from time immemorial to plant trees on graves in order thereby to strengthen the soul of the deceased and thus to save his body from corruption; and as the evergreen cypress and pine are deemed to be fuller of vitality than other trees, they have been chosen by preference for this purpose. Hence the trees that grow on graves are sometimes identified with the souls of the departed. Among the Miao-Kia, an aboriginal race of southern and western China, a sacred tree stands at the entrance of every village, and the inhabitants believe that it is tenanted by the soul of their first ancestor and that it rules their destiny. Sometimes there is a sacred grove near a village, where the trees are suffered to rot and die on the spot. Their fallen branches cumber the ground, and no one may remove them unless he has first asked leave of the spirit of the tree and offered him a sacrifice. Among the Maraves of southern Africa the burial-ground is always regarded as a holy place where neither a tree may be felled nor a beast killed, because everything there is supposed to be tenanted by the souls of the dead.

In most, if not all, of these cases the spirit is viewed as incorporate in the tree; it animates the tree and must suffer and die with it. But, according to another and probably later opinion, the tree is not the body, but merely the abode of the tree-spirit, which can quit it and return to it at pleasure. The inhabitants of Siaoo, an East Indian island, believe in certain sylvan spirits who dwell in forests or in great solitary trees. At full moon the spirit comes forth from his lurking-place and roams about. He has a big head, very long arms and legs, and a ponderous body. In order to propitiate the wood-spirits people bring offerings of food, fowls, goats, and so forth to the places which they are supposed to haunt. The people of Nias think that, when a tree dies, its liberated spirit becomes a demon, which can kill a cocoanut palm by merely lighting on its branches, and can cause the death of all the children in a house by perching on one of the posts that support it. Further, they are of opinion that certain trees are at all times inhabited by roving demons who, if the trees were damaged, would be set free to go about on errands of mischief. Hence the people respect these trees, and are careful not to cut them down.

Not a few ceremonies observed at cutting down haunted trees are based on the belief that the spirits have it in their power to quit the trees at pleasure or in case of need. Thus when the Pelew Islanders are felling a tree, they conjure the spirit of the tree to leave it and settle on another. The wily Negro of the Slave Coast, who wishes to fell an ashorin tree, but knows that he cannot do it so long as the spirit remains in the tree, places a little palm-oil on the ground as a bait, and then, when the unsuspecting spirit has quitted the tree to partake of this dainty, hastens to cut down its late abode. When the Toboongkoos of Celebes are about to clear a piece of forest in order to plant rice, they build a tiny house and furnish it with tiny clothes and some food and gold. Then they call together all the spirits of the wood, offer them the little house with its contents, and beseech them to quit the spot. After that they may safely cut down the wood without fearing to wound themselves in so doing. Before the Tomori, another tribe of Celebes, fell a tall tree they lay a quid of betel at its foot, and invite the spirit who dwells in the tree to change his lodging; moreover, they set a little ladder against the trunk to enable him to descend with safety and comfort. The Mandelings of Sumatra endeavour to lay the blame of all such misdeeds at the door of the Dutch authorities. Thus when a man is cutting a road through a forest and has to fell a tall tree which blocks the way, he will not begin to ply his axe until he has said: "Spirit who lodgest in this tree, take it not ill that I cut down thy dwelling, for it is done at no wish of mine but by order of the Controller." And when he wishes to clear a piece of forest-land for cultivation, it is necessary that he should come to a satisfactory understanding with the woodland spirits who live there before he lays low their leafy dwellings. For this purpose he goes to the middle of the plot of ground, stoops down, and pretends to pick up a letter. Then unfolding a bit of paper he reads aloud an imaginary letter from the Dutch Government, in which he is strictly enjoined to set about clearing the land without delay. Having done so, he says: "You hear that, spirits. I must begin clearing at once, or I shall be hanged."

Even when a tree has been felled, sawn into planks, and used to build a house, it is possible that the woodland spirit may still be lurking in the timber, and accordingly some people seek to propitiate him before or after they occupy the new house. Hence, when a new dwelling is ready the Toradjas of Celebes kill a goat, a pig, or a buffalo, and smear all the woodwork with its blood. If the building is a lobo or spirit-house, a fowl or a dog is killed on the ridge of the roof, and its blood allowed to flow down on both sides. The ruder Tonapoo in such a case sacrifice a human being on the roof. This sacrifice on the roof of a lobo or temple serves the same purpose as the smearing of blood on the woodwork of an ordinary house. The intention is to propitiate the forest-spirits who may still be in the timber; they are thus

Above: *A Maori carving of a Tekoteko as a house-guardian, at Shakare Wasrewa Botorua, New Zealand.*

Opposite: *A twentieth-century mask of wood, fibre, bells and ammunition cases, thought to represent a forest spirit. From the Dan-Ngere tribal complex, West African coast.* Schindler Collection, New York.

put in good humour and will do the inmates of the house no harm. For a like reason people in Celebes and the Moluccas are much afraid of planting a post upside down at the building of a house; for the forest-spirit, who might still be in the timber, would very naturally resent the indignity and visit the inmates with sickness. The Kayans of Borneo are of opinion that tree-spirits stand very stiffly on the point of honour and visit men with their displeasure for any injury done to them. Hence after building a house, whereby they have been forced to ill-treat many trees, these people observe a period of penance for a year during which they must abstain from many things, such as the killing of bears, tiger-cats, and serpents.

When a tree comes to be viewed, no longer as the body of the tree-spirit, but simply as its abode which it can quit at pleasure, an important advance has been made in religious thought. Animism is passing into polytheism. In other words, instead of regarding each tree as a living and conscious being, man now sees in it merely a lifeless, inert mass, tenanted for a longer or shorter time by a supernatural being who, as he can pass freely from tree to tree, thereby enjoys a certain right of possession or lordship over the trees, and, ceasing to be a tree-soul, becomes a forest god. As soon as the tree-spirit is thus in a measure disengaged from each particular tree, he begins to change his shape and assume the body of a man, in virtue of a general tendency of early thought to clothe all abstract spiritual beings in concrete human form. Hence in classical art the sylvan deities are depicted in human shape, their woodland character being denoted by a branch or some equally obvious symbol. But this change of shape does not affect the essential character of the tree-spirit. The powers which he exercised as a tree-soul incorporate and dwelling in a tree, he still continues to wield as a god of trees. This I shall now attempt to prove in detail. Thus, trees considered as animate beings are credited with the power of making the rain to fall, the sun to shine, flocks and herds to multiply, and women to bring forth easily; and, equally, the very same powers are attributed to tree-gods conceived as anthropomorphic beings or as actually incarnate in living men.

First, then, trees or tree-spirits are believed to give rain and sunshine. When the missionary Jerome of Prague was persuading the heathen Lithuanians to fell their sacred groves, a multitude of women besought the Prince of Lithuania to stop him, saying that with the woods he was destroying the house of god from which they had been wont to get rain and sunshine. The Mundaris in Assam think that if a tree in the sacred grove is felled the sylvan gods evince their displeasure by withholding rain. In order to procure rain the inhabitants of Monyo, a village in the Sagaing district of Upper Burma, chose the largest tamarind-tree near the village and named it the haunt of the spirit (nat) who

Above: *Exotic animals and plants climb in the branches of a tree in the manunuscipt of a thirteenth-century Arab traveller.* Arab book painting, Baghdad, 1237. Bibliothèque Nationale, Paris.

Opposite: *An alchemical painting featuring the Tree of Life, under which stand the figures Senior and Adept.* From *Splendor Solis,* Augsburg, thought to be sixteenth century.

controls the rain. Then they offered bread, cocoanuts, plantains, and fowls to the guardian spirit of the village and to the spirit who gives rain, and they prayed, "O Lord nat have pity on us poor mortals, and stay not the rain. Inasmuch as our offering is given ungrudgingly, let the rain fall day and night." Afterwards libations were made in honour of the spirit of the Tamarind-tree; and still later three elderly women, dressed in fine clothes and wearing necklaces and earrings, sang the rain song.

Again, tree-spirits make the crops to grow. Amongst the Mundaris every village has its sacred grove, and "the grove deities are held responsible for the crops, and are especially honoured at all the great agricultural festivals." The Negroes of the Gold Coast are in the habit of sacrificing at the foot of certain tall trees, and they think that if one of these were felled all the fruits of the earth would perish. The Gallas dance in couples round sacred trees, praying for a good harvest. Every couple consists of a man and woman, who are linked together by a stick, of which each holds one end. Under their arms they carry green corn or grass. Swedish peasants stick a leafy branch in each furrow of their cornfields, believing that this will ensure an abundant crop. The same idea comes out in the German and French custom of the Harvest-May. This is a large branch or a whole tree, which is decked with ears of corn, brought home on the last waggon from the harvest-field, and fastened on the roof of the farmhouse or of the barn, where it remains for a year. Mannhardt has proved that this branch or tree embodies the tree-spirit conceived as the spirit of vegetation in general, whose vivifying and fructifying influence is thus brought to bear upon the corn in particular. Hence in Swabia the Harvest-May is fastened amongst the last stalks of corn left standing on the field; in other places it is planted on the corn-field and the last sheaf cut is attached to its trunk.

Again, the tree-spirit makes the herds to multiply and blesses women with offspring. In northern India the Emblica officinalis is a sacred tree. On the eleventh of the month Phalgun (February) libations are poured at the foot of the tree, a red or yellow string is bound about the trunk, and prayers are offered to it for the fruitfulness of women, animals, and crops. Again, in northern India the cocoanut is esteemed one of the most sacred fruits, and is called Sriphala, or the fruit of Sri, the goddess of prosperity. It is the symbol of fertility, and all through Upper India is kept in shrines and presented by the priests to women who desire to become mothers. In the town of Qua, near Old Calabar, there used to grow a palm-tree which ensured conception to any barren woman who ate a nut from its branches. In Europe the May-tree or May-pole is apparently supposed to possess similar powers over both women and cattle. Thus in some parts of Germany on the first of May the peasants set up May-trees or May-

bushes at the doors of stables and byres, one for each horse and cow; this is thought to make the cows yield much milk. Of the Irish we are told that "they fancy a green bough of a tree, fastened on May Day against the house, will produce plenty of milk that summer."

On the second of July some of the Wends used to set up an oak tree in the middle of the village with an iron cock fastened to its top; then they danced round it, and drove the cattle round it to make them thrive. The Circassians regard the pear-tree as the protector of cattle. So they cut down a young pear-tree in the forest, branch it, and carry it home, where it is adored as a divinity. Almost every house has one such pear-tree. In autumn, on the day of the festival, the tree is carried into the house with great ceremony to the sound of music and amid the joyous cries of all the inmates, who compliment it on its fortunate arrival. It is covered with candles, and a cheese is fastened to its top. Round about it they eat, drink, and sing. Then they bid the tree good-bye and take it back to the courtyard, where it remains for the rest of the year, set up against the wall - without receiving any mark of respect.

In the Tuhoe tribe of Maoris "the power of making women fruitful is ascribed to trees. These trees are associated with the navel-strings of definite mythical ancestors, as indeed the navel-strings of all children used to be hung upon them down to quite recent times. A barren woman had to embrace such a tree with her arms, and she received a male or a female child according as she embraced the east or the west side." The common European custom of placing a green bush on May Day before or on the house of a beloved maiden probably originated in the belief of the fertilising power of the tree-spirit. In some parts of Bavaria such bushes are set up also at the houses of newly-married pairs, and the practice is only omitted if the wife is near her confinement; for in that case they say that the husband has "set up a May-bush for himself." Among the South Slavonians a barren woman, who desires to have a child, places a new chemise upon a fruitful tree on the eve of St. George's Day. Next morning before sunrise she examines the garment, and if she finds that some living creature has crept

on it, she hopes that her wish will be fulfilled within the year. Then she puts on the chemise, confident that she will be as fruitful as the tree on which the garment has passed the night. Among the Kara-Kirghiz barren women roll themselves on the ground under a solitary apple-tree, in order to obtain offspring. Lastly, the power of granting to women an easy delivery at childbirth is ascribed to trees both in Sweden and Africa. In some districts of Sweden there was formerly a bardtrad or guardian-tree (lime, ash, or elm) in the neighbourhood of every farm. No one would pluck a single leaf of the sacred tree, any injury to which was punished by ill-luck or sickness. Pregnant women used to clasp the tree in their arms in order to ensure an easy delivery. In some Negro tribes of the

Above: *Raising the Maypole. This annual English festival featured a May-pole or May-tree, which was meant to impart fertility to women and cattle. Originally, such poles are thought to have functioned as gnomons for measuring solar shadows during Megalithic times (prior to 1,000 B.C.).* Engraving by E. Goodall, *Art Journal*, 1854.

Congo region pregnant women make themselves garments out of the bark of a certain sacred tree, because they believe that this tree delivers them from the dangers that attend child-bearing. The story that Leto clasped a palm-tree and an olive-tree, or two laurel-trees, when she was about to give birth to the divine twins Apollo and Artemis, perhaps points to a similar Greek belief in the efficacy of certain trees to facilitate delivery.

Chapter Seven

THE PERILS OF THE SOUL

WHAT DOES EARLY man understand by death? To what causes does he attribute it? And how does he think it may be guarded against?

As the savage commonly explains the processes of inanimate nature by supposing that they are produced by living beings working in or behind the phenomena, so he explains the phenomena of life itself. If an animal lives and moves, it can only be, he thinks, because there is a little animal inside which moves it: if a man lives and moves, it can only be because he has a little man or animal inside who moves him. The animal inside the animal, the man inside the man, is the soul. And as the activity of an animal or man is explained by the presence of the soul, so the repose of sleep or death is explained by its absence; sleep or trance being the temporary, death being the permanent absence of the soul. Hence if death be the permanent absence of the soul, the way to guard against it is either to prevent the soul from leaving the body, or, if it does depart, to ensure that it shall return. The precautions adopted by savages to secure one or other of these ends take the form of certain prohibitions or taboos, which are nothing but rules intended to ensure either the continued presence or the return of the soul. In short, they are life-preservers or life-guards. These general statements will now be illustrated by examples.

Addressing some Australian aborigines, a European missionary said, "I am not one, as you think, but two." Upon this they laughed. "You may laugh as much as you

Above: *The human-headed Ba bird, representing the soul or breath of life, hovers over the mummy. In Egyptian burial ceremonies the Ba was breathed back into the mouth of the mummy to ensure the survival of the dead person in the afterlife.* From *The Papyrus of Ani*, 1250 B.C. British Museum, London.

Opposite: *A painted wooden statue of the Ba bird.* Egyptian, Ptolemaic period of 332-330 B.C. Freud Museum, London.

like," continued the missionary, "I tell you that I am two in one; this great body that you see is one; within that there is another little one which is not visible. The great body dies, and is buried, but the little body flies away when the great one dies." To this some of the aborigines replied, "Yes, yes. We also are two, we also have a little body within the breast." On being asked where the little body went after death, some said it went behind the bush, others said it went into the sea, and some said they did not know.

The Hurons thought that the soul had a head and body, arms and legs; in short, that it was a complete little model of the man himself. The Esquimaux believe that "the soul exhibits the same shape as the body it belongs to, but is of a more subtle and ethereal nature." According to the Nootkas the soul has the shape of a tiny man; its seat is the crown of the head. So long as it stands erect, its owner is hale and hearty; but when from any cause it loses its upright position, he loses his senses. Among the Indian tribes of the Lower Fraser River, man is held to have four souls, of which the principal one has the form of a mannikin, while the other three are shadows of it. The Malays conceive the human soul as a little man, mostly invisible and of the bigness of a thumb, who corresponds exactly in shape, proportion, and even in complexion to the man in whose body he resides. This mannikin is of a thin, unsubstantial nature, though not so impalpable but that it may cause displacement on entering a physical object, and it can flit quickly from place to place; it is temporarily absent from the body in sleep, trance, and disease, and permanently absent after death.

So exact is the resemblance of the mannikin to the man, in other words, of the soul to the body, that, as there are fat bodies and thin bodies, so there are fat souls and thin souls; as there are heavy bodies and light bodies, long bodies and short bodies, so there are heavy souls and light souls, long souls and short souls. The people of Nias think that every man, before he is born, is asked how long or how heavy a soul he would like, and a soul of the desired weight or length is measured out to him. The heaviest soul ever given out weighs about ten grammes. The length of a man's life is proportioned to the length of his soul; children who die young had short

souls. The Fijian conception of the soul as a tiny human being comes out clearly in the customs observed at the death of a chief among the Nakelo tribe. When a chief dies, certain men, who are the hereditary undertakers, call him, as he lies, oiled and ornamented, on fine mats, saying, "Rise, sir, the chief, and let us be going. The day has come over the land." Then they conduct him to the river side, where the ghostly ferryman comes to ferry Nakelo ghosts across the stream. As they thus attend the chief on his last journey, they hold their great fans close to the ground to shelter him, because, as one of them explained to a missionary, "His soul is only a little child."

People in the Punjab who tattoo themselves believe that at death the soul, "the little entire man or woman" inside the mortal frame, will go to heaven blazoned with the same tattoo patterns which adorned the body in life. Sometimes, however, as we shall see, the human soul is conceived not in human but in animal form.

The soul is commonly supposed to escape by the natural openings of the body, especially the mouth and nostrils. Hence in Celebes they sometimes fasten fish-hooks to a sick man's nose, navel, and feet, so that if his soul should try to escape it may be hooked and held fast. A Turik on the Baram River, in Borneo, refused to part with some hook-like stones, because they, as it were, hooked his soul to his body, and so prevented the spiritual portion of him from becoming detached from the material. When a Sea Dyak sorcerer or medicine-man is initiated, his fingers are supposed to be furnished with fish-hooks, with which he will thereafter clutch the human soul in the act of flying away, and restore it to the body of the sufferer. But hooks, it is plain, may be used to catch the souls of enemies as well as of friends. Acting on this principle head-hunters in Borneo hang wooden hooks beside the skulls of their slain enemies in the belief that this helps them on their forays to hook in fresh heads. One of the implements of a Haida medi-cine-man is a hollow bone, in which he bottles up departing souls, and so restores them to their owners. When anyone yawns in their presence the Hindoos always snap their thumbs, believing that this will hinder the soul from issuing through the open mouth. The Marquesans used to hold the mouth and nose of a dying man, in order to keep him in life by preventing his soul from escaping; the same custom is reported of the New Caledonians; and with the like intention the Bagobos of the Philippine Islands put rings of brass wire on the wrists or ankles of their sick. On the other hand, the Itonamas of South America seal up the eyes, nose, and mouth of a dying person, in case his ghost should get out and carry off others; and for a similar reason the people of Nias, who fear the spirits of the recently deceased and identify them with the breath, seek to confine the vagrant soul in its earthly tabernacle by bunging up the nose or tying up the jaws of the corpse. Before leaving a corpse the Wakelbura of Australia used to place hot coals in its ears in order to keep the ghost in the body, until they had got such a good start that he could not overtake them. In southern Celebes, to hin-der the escape of a woman's soul in childbed, the nurse ties a band as tightly as possible round the body of the expectant mother. The Minangkabauers of Sumatra observe a similar custom; a skein of thread or a string is sometimes fastened round the wrist or loins of a woman in childbed, so that when her soul seeks to depart in her hour of travail it may find the egress barred. And lest the soul of a babe should escape and be lost as soon as it is born, the Alfoors of Celebes, when a birth is about to take place, are careful to close every opening in the house, even the keyhole; and they stop up every chink and cranny in the walls. Also they tie up the mouths of all animals inside and outside the house, for fear one of them might swallow the child's soul. For a similar reason all persons present in the house, even the mother herself, are obliged to keep their mouths shut the whole time the birth is taking place. When the question was put, Why they did not hold their noses also, lest the child's soul should get into one of them? the answer was that breath being exhaled as well as

Opposite: *A shaman's spirit trap, with magic knife and print-block with magical characters. This is an ancient object of unknown date, which was still being used in the early twentieth century. From the Laotian-Thai border area. Reece Collection, Knaresborough, Yorkshire, England.*

inhaled through the nostrils, the soul would be expelled before it could have time to settle down. Popular expressions in the language of civilised peoples, such as to have one's heart in one's mouth, or the soul on the lips or in the nose, show how natural is the idea that the life or soul may escape by the mouth or nostrils.

Often the soul is conceived as a bird ready to take flight. This conception has probably left traces in most

Above: *A Laotian shaman's magical cloth containing spirit-trap designs. From the Tai Daeng tribe, Nam Ma River, Hua Phan Province, Laos.* Reece Collection, Knaresborough, Yorkshire, England.

Opposite: *A baby being held in the smoke as part of a birth purification ritual by the Azande tribe of southern Sudan.*

languages, and it lingers as a metaphor in poetry. The Malays carry out the conception of the bird-soul in a number of odd ways. If the soul is a bird on the wing, it may be attracted by rice, and so is either prevented from flying away or lured back again from its perilous flight. Thus in Java when a child is placed on the ground for the first time (a moment which uncultured people seem to regard as especially dangerous), it is put in a hencoop and the mother makes a clucking sound, as if she were calling hens. And in Sintang, a district of Borneo, when a person, whether man, woman, or child, has fallen out of a house or off a tree, and has been brought home, his wife or other kinswoman goes as speedily as possible to the spot where the accident happened, and there strews rice, which has been coloured yellow, while she utters the words, "Cluck! cluck! soul! So-and-so is in his house again. Cluck! cluck! soul!" Then she gathers up the rice in a basket, carries it to the sufferer, and drops the grains from her hand on his head, saying again, "Cluck! cluck! soul!" Here the intention clearly is to decoy back the loitering bird-soul and replace it in the head of its owner.

The soul of a sleeper is supposed to wander away from his body and actually to visit the places, to see the persons, and to perform the acts of which he dreams. For example, when an Indian of Brazil or Guiana wakes up from a sound sleep, he is firmly convinced that his soul has really been away hunting, fishing, felling trees, or whatever else he has dreamed of doing, while all the time his body has been lying motionless in his hammock. A whole Bororo village has been thrown into a panic and nearly deserted because somebody had dreamed that he saw enemies stealthily approaching it. A Macusi Indian in weak health, who dreamed that his employer had made him haul the canoe up a series of difficult cataracts, bitterly reproached his master next morning for his want of consideration in thus making a poor invalid go out and toil during the night. The Indians of the Gran Chaco are often heard to relate the most incredible stories as things which they have themselves seen and heard; hence strangers who do not know them intimately say in their haste that these Indians are liars.

In point of fact the Indians are firmly convinced of the truth of what they relate; for these wonderful adventures are simply their dreams, which they do not distinguish from waking realities.

Now the absence of the soul in sleep has its dangers, for if from any cause the soul should be permanently detained away from the body, the person thus deprived of the vital principle must die. There is a German belief that the soul escapes from a sleeper's mouth in the form of a white mouse or a little bird, and that to prevent the return of the bird or animal would be fatal to the sleeper. Hence in Transylvania they say that you should not let a child sleep with its mouth open, or its soul will slip out in the shape of a mouse, and the child will never wake. Many causes may detain the sleeper's soul. Thus, his soul may meet the soul of another sleeper and the two souls may fight; if a Guinea Negro wakens with sore bones in the morning, he thinks that his soul has been thrashed by another soul in sleep. Or it may meet the soul of a person just deceased and be carried off by it;

hence in the Aru Islands the inmates of a house will not sleep the night after a death has taken place in it, because the soul of the deceased is supposed to be still in the house and they fear to meet it in a dream. Again, the soul of the sleeper may be prevented by an accident or by physical force from returning to his body. When a Dyak dreams of falling into the water, he supposes that this accident has really befallen his spirit, and he sends for a wizard, who fishes for the spirit with a hand-net in a basin of water till he catches it and restores it to its owner. The Santals tell how a man fell asleep, and growing very thirsty, his soul, in the form of a lizard, left his body and entered a pitcher of water to drink. Just then the owner of the pitcher happened to cover it; so the soul could not return to the body and the man died. While his friends were preparing to burn the body some one uncovered the pitcher to get water. The lizard thus escaped and returned to the body, which immediately revived; so the man rose up and asked his friends why they were weeping. They told him they thought he was

fantastic colours or giving moustaches to a sleeping woman. For when the soul returns it will not know its own body, and the person will die.

But in order that a man's soul should quit his body, it is not necessary that he should be asleep. It may quit him in his waking hours, and then sickness, insanity, or death will be the result. Thus a man of the Wurun-jeri tribe in Australia lay at his last gasp because his spirit had departed from him. A medicine-man went in pursuit and caught the spirit by the middle just as it was about to plunge into the sunset glow, which is the light cast by the souls of the dead as they pass in and out of the under-world, where the sun goes to rest. Having captured the vagrant spirit, the doctor brought it back under his opossum rug, laid himself down on the dying man, and put the soul back into him, so that after a time he revived. The Karens of Burma are perpetually anxious about their souls, lest these should go roving from their bodies, leaving the owners to die. When a man has reason to fear that his soul is about to take this fatal step, a ceremony is performed to retain or recall it, in which the whole family must take part. A meal is prepared consisting of a cock and hen, a special kind of rice, and a bunch of bananas. Then the head of the family takes the bowl which is used to skim rice, and knocking with it thrice on the top of the house-ladder says: "Prrroo! Come back, soul, do not tarry outside! If it rains, you will be wet. If the sun shines, you will be hot. The gnats will sting you, the leeches will bite you, the tigers will devour you, the thunder will crush you. Prrroo! Come back, soul! Here it will be well with you. You shall want for nothing. Come and eat under shelter from the wind and the storm." After that the family partakes of the meal, and the ceremony ends with everybody tying their right wrist with a string which has been charmed by a sorcerer. Similarly the Lolos of south-western China believe that the soul leaves the body in chronic illness. In that case they read a sort of elaborate litany, calling on the soul by name and beseeching it to return from the hills, the vales, the rivers, the forests, the fields, or from

dead and were about to burn his body. He said he had been down a well to get water, but had found it hard to get out and had just returned. So they saw it all.

It is a common rule with primitive people not to waken a sleeper, because his soul is away and might not have time to get back; so if the man wakened without his soul, he would fall sick. If it is absolutely necessary to rouse a sleeper, it must be done very gradually, to allow the soul time to return. A Fijian in Matuku, suddenly wakened from a nap by somebody treading on his foot, has been heard bawling after his soul and imploring it to return. He had just been dreaming that he was far away in Tonga, and great was his alarm on suddenly wakening to find his body in Matuku. Death stared him in the face unless his soul could be induced to speed at once across the sea and reanimate its deserted tenement. The man would probably have died of fright if a missionary had not been at hand to allay his terror.

Still more dangerous is it in the opinion of primitive man to move a sleeper or alter his appearance, for if this were done the soul on its return might not be able to find or recognise its body, and so the person would die. The Minangkabauers deem it highly improper to blacken or dirty the face of a sleeper, lest the absent soul should shrink from re-entering a body thus disfigured. Patani Malays fancy that if a person's face be painted while he sleeps, the soul which has gone out of him will not recognise him, and he will sleep on till his face is washed. In Bombay it is thought equivalent to murder to change the aspect of a sleeper, as by painting his face in

wherever it may be straying. At the same time cups of water, wine, and rice are set at the door for the refreshment of the weary wandering spirit. When the ceremony is over, they tie a red cord round the arm of the sick man to tether the soul, and this cord is worn by him until it decays and drops off.

Some of the Congo tribes believe that when a man is ill, his soul has left his body and is wandering at large. The aid of the sorcerer is then called in to capture the vagrant spirit and restore it to the invalid. Generally the physician declares that he has successfully chased the soul into the branch of a tree. The whole town thereupon turns out and accompanies the doctor to the tree, where the strongest men are deputed to break off the branch in which the soul of the sick man is supposed to be lodged. This they do and carry the branch back to the town, insinuating by their gestures that the burden is heavy and hard to bear. When the branch has been brought to the sick man's hut, he is placed in an upright position by its side, and the sorcerer performs the enchantments by which the soul is believed to be restored to its owner.

Opposite: *An Inuit (Eskimo) "soul-boat" from Alaska.*

Below: *A Native American shaman's soul-catcher, from the Tlingit tribe of the northwest coast of the United States and Canada. Made of bone inlaid with abalone shell. When the soul left the body because of sickness, a shaman was hired to go out and catch it with this object and then return it to the patient so that he could recover.* Provincial Museum, Victoria, British Columbia, Canada.

Pining, sickness, great fright, and death are ascribed by the Bataks of Sumatra to the absence of the soul from the body. At first they try to beckon the wanderer back, and to lure him, like a fowl, by strewing rice. Then the following form of words is commonly repeated: "Come back, O soul, whether thou art lingering in the wood, or on the hills, or in the dale. See, I call thee with a toemba bras, with an egg of the fowl Rajah moelija, with the eleven healing leaves. Detain it not, let it come straight here, detain it not, neither in the wood, nor on the hill, nor in the dale. That may not be. O come straight home!" Once when a popular traveller was leaving a Kayan village, the mothers, fearing that their children's souls might follow him on his journey, brought him the boards on which they carry their infants and begged him to pray that the souls of the little ones would return to the familiar boards and not go away with him into the far country. To each board was fastened a looped string for the purpose of tethering the vagrant spirits, and through the loop each baby was made to pass a chubby finger to make sure that its tiny soul would not wander away.

In an Indian story a king conveys his soul into the dead body of a Brahman, and a hunchback conveys his soul into the deserted body of the king. The hunchback is now king and the king is a Brahman. However, the hunchback is induced to show his skill by transferring his soul to the dead body of a parrot, and the king seizes the opportunity to regain possession of his own body. A tale of the same type, with variations of detail, reappears

among the Malays. A king has incautiously transferred his soul to an ape, upon which the vizier adroitly inserts his own soul into the king's body and so takes possession of the queen and the kingdom, while the true king languishes at court in the outward semblance of an ape. But one day the false king, who played for high stakes, was watching a combat of rams, and it happened that the animal on which he had laid his money fell down dead. All efforts to restore animation proved unavailing till the false king, with the instinct of a true sportsman, transferred his own soul to the body of the deceased ram, and thus renewed the fray. The real king in the body of the ape saw his chance, and with great presence

Above: *A traditional "dream-catcher" of the Canadian Indians, used by the shaman to snare the elusive visions of the night.* Hull Museum of Civilization, Quebec, Canada.

Opposite: *A Burmese town spirit-shrine in Arakan State.*

of mind darted back into his own body, which the vizier had rashly vacated. So he came to his own again, and the usurper in the ram's body met with the fate he richly deserved. Similarly the Greeks told how the soul of Hermotimus of Clazomenae used to quit his body and roam far and wide, bringing back intelligence of what he had seen on his rambles to his friends at home; until one day, when his spirit was abroad, his enemies contrived to seize his deserted body and committed it to the flames.

The departure of the soul is not always voluntary. It may be extracted from the body against its will by ghosts, demons, or sorcerers. Hence, when a funeral is passing the house, the Karens tie their children with a special kind of string to a particular part of the house, lest the souls of the children should leave their bodies and go into the corpse which is passing. The children are kept tied in this way until the corpse is out of sight. And after the corpse has been laid in the grave, but before the earth has been shovelled in, the mourners and friends range themselves round the grave, each with a bamboo split lengthwise in one hand and a little stick in the other; each man thrusts his bamboo into the grave, and drawing the stick along the groove of the bamboo points out to his soul that in this way it may easily climb up out of the tomb. While the earth is being shovelled in, the bamboos are kept out of the way, lest the souls should be in them, and so should be inadvertently buried with the earth as it is being thrown into the grave; and when the people leave the spot they carry away the bamboos, begging their souls to come with them. Further, on returning from the grave each Karen provides himself with three little hooks made of branches of trees, and calling his spirit to follow him, at short intervals, as he returns, he makes a motion as if hooking it, and then thrusts the hook into the ground. This is done to prevent the soul of the living from staying behind with the soul of the dead. When the Karo-Bataks have buried somebody and are filling in the grave, a sorceress runs about beating the air with a stick. This she does in order to drive away the souls of the survivors, for if one of these souls hap-

Above: *A modern fabric-print evoking incantational witchcraft and showing shamans with musical instruments.* From *The Singing Tadpole, or The Pig in the Pond*, by Thessalonius Loyola, 1987.

Opposite: *The image and sigil (personal sign) of a "cardinal demon" known in black magical tradition as Gaap, said to be the Ruler of the West.* From a manuscript derived from *Dictionaire Infernale* by Collin de Plancy, 1864.

pened to slip into the grave and to be covered up with earth, its owner would die.

In Uea, one of the Loyalty Islands, the souls of the dead seem to have been credited with the power of stealing the souls of the living. For when a man was sick the soul-doctor would go with a large troop of men and women to the graveyard. Here the men played on flutes and the women whistled softly to lure the soul home. After this had gone on for some time they formed in procession and moved homewards, the flutes playing and the women whistling all the way, while they led back the wandering soul and drove it gently along with open palms. On entering the patient's dwelling they commanded the soul in a loud voice to enter his body.

Often the abduction of a man's soul is set down to demons. Thus fits and convulsions are generally ascribed by the Chinese to the agency of certain mischievous spirits who love to draw men's souls out of their bodies. At Amoy the spirits who serve babies and children in this way rejoice in the high-sounding titles of "celestial agencies bestriding galloping horses" and "literary graduates residing halfway up in the sky."

When an infant is writhing in convulsions, the frightened mother hastens to the roof of the house, and, waving about a bamboo pole to which one of the child's garments is attached, cries out several times "My child so-and-so, come back, return home!" Meantime, another inmate of the house bangs away at a gong in the hope of attracting the attention of the strayed soul, which is supposed to recognise the familiar garment and to slip into it. The garment containing the soul is then placed on or beside the child, and if the child does not die recovery is sure to follow, sooner or later. Similarly some Indians catch a man's lost soul in his boots and restore it to his body by putting his feet into them.

In the Moluccas when a man is unwell it is thought that some devil has carried away his soul to the tree, mountain, or hill where he (the devil) resides. A sorcerer having pointed out the devil's abode, the friends of the patient carry thither cooked rice, fruit, fish, raw eggs, a hen, a chicken, a silken robe, gold, armlets, and so forth. Having set out the food in order they pray, saying: "We come to offer to you, O devil, this offering of food, clothes, gold, and so on; take it and release the soul of the patient for whom we pray. Let it return to his body, and he who now is sick shall be made whole." Then they eat a little and let the hen loose as a ransom for the soul of the patient; also they put down the raw eggs; but the silken robe, the gold, and the armlets they take home with them. As soon as they are come to the house they place a flat bowl containing the offerings which have been brought back at the sick man's head, and say to him: "Now is your soul released, and you shall fare well and live to grey hairs on the earth."

Demons are especially feared by persons who have just entered a new house. Hence at a house-warming among the Alfoors of Minahassa in Celebes the priest performs a ceremony for the purpose of restoring their souls to the inmates. He hangs up a bag at the place of sacrifice and then goes through a list of the gods. There are so many of them that this takes him the whole night through without stopping. In the morning he offers the gods an egg and some rice. By this time the souls of the

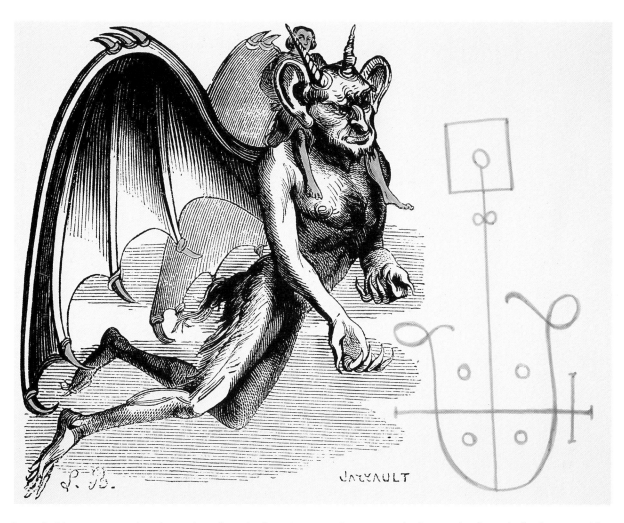

household are supposed to be gathered in the bag. So the priest takes the bag, and holding it on the head of the master of the house, says, "Here you have your soul; go (soul) tomorrow away again." He then does the same, saying the same words, to the housewife and all the other members of the family. Amongst the same Alfoors one way of recovering a sick man's soul is to let down a bowl by a belt out of a window and fish for the soul till it is caught in the bowl and hauled up. And among the same people, when a priest is bringing back a sick man's soul which he has caught in a cloth, he is preceded by a girl holding the large leaf of a certain palm over his head as an umbrella to keep him and the soul from getting wet, in case it should rain; and he is followed by a man brandishing a sword to deter other souls from any attempt at rescuing the captured spirit.

Sometimes the lost soul is brought back in a visible shape. The Salish or Flathead Indians of Oregon believe that a man's soul may be separated for a time from his body without causing death and without the man being aware of his loss. It is necessary, however, that the lost soul should be soon found and restored to its owner or he will die. The name of the man who has lost his soul is revealed in a dream to the medicine-man, who hastens to inform the sufferer of his loss. Generally a number of men have sustained a like loss at the same time; all their names are revealed to the medicine-man, and all employ him to recover their souls. The whole night long these soulless men go about the village from lodge to lodge, dancing and singing. Towards daybreak they go into a separate lodge, which is closed up so as to be totally dark. A small hole is then made in the roof, through

which the medicine-man, with a bunch of feathers, brushes in the souls, in the shape of bits of bone and the like, which he receives on a piece of matting. A fire is next kindled, by the light of which the medicine-man sorts out the souls. First he puts aside the souls of dead people, of which there are usually several; for if he were to give the soul of a dead person to a living man, the man would die instantly. Next he picks out the souls of all the persons present, and making them all to sit down before him, he takes the soul of each, in the shape of a splinter of bone, wood, or shell, and placing it on the owner's head, pats it with many prayers and contortions till it descends into the heart and so resumes its proper place.

Again, souls may be extracted from their bodies or detained on their wanderings not only by ghosts and demons but also by men, especially by sorcerers. In Fiji, if a criminal refused to confess, the chief sent for a scarf with which "to catch away the soul of the rogue." At the sight or even at the mention of the scarf the culprit generally made a clean breast. For if he did not, the scarf would be waved over his head till his soul was caught in it, when it would be carefully folded up and nailed to the end of a chief's canoe; and for want of his soul the criminal would pine and die. The sorcerers of Danger Island used to set snares for souls. The snares were made of stout cinet, about fifteen to thirty feet long, with loops on either side of different sizes, to suit the different sizes of souls; for fat souls there were large loops, for thin souls there were small ones. When a man was sick against whom the sorcerers had a grudge, they set up these soul-snares near his house and watched for the flight of his soul. If in the shape of a bird or an insect it was caught in the snare, the man would infallibly die. In some parts of West Africa, indeed, wizards are continually setting traps to catch souls that wander from their bodies in sleep; and when they have caught one, they tie it up over the fire, and as it shrivels in the heat the owner sickens. This is done, not out of any grudge towards the sufferer, but purely as a matter of business. The wizard does not care whose soul he has captured, and will readily restore it to its owner, if only he is paid for doing so. Some sorcerers keep regular asylums for strayed souls, and anybody who has lost or mislaid his own soul can always have another one from the asylum on payment of the usual fee. No blame whatever attaches to men who keep these private asylums or set traps for passing souls; it is their profession, and in the exercise of it they are actuated by no harsh or unkindly feelings. But there are also wretches who from pure spite or for the sake of lucre set and bait traps with the deliberate purpose of catching the soul of a particular man; and in the bottom of the pot, hidden by the bait, are knives and sharp hooks which tear and rend the poor soul, either killing it outright or mauling it so as to impair the health of its owner when it succeeds in escaping and returning to him. Miss Kingsley knew a Kruman who became very anxious about his soul, because for several nights he had smelt in his dreams the savoury smell of smoked crawfish seasoned with red pepper. Clearly some ill-wisher had set a trap baited with this dainty for his dream-soul, intending to do him grievous bodily, or rather spiritual, harm; and for the next few nights great pains were taken to keep his soul from straying abroad in his sleep. In the sweltering heat of the tropical night he lay sweating and snorting under a blanket, his nose and mouth tied up with a handkerchief to prevent the escape of his precious soul. In Hawaii there were sorcerers who caught souls of living people, shut them up in calabashes, and gave them to people to eat. By squeezing a captured soul

Above: *An Alaskan Inuit arrow shaft straightener with carvings of caribou heads. It was also believed to massage caribou souls, making the animal more amenable to being caught.* Museum of Mankind, London.

Opposite: *Miniature houses built for spirits, situated at the base of a cliff in Torajaland, Sulawesi, Indonesia.*

in their hands they discovered the place where people had been secretly buried.

Nowhere perhaps is the art of abducting human souls more carefully cultivated or carried to higher perfection than in the Malay Peninsula. Here the methods by which the wizard works his will are various, and so too are his motives. Sometimes he desires to destroy an enemy, sometimes to win the love of a cold or bashful beauty. Thus, to take an instance of the latter sort of charm, the following are the directions given for securing the soul of one whom you wish to render distraught. When the moon, just risen, looks red above the eastern horizon, go out, and standing in the moonlight, with the big toe of your right foot on the big toe of your left, make a speaking-trumpet of your right hand and recite through it the following words:

OM. I loose my shaft, I loose it and the moon clouds over,
I loose it, and the sun is extinguished.
I loose it, and the stars burn dim.
But it is not the sun, moon, and stars that I shoot at,
It is the stalk of the heart of that child of the congreg-
  ation, So-and-so.
Cluck! cluck! soul of So-and-so, come and walk with me.
Come and sit with me,
Come and sleep and share my pillow.
Cluck! cluck! soul.

Repeat this thrice and after every repetition blow through your hollow fist. Or you may catch the soul in your turban, thus. Go out on the night of the full moon and the two succeeding nights; sit down on an ant-hill facing the moon, burn incense, and recite the following incantation:

I bring you a betel leaf to chew,
Dab the lime on to it, Prince Ferocious,
For Somebody, Prince Distraction's daughter, to chew.
Somebody at sunrise be distraught for love of me,
Somebody at sunset be distraught for love of me.
As you remember your parents, remember me;
As you remember your house and house-ladder,
    remember me;
When thunder rumbles, remember me;
When wind whistles, remember me;
When the heavens rain, remember me;
When cocks crow, remember me;
When the dial-bird tells its tales, remember me;
When you look up at the sun, remember me;
When you look up at the moon, remember me,
For in that self-same moon I am there.
Cluck! cluck! soul of Somebody come hither to me.
I do not mean to let you have my soul,
Let your soul come hither to mine.

Now wave the end of your turban towards the moon seven times each night. Go home and put it under your pillow, and if you want to wear it in the day-time, burn incense and say, "It is not a turban that I carry in my girdle, but the soul of Somebody."

The Indians of the Nass River, in British Columbia, are impressed with a belief that a physician may swallow his patient's soul by mistake. A doctor who is believed to have done so is made by the other members of the faculty to stand over the patient, while one of them thrusts his fingers down the doctor's throat, another kneads him in the stomach with his knuckles, and a third slaps him on the back. If the soul is not in him after all, and if the same process has been repeated

Above (right): *A West African wooden spirit mask called Tankagle, of the Dan-Ngere coastal tribal complex. The mask represents a handsome young man and embodies a spirit called Du, who normally lives outside the village in the bush or hills.* Entwistle Gallery, London.

Opposite: *Shamans of Lapland in the eighteenth century, in a divinatory trance.* From *Picart's Religious Ceremonies,* Paris, 1730.

upon all the medical men without success, it is concluded that the soul must be in the head-doctor's box. A party of doctors, therefore, waits upon him at his house and requests him to produce his box. When he has done so and arranged its contents on a new mat, they take the votary of Aesculapius and hold him up by the heels with his head in a hole in the floor. In this position they wash his head, and "any water remaining from the ablution is taken and poured upon the sick man's head." No doubt the lost soul is in the water.

But the spiritual dangers I have enumerated are not the only ones which beset the savage. Often he regards his shadow or reflection as his soul, or at all events as a vital part of himself, and as such it is necessarily a source of danger to him. For if it is trampled upon, struck, or stabbed, he will feel the injury as if it were done to his person; and if it is detached from him entirely (as he believes that it may be) he will die. In the island of Wetar there are magicians who can make a man ill by stabbing his shadow with a pike or hacking it with a sword. After Sankara had destroyed the Buddhists in India, it is said that he journeyed to Nepal, where he had some difference of opinion with the Grand Lama. To prove his supernatural powers, he soared into the air. But as he mounted up the Grand Lama, perceiving his shadow swaying and wavering on the ground, struck his knife into it and down fell Sankara and broke his neck.

In the Banks Islands there are some stones of a remarkably long shape which go by the name of "eating ghosts," because certain powerful and dangerous ghosts are believed to lodge in them. If a man's shadow falls on one of these stones, the ghost will draw his soul out from him, so that he will die. Such stones, therefore, are set in a house to guard it; and a messenger sent to a house by the absent owner will call out the name of the

Above: *This Native American totem pole depicts tribe or spirit guardians. It stands in the center of Vancouver, British Columbia.*

Opposite: *The empty house of a dead man among the Azande tribe of southern Sudan, with all his possessions displayed outside. No Azande is believed to have died of natural causes; all die as a result of curses. Having been emptied to clear it of its curse, the house will eventually be burned.*

sender, lest the watchful ghost in the stone should fancy that he came with evil intent and should do him a mischief. At a funeral in China, when the lid is about to be placed on the coffin, most of the bystanders, with the exception of the nearest kin, retire a few steps or even retreat to another room, for a person's health is believed to be endangered by allowing his shadow to be enclosed in a coffin. And when the coffin is about to be lowered into the grave most of the spectators recoil to a little distance lest their shadows should fall into the grave and harm should thus be done to their persons. The geomancer and his assistants stand on the side of the grave which is turned away from the sun; and the grave-diggers and coin-bearers attach their shadows firmly to their persons by tying a strip of cloth tightly round their waists. Nor is it human beings alone who are thus liable to be injured by means of their shadows. Animals are to some extent in the same predicament. A small snail, which frequents the neighbourhood of the limestone hills in Perak, is believed to suck the blood of cattle through their shadows; hence the beasts grow lean and sometimes die from loss of blood. The ancients supposed that in Arabia, if a hyaena trod on a man's shadow, it deprived him of the power of speech and motion; and that if a dog, standing on a roof in the moonlight, cast a shadow on the ground and a hyaena trod on it, the dog would fall down as if dragged with a rope. Clearly in these cases the shadow, if not equivalent to the soul, is at least regarded as a living part of the man or the animal, so that injury done to the shadow is felt by the person or animal as if it were done to his body.

Conversely, if the shadow is a vital part of a man or an animal, it may under certain circumstances be as hazardous to be touched by it as it would be to come into contact with the person or animal. Hence the savage makes it a rule to shun the shadow of certain persons whom for various reasons he regards as sources of dangerous influence. Amongst the dangerous classes he commonly ranks mourners and women in general, but especially his mother-in-law. The Shuswap Indians think that the shadow of a mourner falling upon a person would make him sick. Amongst the Kurnai of Victoria novices at initiation were cautioned not to let a woman's shadow fall across them, as this would make them thin, lazy, and stupid. An Australian native is said to have once nearly died of fright because the shadow of his mother-in-law fell on his legs as he lay asleep under a tree. The awe and dread with which the untutored savage contemplates his mother-in-law are amongst the most familiar facts of anthropology. In the Yuin tribes of New South Wales the rule which forbade a man to hold

Above: *The deceased's heart is being weighed in the scales against the feather of truth by the dog-headed god Anubis, whilst the divine scribe Thoth, with the ibis-head, records the result, and the hawk-headed god Horus look on.* Illustration from the Egyptian *Book of the Dead Papyrus* of Anhai (circa 1100 B.C.). British Museum, London.

any communication with his wife's mother was very strict. He might not look at her or even in her direction. It was a ground of divorce if his shadow happened to fall on his mother-in-law: in that case he had to leave his wife, and she returned to her parents. In New Britain the native imagination fails to conceive the extent and nature of the calamities which would result from a man's accidentally speaking to his wife's mother; suicide of one or both would probably be the only course open to them. The most solemn form of oath a New Briton can take is, "Sir, if I am not telling the truth, I hope I may shake hands with my mother-in-law."

Where the shadow is regarded as so intimately bound up with the life of the man that its loss entails debility or death, it is natural to expect that its diminution should be regarded with solicitude and apprehension, as betokening a corresponding decrease in the vital energy of its owner. In Amboyna and Uliase, two islands near the equator, where necessarily there is little or no shadow cast at noon, the people make it a rule not to go out of the house at midday, because they fancy that by doing so a man may lose the shadow of his soul. The Mangaians tell of a mighty warrior, Tukaitawa, whose strength waxed and waned with the length of his shadow. In the morning, when his shadow fell longest, his strength was greatest; but as the shadow shortened towards noon his strength ebbed with it, till exactly at noon it reached its lowest point; then, as the shadow stretched out in the afternoon, his strength returned. A certain hero discovered the secret of Tukaitawa's strength and slew him at noon. The savage Besisis of the Malay Peninsula fear to bury their dead at noon, because they fancy that the shortness of their shadows at that hour would sympathetically shorten their own lives.

Nowhere, perhaps, does the equivalence of the shadow to the life or soul come out more clearly than in some customs practised to this day in southeastern Europe. In modern Greece, when the foundation of a new building is being laid, it is the custom to kill a cock, a ram, or a lamb, and to let its blood flow on the foundation-stone, under which the animal is afterwards buried. The object of the sacrifice is to give strength and stability to the building. But sometimes, instead of killing an animal, the builder entices a man to the foundation-stone, secretly measures his body, or a part of it, or his shadow, and buries the measure under the foundation-stone; or he lays the foundation-stone upon the man's shadow. It is believed that the man will die within the year. The Roumanians of Transylvania think that he whose shadow is thus immured will die within forty days; so persons passing by a building which is in course of erection may hear a warning cry, "Beware lest they take thy shadow!" Not long ago there were still shadow-traders whose business it was to provide architects with the shadows necessary for securing their walls. In these cases the measure of the shadow is looked on as equivalent to the shadow itself, and to bury it is to bury the life or soul of the man, who, deprived of it, must die. Thus the custom is a substitute for the old practice of immuring a living person in the walls, or crushing him under the foundation-stone of a new building, in order to give strength and durability to the structure, or more definitely in order that the angry ghost may haunt the place and guard it against the intrusion of enemies.

As some peoples believe a man's soul to be in his shadow, so other (or the same) peoples believe it to be in his reflection in water or a mirror. Thus "the Andamanese do not regard their shadows but their reflections (in any mirror) as their souls." When the Motumotu of New Guinea first saw their likenesses in a looking-glass, they thought that their reflections were their souls. In New Caledonia the old men are of the opinion that a person's reflection in water or a mirror is his soul; but the younger men, taught by the Catholic priests, maintain that it is a reflection and nothing more, just like the reflection of palm trees in the water. The reflection-soul, being external to the man, is exposed to much the same dangers as the shadow-soul. The Zulus will not look into a dark pool because they think there is a beast in it which will take away their reflections, so that they die. The Basutos say that crocodiles have the power of thus killing a man by dragging his reflection under water. When one of them dies suddenly and from no apparent cause, his relatives will allege that a crocodile must have taken his shadow some time when he crossed a stream. In Saddle Island, Melanesia, there is a pool "into which if anyone looks he dies; the malignant spirit takes hold upon his life by means of his reflection on the water."

We can now understand why it was a maxim both in ancient India and ancient Greece not to look at one's reflection in water, and why the Greeks regarded it as an omen of death if a man dreamed of seeing himself so reflected. They feared that the water-spirits would drag the person's reflection or soul under water, leaving him soulless to perish. This was probably the origin of the classical story of the beautiful Narcissus, who languished and died through seeing his reflection in the water.

Further, we can now explain the widespread custom of covering up mirrors or turning them to the wall after a death has taken place in the house. It is feared that the soul, projected out of the person in the shape of his reflection in the mirror, may be carried off by the ghost of the departed, which is commonly supposed to linger about the house till the burial. The custom is thus exactly parallel to the Aru custom of not sleeping in a house after a death for fear that the soul, projected out of the body in a dream, may meet the

THE PERILS OF THE SOUL

Above: *Homer describes the souls of Penelope's slain suitors "rustling like bats" as they are led by Hermes to the underworld. The Song of Phemius and the Sorrow of Penelope,* a scene from *The Odyssey,* by Thomas Ralph Spence, 1897.

Opposite: *In ancient Greece, it was an omen of death to see one's reflection in water. Here Narcissus gazes in a forest pool and falls in love with himself.* Seventeenth-century painting by Jan Moreelse.

ghost and be carried off by it. The reason why sick people should not see themselves in a mirror, and why the mirror in a sick-room is therefore covered up, is also plain; in time of sickness, when the soul might take flight so easily, it is particularly dangerous to project it out of the body by means of the reflection in a mirror. The rule is therefore precisely parallel to the rule observed by some peoples of not allowing sick people to sleep; for in sleep the soul is projected out of the body, and there is always a risk that it may not return.

As with shadows and reflections, so with portraits; they are often believed to contain the soul of the person portrayed. People who hold this belief are naturally loth to have their likenesses taken; for if the portrait is the soul, or at least a vital part of the person portrayed, whoever possesses the portrait will be able to exercise a fatal influence over the original of it. Thus the Esquimaux of Bering Strait believe that persons dealing in witchcraft have the power of stealing a person's shade, so that without it he will pine away and die. Once at a village on the lower Yukon River an explorer had set up his camera to get a picture of the people as they were moving about among their houses. While he was focusing the instrument, the headman of the village came up and insisted on peeping under the cloth. Being allowed to do so, he gazed intently for a minute at the moving figures on the ground glass, then suddenly withdrew his head and bawled at the top of his voice to the people, "He has all of your shades in this box."

Above: *In some parts of the world it was thought that the camera had the power to take away souls and photographers were regarded with suspicion. Here a woman in the town of Guanajuato, Mexico, hides her face from the camera.*

Opposite: *A shrine to the gods of the land, before which sacrifices are made, from the Bouya Minority tribe in Anshan District of Guizhou Province, China.*

A panic ensued among the group, and in an instant they disappeared helter-skelter into their houses. The Tepehuanes of Mexico stood in mortal terror of the camera, and five days' persuasion was necessary to induce them to pose for it. When at last they consented, they looked like criminals about to be executed. They believed that by photographing people the artist could carry off their souls and devour them at his leisure moments. They said that, when the pictures reached his country, they would die or some other evil would befall them. When Dr. Catat and some companions were exploring the Bara country on the west coast of Madagascar, the people suddenly became hostile. The day before the travellers, not without difficulty, had photographed the royal family, and now found themselves accused of taking the souls of the natives for the purpose of selling them when they returned to France. Denial was vain; in compliance with the custom of the country they were obliged to catch the souls, which were then put into a basket and ordered by Dr. Catat to return to their respective owners.

Some villagers in Sikkim betrayed a lively horror and hid away whenever the lens of a camera, or "the evil eye of the box" as they called it, was turned on them. They thought it took away their souls with their pictures, and so put it in the power of the owner of the pictures to cast spells on them, and they alleged that a photograph of the scenery blighted the landscape. Until the reign of the late King of Siam no Siamese coins were ever stamped with the image of the king, "for at that time there was a strong prejudice against the making of portraits in any medium. Europeans who travel into the jungle have, even at the present time, only to point a camera at a crowd to procure its instant dispersion. When a copy of the face of a person is made and taken away from him, a portion of his life goes with the picture. Unless the sovereign had been blessed with the years of a Methusaleh he could scarcely have permitted his life to be distributed in small pieces together with the coins of the realm."

Beliefs of the same sort still linger in various parts of Europe. Not very many years ago some old women in the Greek island of Carpathus were very angry at having their likenesses drawn, thinking that in consequence they would pine and die. There are persons in the west of Scotland "who refuse to have their likenesses taken lest it prove unlucky; and give as instances the cases of several of their friends who never had a day's health after being photographed."

Chapter Eight

THE TRANSFERENCE OF EVIL

THE NOTION THAT we can transfer our guilt and sufferings to some other being who will bear them for us is familiar to the savage mind. It arises from a very obvious confusion between the physical and the mental, between the material and the immaterial. Because it is possible to shift a load of wood, stones, or what not, from our own back to the back of another, the savage fancies that it is equally possible to shift the burden of his pains and sorrows to another, who will suffer them in his stead. Upon this idea he acts, and the result is an endless number of very unamiable devices for palming off upon someone else the trouble which a man shrinks from bearing himself. In short, the principle of vicarious suffering is commonly understood and practised by races who stand on a low level of social and intellectual culture.

The devices to which the cunning and selfish savage resorts for the sake of easing himself at the expense of his neighbour are manifold; the evil of

Right: *The interior of a witch-doctor's hut in southern Zambia, containing effigies and a replica of a coiled snake.*

Opposite: *A Kota guardian figure of the Gabon, Equatorial Africa. These figures, called mbulu-ngulu, are attached to bark boxes or bundles containing bones and other relics of clan or village ancestors, and serve to protect them or to act as a focus for prayers and sacrifices.* Wood with copper and brass. Entwhistle Gallery, London.

which a man seeks to rid himself need not be transferred to a person; it may equally well be transferred to an animal or a thing, though in the last case the thing is often only a vehicle to convey the trouble to

the first person who touches it. In some of the East Indian islands they think that epilepsy can be cured by striking the patient on the face with the leaves of certain trees and then throwing them away. The disease is believed to have passed into the leaves, and to have been thrown away with them.

To cure toothache some of the Australian aborigines apply a heated spear-thrower to the cheek. The spear-thrower is then cast away, and the toothache goes with it in the shape of a black stone called tamitch. Stones of this kind are found in old mounds and sandhills. They are carefully collected and thrown in the direction of enemies in order to give them toothache. The Bahima, a pastoral people of Uganda, often suffer from deep-seated abscesses: "their cure for this is to transfer the disease to some other person by obtaining herbs from the medicine-man, rubbing them over the place where the swelling is, and burying them in the road where people continually pass; the first person who steps over these buried herbs contracts the disease, and the original patient recovers."

Sometimes in case of sickness the malady is transferred to an effigy as a preliminary to passing it on to a human being. Thus among the Baganda the medicine-man would sometimes make a model of his patient in clay; then a relative of the sick man would rub the image over the sufferer's body and either bury it in the road or hide it in the grass by the wayside. The first person who stepped over the image or passed by it would catch the disease. Sometimes the effigy was made out of a plantain-flower tied up so as to look like a person; it was used in the same way as the clay figure. But the use of images for this maleficent purpose was a capital crime; any person caught in the act of burying one of them in the public road would surely have been put to death.

In the western district of the island of Timor, when men or women are making long and tiring journeys, they fan themselves with leafy branches, which they afterwards throw away on particular spots where their forefathers did the same before them. The fatigue which they felt is thus supposed to have passed into

Above: *Two witches riding on broomsticks to the Witches' sabbath. Such aerial adventures were reputed to have been experienced by witches when they rubbed themselves with a powerful hallucinogenic ointment containing henbane and other herbs.* French sixteenth-century manuscript illustration, Bibliothèque Nationale, Paris.

Opposite: *A Native American medicine man, or shaman, in full regalia, in Alaska in 1904.*

the leaves and to be left behind. Others use stones instead of leaves. Similarly in the Babar Archipelago tired people will strike themselves with stones, believing that they thus transfer to the stones the weariness which they felt in their own bodies. They then throw away the stones in places which are specially set apart for the purpose.

A like belief and practice in many distant parts of the world have given rise to those cairns or heaps of

Above: *The magical herb mandrake, which was said to scream in pain when it was pulled from the earth by dogs tied to its stem. Its root resembles the shape of a miniature human.* From a fourteenth-century Trento herbal. Castello Buonconsiglio, Trento, Italy.

Opposite: *Wooden masks of the Ibibio tribe of southeastern Nigeria, twentieth century, which represent people suffering from various diseases. By embodying the spirits of the diseases, these masks were thought to aid in their cures.* Anspach Collection, New York.

sticks and leaves which travellers often observe beside the path, and to which every passing native adds his contribution in the shape of a stone, or stick, or leaf. Thus in the Solomon and Banks Islands the natives are wont to throw sticks, stones, or leaves upon a heap at a place of steep descent, or where a difficult path begins, saying, "There goes my fatigue." The act is not a religious rite, for the thing thrown on the heap is not an offering to spiritual powers, and the words which accompany the act are not a prayer. It is nothing but a magical ceremony for getting rid of fatigue, which the

simple savage fancies he can embody in a stick, leaf, or stone, and so cast it from him.

Animals are often employed as a vehicle for carrying away or transferring the evil. When a Moor has a headache he will sometimes take a lamb or a goat and beat it till it falls down, believing that the headache will thus be transferred to the animal. In Morocco most wealthy Moors keep a wild boar in their stables, in order that the jinn and evil spirits may be diverted from the horses and enter into the boar. Amongst the Caffres of South Africa, when other remedies have failed, "natives sometimes adopt the custom of taking a goat into the presence of a sick man, and confess the sins of the kraal over the animal. Sometimes a few drops of blood from the sick man are allowed to fall on the head of the goat, which is turned out into an uninhabited part of the veldt. The sickness is supposed to be transferred to the animal, and to become lost in the desert." In Arabia, when the plague is raging, the people will sometimes lead a camel through all the quarters of the town in order that the animal may take the pestilence on itself. Then they strangle it in a sacred place and imagine that they have rid themselves of the camel and of the plague at one blow. It is said that when smallpox is raging the aborigines of Formosa will drive the demon of disease into a sow, then cut off the animal's ears and burn them or it, believing that in this way they rid themselves of the plague.

The Bataks of Sumatra have a ceremony which they call "making the curse to fly away." When a woman is childless, a sacrifice is offered to the gods of three grasshoppers, representing a head of cattle, a buffalo, and a horse. Then a swallow is set free, with a prayer that the curse may fall upon the bird and fly away with it. The Huzuls of the Carpathians imagine that they can transfer freckles to the first swallow they see in spring by washing their face in flowing water and saying, "Swallow, swallow, take my freckles, and give me rosy cheeks."

Indeed, men sometimes play the part of scapegoat by diverting to themselves the evils that threaten others. When a Cingalese is dangerously ill, and the physicians can do nothing, a devil-dancer is called in, who by making offerings to the devils, and dancing in the masks appropriate to them, conjures these demons of disease, one after the other, out of the sick man's body and into his own. Having thus successfully extracted the cause of the malady, the artful dancer lies down on a bier, and shamming death is carried to an open place outside the village. Here, being left to himself, he soon comes to life again, and hastens back to claim his reward. In 1590 a Scottish witch of the name of Agnes Sampson was convicted of curing a certain Robert Kers of a disease "laid upon him by a westland warlock when he was at Dumfries, which sickness she took upon herself, and kept the same with great groaning and torment till the morn, at which time there was a great din heard in the house." The noise was made by the witch in her efforts to shift the disease, by means of clothes, from herself to a cat or dog. Unfortunately the attempt partly miscarried. The disease missed the animal and hit Alexander Douglas of Dalkeith, who died of it, while the original patient, Robert Kers, was made whole.

"In one part of New Zealand when an expiation for sin was felt to be necessary; a service was performed over an individual, by which all the sins of the tribe were supposed to be transferred to him, a fern stalk was previously tied to his person, with which he jumped into the river, and there unbinding it, allowed it to float away to the sea, bearing their sins with it."

In great emergencies the sins of the Rajah of Manipur used to be transferred to somebody else, usually to a criminal, who earned his pardon by his vicarious sufferings. To effect the transference the Rajah and his wife, clad in fine robes, bathed on a scaffold erected in the bazaar, while the criminal crouched beneath it. With the water which dripped from them on him their sins also were washed away and fell on the human scapegoat. To complete the transference the Rajah and his wife made over their fine robes to their substitute, while they themselves, clad in new raiment, mixed with the people till evening. In Travancore, when a Rajah is near his end, they seek out a holy Brahman, who consents to take upon himself the sins of the dying man in consideration of the sum of ten thousand rupees. Thus prepared to immolate himself on the altar of duty, the saint is introduced into the chamber of death, and closely embraces the dying Rajah, saying to him, "O King, I undertake to bear all your sins and diseases. May your Highness live long and reign happily." Having thus taken to himself the sins of the sufferer, he is sent away from the country and never more allowed to return. At Utch Kurgan in Turkestan Mr. Schuyler saw an old man who was said to get his living by taking on himself the sins of the dead, and thenceforth devoting his life to prayer for their souls.

In Uganda, when an army had returned from war, and the gods warned the king by their oracles that some evil had attached itself to the soldiers, it was customary to pick out a woman slave from the captives, together with a cow, a goat, a fowl, and a dog from the booty, and send them back under a strong guard to the borders of the country from which they had come. There their limbs were broken and they were left to die; for they were too crippled to crawl back to Uganda. In order to ensure the transference of the evil to these substitutes, bunches of grass were rubbed over the people and cattle and then tied to the victims. After that the army was pronounced clean and was allowed to return to the capital. So on his accession a new king of Uganda used to wound a man and send him away as a scapegoat to Bunyoro to carry away any uncleanliness that might attach to the king or queen.

The examples of the transference of evil hitherto adduced have been mostly drawn from the customs of savage or barbarous peoples. But similar attempts to shift the burden of disease, misfortune, and sin from one's self to another person, or to an animal or thing, have been common also among the civilised nations of Europe, both in ancient and modern times. A Roman cure for fever was to pare the patient's nails, and stick the parings with wax on a neighbour's door before sunrise: the fever then passed from the sick man to his neighbour. Similar devices must have been resorted to by the Greeks; for in laying down laws for his ideal state, Plato thinks it too much to expect that men should not be alarmed at finding certain wax figures adhering to their doors or to the tombstones of their parents, or lying at cross-roads. In the fourth century of our era Marcellus of Bordeaux prescribed a cure for warts, which has still a great vogue among the superstitious in various parts of Europe. You are to touch your warts with as many little stones as you have warts; then wrap the stones in an ivy leaf, and throw them away in a thoroughfare. Whoever picks them up will get the warts, and you will be rid of them.

People in the Orkney Islands will sometimes wash a sick man, and then throw the water down at a gateway, in the belief that the sickness will leave the patient and be transferred to the first person who passes through the gate. A Bavarian cure for fever is to write upon a piece of paper, "Fever, stay away, I am not at home," and to put the paper in somebody's pocket. The latter then catches the fever, and the patient is rid of it. A Bohemian prescription for the same malady is this. Take an empty pot, go with it to a cross-road, throw it down, and run away. The first person who kicks against the pot will catch your fever, and you will be cured.

Often in Europe, as among savages, an attempt is made to transfer a pain or malady from a man to an animal. Grave writers of antiquity recommended that, if a man be stung by a scorpion, he should sit upon an

Above: *The sacred well in the village of Llandegla in Wales, where falling sickness was cured by being transferred to a fowl.*

Opposite: *Willow trees were believed to offer cures for various ailments.* Detail from a painting by Charles Ernest Butler.

ass with his face to the tail, or whisper in the animal's ear, "A scorpion has stung me," in either case, they thought, the pain would be transferred from the man to the ass. Many cures of this sort are recorded by Marcellus. For example, he tells us that the following is a remedy for toothache. Standing booted under the open sky on the ground, you catch a frog by the head, spit into its mouth, ask it to carry away the ache, and then let it go. But the ceremony must be performed on a lucky day and at a lucky hour.

In Cheshire the ailment known as aphtha or thrush, which affects the mouth or throat of infants, is not uncommonly treated in much the same manner. A young frog is held for a few moments with its head inside the mouth of the sufferer, whom it is supposed to relieve by taking the malady to itself. "I assure you," said an old woman who had often superintended such a cure, "we used to hear the poor frog whooping and coughing, mortal bad, for days after; it would have made your heart ache to hear the poor creature coughing as it did about the garden."

A Northamptonshire, Devonshire, and Welsh cure for a cough is to put a hair of the patient's head between two slices of buttered bread and give the sandwich to a dog. The animal will thereupon catch the cough and the patient will lose it. Sometimes an ailment is transferred to an animal by sharing food with it. Thus in Oldenburg, if you are sick of a fever you set a bowl of sweet milk before a dog and say, "Good luck, you hound! may you be sick and I be sound!" Then when the dog has lapped some of the milk, you take a swig at the bowl; and then the dog must lap again, and then you must swig again; and when you and the dog have done it the third time, he will have the fever and you will be quit of it.

A Bohemian cure for fever is to go out into the forest before the sun is up and look for a snipe's nest. When you have found it, take out one of the young birds and keep it beside you for three days. Then go back into the wood and set the snipe free. The fever will leave you at once. The snipe has taken it away. So in Vedic times the Hindoos of old sent consumption away with a blue jay. They said, "O consumption, fly away, fly away with the blue jay! With the wild rush of the storm and the whirlwind, oh, vanish away!"

In the village of Llandegla in Wales there is a church dedicated to the virgin martyr St. Tecla, where the falling sickness is, or used to be, cured by being transferred to a fowl. The patient first washed his limbs in a sacred well hard by, dropped fourpence into it as an offering, walked thrice round the well, and thrice repeated the Lord's prayer. Then the fowl, which was a cock or a hen according as the patient was a man or a woman, was put into a basket and carried round first the well and afterwards the church. Next the sufferer entered the church and lay down under the communion table till break of day. After that he offered sixpence and departed, leaving the fowl in the church. If the bird died, the sickness was

supposed to have been transferred to it from the man or woman, who was now rid of the disorder. As late as 1855 the old parish clerk of the village remembered quite well to have seen the birds staggering about from the effects of the fits which had been transferred to them.

Often the sufferer seeks to shift his burden of sickness or ill-luck to some inanimate object. In Athens there is a little chapel of St. John the Baptist built against an ancient column. Fever patients resort thither, and by attaching a waxed thread to the inner side of the column believe that they transfer the fever from themselves to the pillar. In the Mark of Brandenburg they say that if you suffer from giddiness you should strip yourself naked and run thrice round a flax-field after sunset; in that way the flax will get the giddiness and you will be rid of it.

But perhaps the thing most commonly employed in Europe as a receptacle for sickness and trouble of all sorts is a tree or bush. A Bulgarian cure for fever is to run thrice around a willow-tree at sunrise, crying, "The fever shall shake thee, and the sun shall warm me." In the Greek island of Karpathos the priest ties a red thread round the neck of a sick person. Next morning the friends of the patient remove the thread and go out to the hillside, where they tie the thread to a tree, thinking that they thus transfer the sickness to the tree. Italians attempt to cure fever in like manner by tethering it to a tree. The sufferer ties a thread round his left wrist at night, and hangs the thread on a tree next morning. The fever is thus believed to be tied up to the tree, and the patient to be rid of it; but he must be careful not to pass by that tree again, otherwise the fever would break loose from its bonds and attack him afresh.

A Flemish cure for the ague is to go early in the morning to an old willow, tie three knots in one of its branches, say, "Good-morrow, Old One, I give thee the cold; good-morrow, Old One," then turn and run away without looking round. In Sonnenberg, if you would rid yourself of gout you should go to a young fir-tree and tie a knot in one of its twigs, saying, "God greet thee, noble fir. I bring thee my gout. Here will I tie a knot and bind my gout into it. In the name," etc.

Another way of transferring gout from a man to a tree is this. Pare the nails of the sufferer's fingers and clip some hairs from his legs. Bore a hole in an oak, stuff the nails and hair in the hole, stop up the hole again, and smear it with cow's dung. If, for three months thereafter, the patient is free of gout, you may be sure the oak has it in his stead. In Cheshire if you would be rid of warts, you have only to rub them with a piece of bacon, cut a slit in the bark of an ash tree, and slip the bacon under the bark. Soon the warts will disappear from your hand, only however to reappear in the shape of rough excrescences or knobs on the bark of the tree. At Berkhampstead, in Hertfordshire, there used to be certain oak trees which were long celebrated for the cure of ague. The transference of the malady to the tree was simple but painful. A lock of the sufferer's hair was pegged into an oak; then by a sudden wrench he left his hair and his ague behind him in the tree.

But similar means have been adopted to free a whole community from diverse evils that afflict it. Such attempts to dismiss at once the accumulated sorrows of a people are by no means rare or exceptional; on the contrary they have been made in many lands, and from being occasional they tend to become periodic and annual.

It needs some effort on our part to realise the frame of mind which prompts these attempts. Bred in a philosophy which strips nature of personality and reduces it to the unknown cause of an orderly series of impressions on our senses, we find it hard to put ourselves in the place of the savage, to whom the same impressions appear in the guise of spirits or the handiwork of spirits. For ages the army of spirits, once so near, has been receding farther and farther from us, banished by the magic wand of science from hearth and home, from ruined cell and ivied tower, from haunted glade and lonely mere, from the riven murky cloud that belches forth the lightning, and from those

Above: *The purpose of magic was to keep an army of unseen spirits at bay. A Rabbit among the Fairies* by John Anster Fitzgerald.

Opposite: *By hunting out ghosts and demons, primitive people believed they could restore a golden age. This picture shows how the golden age was imagined in classical times, based upon accounts by the Greek poet Hesiod and the Roman poet Ovid.* Painting on wood, circa 1530, by Lucas Cranach. The Old Picture Gallery, Munich.

fairer clouds that pillow the silvery moon or fret with flakes of burning red the golden eve. The spirits are gone even from their last stronghold in the sky, whose blue arch no longer passes, except with children, for the screen that hides from mortal eyes the glories of the celestial world. Only in poets' dreams or impassioned flights of oratory is it given to catch a glimpse of the last flutter of the standards of the retreating host, to hear the beat of their invisible wings, the sound of their mocking laughter, or the swell of angel music dying away in the distance. Far otherwise is it with the savage. To his imagination the world still teems with those motley beings whom a more sober philosophy has discarded. Fairies and goblins, ghosts and demons, still hover about him both waking and sleeping. They dog his footsteps, dazzle his senses, enter into him, harrass and deceive and torment him in a thousand freakish and mischievous ways. The mishaps that befall him, the losses he sustains, the pains he has to endure, he commonly sets down, if not to the magic of his enemies, to the spite or anger or caprice of the spirits. Their constant presence wearies him, their sleepless malignity exasperates him; he longs with an unspeakable longing to be rid of them altogether, and from time to time, driven to bay, his patience utterly exhausted, he turns fiercely on his persecutors and makes a desperate effort to chase the whole pack of them from the land, to clear the air of their swarming multitudes, that he may breathe more freely and go on his way unmolested, at least for a time. Thus it comes about that the endeavour of primitive people to make a clean sweep of all their troubles generally takes the form of a grand hunting out and expulsion of devils or ghosts. They think that if they can only shake off these their accursed tormentors, they will make a fresh start in life, happy and innocent; the tales of Eden and the old poetic golden age will come true again.

We can therefore understand why those general clearances of evil, to which from time to time the savage resorts, should commonly take the form of a forcible expulsion of devils. In these evil spirits primitive man sees the cause of many if not of most of his troubles, and he fancies that if he can only deliver himself from them, things will go better with him. The public attempts to expel the accumulated ills of a whole community may be divided into two classes, according as the expelled evils are immaterial and invisible or are embodied in a material vehicle or scapegoat. The former may be called the direct or immediate expulsion of evils; the latter the indirect or mediate expulsion, or the expulsion by scapegoat. We begin with examples of the former.

In the island of Rook, between New Guinea and New Britain, when any misfortune has happened, all the people run together, scream, curse, howl, and beat the air with sticks to drive away the devil, who is supposed to be the author of the mishap. From the spot where the mishap took place they drive him step by step to the sea, and on reaching the shore they redouble their shouts and blows in order to expel him from the island. He generally retires to the sea or to the island of Lottin. The natives of New Britain ascribe sickness, drought, the failure of crops, and in short all misfortunes, to the influence of wicked spirits. So at

times when many people sicken and die, as at the beginning of the rainy season, all the inhabitants of a district, armed with branches and clubs, go out by moonlight to the fields, where they beat and stamp on the ground with wild howls till morning, believing that this drives away the devils; and for the same purpose they rush through the village with burning torches.

The natives of New Caledonia are said to believe that all evils are caused by a powerful and malignant

Above: *Witches have been regarded as a threat through much of human history. Here a hallucinogenic potion is being prepared. The Witches' Sabbath, a woodcut of 1510 by Hans Baldung.*

Opposite: *Witches gather for an exorcism. Conjuro painted by Goya in 1798 for the study of the royal summer residence at Alameda. Museo Lazaro Galdiano, Madrid.*

Above: *In the Balinese Barong dance, often used as an exorcism, the hideous witch Rangda battles against the Barong, a dragon-like holy creature whose role is to protect humanity against her evil schemes.*

Opposite: *During a Hindu cremation ceremony in Bali, the body is burned and the ashes taken to a river or the sea, so that they can be cleansed of sin.*

spirit; hence in order to rid themselves of him they will from time to time dig a great pit, round which the whole tribe gathers. After cursing the demon, they fill up the pit with earth, and trample on the top with loud shouts. This they call burying the evil spirit. Among the Dieri tribe of Central Australia, when a serious illness occurs, the medicine-men expel Cootchie or the devil by beating the ground in and outside of the camp with the stuffed tail of a kangaroo, until they have chased the demon away to some distance from the camp.

When a village has been visited by a series of disasters or a severe epidemic, the inhabitants of Minahassa in Celebes lay the blame upon the devils who are infesting the village and who must be expelled from it. Accordingly, early one morning all the people, men, women, and children, quit their homes, carrying their household goods with them, and take up their quarters in temporary huts which have been erected outside the village. Here they spend several days, offering sacrifices and preparing for the final ceremony. At last the men, some wearing masks, others with their faces blackened, and so on, but all armed with swords, guns, pikes, or brooms, steal cautiously and silently back to the deserted village. Then, at a signal from the priest, they rush furiously up and down the streets and into and under the houses (which are raised on piles above the ground), yelling and striking on walls, doors, and windows, to drive away the devils. Next, the priests and the rest of the people come with the holy fire and march nine times round each house and thrice round the ladder that leads up to it, carrying the fire with them. Then they take the fire into the kitchen, where it must burn for three days continuously. The devils are now driven away, and great and general is the joy.

Sometimes, instead of chasing the demon of disease from their homes, savages prefer to leave him in peaceable possession, while they themselves take to flight and attempt to prevent him from following in their tracks. Thus when the Patagonians were attacked by smallpox, which they attributed to the machinations of an evil spirit, they used to abandon their sick and flee, slashing the air with their weapons and throwing water about in order to keep off the dreadful pursuer; and when after several days' march they reached a place where they hoped to be beyond his reach, they used by way of precaution to plant all their cutting weapons with the sharp edges turned towards the quarter from which they had come, as if they were repelling a charge of cavalry. Similarly, when the Lules or Tonocotes Indians of the Gran Chaco were attacked by an epidemic, they regularly sought to evade it by flight, but in so doing they always followed a sinuous, not a straight, course; because they said that when the disease made after them he would be so exhausted by the turnings and windings of the route that he would never be able to come up with them. When the Indians of New Mexico were decimated by smallpox or other infectious disease, they used to shift their quarters every day, retreating into the most sequestered parts of the mountains and choosing the thorniest thickets they could find, in the hope that the smallpox would be too afraid of scratching himself on the thorns to follow them. When some Chins on a visit to Rangoon were attacked by cholera, they went about with drawn swords to scare away the demon,

and they spent the day hiding under bushes so that he might not be able to find them.

The expulsion of evils, from being occasional, tends to become periodic. It comes to be thought desirable to have a general riddance of evil spirits at fixed times, usually once a year, in order that the people may make a fresh start in life, freed from all the malignant influences which have been long accumulating about them. Some of the Australian aborigines annually expelled the ghosts of the dead from their territory. The ceremony was witnessed by the Rev. W. Ridley on the banks of the River Barwan: "A chorus of twenty, old and young, were singing and beating time

Below: *In Penang, Malayisa, the Hungry Ghosts ceremony is held annually to appease the souls of the dead when they are released from purgatory.*

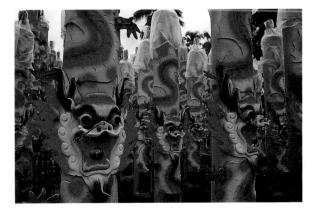

Above: *Saint Zeno exorcizing a woman of a demon.* From the twelfth-century bronze doorway of the San Zeno church in Verona, Italy.

Opposite: *A sorcerer performing a ceremony to drive out evil spirits, in Bunhan, Bhutan.*

with boomerangs . . . Suddenly, from under a sheet of bark darted a man with his body whitened by pipeclay, his head and face coloured with lines of red and yellow, and a tuft of feathers fixed by means of a stick two feet above the crown of his head. He stood twenty minutes perfectly still, gazing upwards. An aboriginal who stood by told me he was looking for the ghosts of dead men. At last he began to move very slowly, and soon rushed to and fro at full speed, flourishing a branch as if to drive away some foes invisible to us. When I thought this pantomime must be almost over, ten more, similarly adorned, suddenly appeared from behind the trees, and the whole party joined in a brisk conflict with their mysterious assailants. At last, after some rapid evolutions in which they put forth all their strength, they rested from the exciting toil which they had kept up all night and for some hours after sunrise; they seemed satisfied that the ghosts were driven away for twelve months. They were performing the same ceremony at every station along the river, and I am told it is an annual custom."

Certain seasons of the year mark themselves naturally out as appropriate moments for a general expulsion of devils. Such a moment occurs towards the close of an Arctic winter, when the sun reappears on the horizon after an absence of weeks or months. Accordingly, at Point Barrow, the most northerly extremity of Alaska, and nearly of America, the Esquimaux choose the moment of the sun's reappearance to hunt the mischievous spirit Tuna from every house. The ceremony was witnessed by the members of the United States Polar Expedition, who wintered at Point Barrow. A fire was built in front of the council-house, and an old woman was posted at the entrance to every house. The men gathered round the council-house while the young women and girls drove the spirit out of every house with their knives, stabbing viciously under the bunk and deer-skins and calling upon Tuna to be gone. When they thought he had been driven out of every hole and corner, they thrust him down through the hole in the floor and chased him into the open air with loud cries and frantic gestures. Meanwhile the old woman at the entrance of the house made passes with a long knife in the air to keep him from returning. Each party drove the spirit towards the fire and invited him to go into it. All were by this time drawn up in a semicircle round the fire, when several of the leading men made specific charges against the spirit; and each after his speech brushed his clothes violently, calling on the spirit to leave him and go into the fire. Two men now stepped forward with rifles loaded with blank cartridges, while a third brought a vessel of urine and flung it on the flames. At the same time one of the men fired a shot into the fire; and as the cloud of steam rose it received the other shot, which was supposed to finish Tuna for the time being.

Sometimes the date of the annual expulsion of devils is fixed with reference to the agricultural seasons. Thus among the Hos of Togoland, in West Africa, the expulsion is performed annually before the people partake of the new yams. The chiefs summon the

priests and magicians and tell them that the people are now to eat the new yams and be merry, therefore they must cleanse the town and remove the evils. Accordingly the evil spirits, witches, and all the ills that infest the people are conjured into bundles of leaves and creepers, fastened to poles, which are carried away and set up in the earth on various roads outside the town. During the following night no fire may be lit and no food eaten. Next morning the women sweep out their hearths and houses, and deposit the sweepings on broken wooden plates. Then the people pray, saying, "All ye sicknesses that are in our body and plague us, we are come to-day to throw you out." Thereupon they run as fast as they can in the direction of Mount Adaklu, smiting their mouths and screaming: "Out to-day! Out to-day!" That which kills anybody, out to-day! Ye evil spirits, out to-day! And all that causes our heads to ache, out to-day! Anlo and Adaklu are the places to which all ill shall betake itself!" When they have come to a certain tree on Mount Adaklu, they throw everything away and return home.

At Kiriwina, in southeastern New Guinea, when the new yams had been harvested, the people feasted and danced for many days, and a great deal of property, such as armlets, native money, and so forth, was displayed conspicuously on a platform erected for the purpose. When the festivities were over, all the people gathered together and expelled the spirits from the village by shouting, beating the posts of the houses, and overturning everything under which a wily spirit might be supposed to lurk. The explanation which the people gave to a missionary was that they had entertained and feasted the spirits and provided them with

riches, and it was now time for them to take their departure. Had they not seen the dances, and heard the songs, and gorged themselves on the souls of the yams, and appropriated the souls of the money and all the other fine things set out on the platform? What more could the spirits want? So out they must go.

Amongst some of the Hindoo Koosh tribes, as among the Hos and Mundaris, the expulsion of devils takes place after harvest. When the last crop of autumn has been got in, it is thought necessary to drive away evil spirits from the granaries. A kind of porridge is eaten, and the head of the family takes his matchlock and fires it into the floor. Then, going outside, he sets to work loading and firing till his powder-horn is exhausted, while all his neighbours are similarly employed. The next day is spent in rejoicings. In Chitral this festival is called "devil-driving."

The people of Bali, an island to the east of Java, have periodical expulsions of devils upon a great scale. Generally the time chosen for the expulsion is the day of the "dark moon" in the ninth month. When the demons have been long unmolested the country is said to be "warm," and the priest issues orders to expel them by force, lest the whole of Bali should be rendered uninhabitable. On the day appointed the people of the village or district assemble at the principal temple. Here at a crossroad offerings are set out for the devils. After prayers have been recited by the priests, the blast of a horn summons the devils to partake of the meal which has been prepared for them. At the same time a number of men step forward and light their torches at the holy lamp which burns before the chief priest. Immediately afterwards, followed by the by-standers, they spread in all directions and march through the streets and lanes crying, "Depart! go away!" Wherever they pass, the people who have stayed at home hasten, by a deafening clatter on doors, beams, rice-blocks, and so forth, to take their share in the expulsion of devils. Thus chased from the houses, the fiends flee to the banquet which has been set out for them; but here the priest receives them with curses which finally drive them from the district.

When the last devil has taken his departure, the uproar is succeeded by a dead silence, which lasts during the next day also. The devils, it is thought, are anxious to return to their old homes, and in order to make them think that Bali is not Bali but some desert island, no one may stir from his own abode for twenty-four hours. Even ordinary household work, includ-

Opposite: *Helmet mask used by the Ngongtang society in anti-witchcraft rituals.* Fang tribe, Gabon, Equatorial Africa.

Below: *Among the Dinkas of North Africa, each family owns a sacred cow. In times of disaster, they may be called upon to supply the cow to act as a scapegoat for the village.*

ing cooking, is discontinued. Only the watchmen may show themselves in the streets. Wreaths of thorns and leaves are hung at all the entrances to warn strangers from entering. Not till the third day is this state of siege raised, and even then it is forbidden to work at the rice-fields or to buy and sell in the market. Most people still stay at home, whiling away the time with cards and dice.

In Christian Europe the old heathen custom of expelling the powers of evil at certain times of the year has survived to modern times. Thus in some villages of Calabria the month of March is inaugurated with the expulsion of the witches. It takes place at

night to the sound of the church bells, the people running about the streets and crying, "March is come." They say that the witches roam about in March, and the ceremony is repeated every Friday evening during the month. Often, as might have been anticipated, the ancient pagan rite has attached itself to church festivals. In Albania on Easter Eve the young people light torches of resinous wood and march in procession, swinging them, through the village. At last they throw the torches into the river, crying, "Ha, Kore! we throw you into the river, like these torches, that you may never return." Silesian peasants believe that on Good Friday the witches go their rounds and have great power for mischief. Hence about Oels, near Strehlitz, the people on that day arm themselves with old brooms and drive the witches from house and home, from farmyard and cattle-stall, making a great uproar and clatter as they do so.

Thus far we have dealt with the class of the general expulsion of evils which I have called direct or immediate. In this class the evils are invisible, at least to common eyes, and the mode of deliverance consists for the most part in beating the empty air and raising such a hubbub as may scare the mischievous spirits and put them to flight. It remains to illustrate the second class of expulsions, in which the evil influences are embodied in a visible form or at least supposed to be loaded upon a material medium, which acts as a vehicle to draw them off from the people of the village or the town.

Often the vehicle which carries away the collected demons or ills of a whole community is an animal or scapegoat. In the Central Provinces of India, when cholera breaks out in a village, everyone retires after sunset to his house. The priests then parade the streets, taking from the roof of each house a straw, which is burnt with an offering of rice, ghee, and turmeric, at some shrine to the east of the village. Chickens daubed with vermilion are driven away in the direction of the smoke, and are believed to carry the disease with them. If they fail, goats are tried, and last of all pigs. When cholera rages among the Bhars, Mallans, and

Above: *Silenus, a spirit of the wild, offering a sacrifice at a blazing altar.* Fragment of a Roman marble relief. Scavi di Ostia, Italy.

Opposite: *The ancient Greek Eumenides, also called the Erinyes, were goddesses who avenged blood guilt within families. Often those who had murdered a relative were driven mad by a sense of guilt, and it was said that the Erinyes had taken their blood-revenge.* Woodcut from *Natalis Comities, Mythologiae.*

Kurmis of India, they take a goat or a buffalo—in either case the animal must be a female, and as black as possible—then having tied some grain, cloves, and red lead in a yellow cloth on its back they turn it out of the village. The animal is conducted beyond the boundary and not allowed to return. Sometimes the buffalo is marked with a red pigment and driven to the next village, where he carries the plague with him.

Amongst the Dinkas, a pastoral people of the White Nile, each family possesses a sacred cow. When the country is threatened with war, famine, or any other public calamity, the chiefs of the village require a particular family to surrender their sacred cow to serve as a scapegoat. The animal is driven by the women to the brink of the river and across it to the other bank, there to wander in the wilderness and fall a prey to ravening beasts. Then the women return in silence and without looking behind them; were they to cast a backward glance, they imagine that the ceremony would have no effect. In 1857, when the Aymara Indians of Bolivia and Peru were suffering from a plague, they loaded a black llama with the clothes of the plague-stricken people, sprinkled brandy on the clothes, and then turned the animal loose on the mountains, hoping that it would carry the pest away with it.

Occasionally the scapegoat is a man. For example, from time to time the gods used to warn the King of Uganda that his foes the Banyoro were working magic against him and his people to make them die of disease. To avert such a catastrophe the king would send a scapegoat to the frontier of Bunyoro, the land of the enemy. The scapegoat consisted of either a man and a boy or a woman and her child, chosen because of some mark or bodily defect, which the gods had noted and by which the victims were to be recognised. With the human victims were sent a cow, a goat, a fowl, and a dog; and a strong guard escorted them to the land which the god had

indicated. There the limbs of the victims were broken and they were left to die a lingering death in the enemy's country, being too crippled to crawl back to Uganda. The disease or plague was thought to have been thus transferred to the victims and to have been conveyed back in their persons to the land from which it came.

Some of the aboriginal tribes of China, as a protection against pestilence, select a man of great muscular strength to act the part of scapegoat. Having besmeared his face with paint, he performs many antics with the view of enticing all pestilential and noxious influences to attach themselves to him only. He is assisted by a priest. Finally the scapegoat, hotly pursued by men and women beating gongs and tom-toms, is driven with great haste out of the town or village. In the Punjab a cure for the murrain is to hire a man of the Chamar caste, turn his face away from

Above: *The butchers who worked for the oba, or king, of Benin sacrifice a cow, the most prestigious animal.* Brass plaque from the palace of the Benin kings, Nigeria, early seventeenth century. British Museum, London.

Opposite: *Detail of demonic figures from an Indian Buddhist painting of the mid-nineteenth century.*

the village, brand him with a red-hot sickle, and let him go out into the jungle taking the murrain with him. He must not look back.

The scapegoat may be a divine man. Thus, in November the Gonds of India worship Ghansyam Deo, the protector of the crops, and at the festival the god himself is said to descend on the head of one of the worshippers, who is suddenly seized with a kind of fit and, after staggering about, rushes off into the jungle, where it is believed that, if left to himself, he would die mad. However, they bring him back, but he does not recover his senses for one or two days. The people think that one man is thus singled out as a scapegoat for the sins of the rest of the village.

In the temple of the Moon the Albanians of the eastern Caucasus kept a number of sacred slaves, of whom many were inspired and prophesied. When one of these men exhibited more than usual symptoms of inspiration or insanity, and wandered solitary up and down the woods, like the Gond in the jungle, the high priest had him bound with a sacred chain and maintained him in luxury for a year. At the end of the year he was anointed with unguents and led forth to be sacrificed. A man whose business it was to slay these human victims and to whom practice had given dexterity, advanced from the crowd and thrust a sacred spear into the victim's side, piercing his heart. From the manner in which the slain man fell, omens were drawn as to the welfare of the commonwealth. Then the body was carried to a certain spot where all the people stood upon it as a purificatory ceremony. This last circumstance clearly indicates that the sins of the people were transferred to the victim, just as the Jewish priest transferred the sins of the people to the scapegoat by laying his hands on the animal's head; and since the man was believed to be possessed by the divine spirit, we have here an undoubted example of a man-god slain to take away the sins and misfortunes of the people.

The employment of a divine man or animal as a scapegoat is especially to be noted; indeed, we are here directly concerned with the custom of banishing

Above: *A medicine bundle of the Crow Eagle tribe of the American plains. When a bird or animal appeared in a shamanic vision, its skin had to be procured and used as a medium to realize its power.*

Opposite: *An animal was chosen as a vehicle to carry away the collected ills of a community. The Scapegoat, painting by William Holman Hunt. (1827-1910.) Lady Lever Art Gallery, Port Sunlight.*

evils only in so far as these evils are believed to be transferred to a god who is afterwards slain. If we ask why a dying god should be chosen to take upon himself and carry away the sins and sorrows of the people, it may be suggested that in the practice of using the divinity as a scapegoat we have a combination of two customs which were at one time distinct and independent. On the one hand it was customary to kill the human or animal god in order to save his divine life from being weakened by the inroads of age. On the other hand we have seen that it has been customary to have a general expulsion of evils and sins once a year. Now, if it occurred to people to

combine these two customs, the result would be the employment of the dying god as a scapegoat. He was killed, not originally to take away sin, but to save the divine life from the degeneracy of old age; but, since he had to be killed at any rate, people may have thought that they might as well seize the opportunity to lay upon him the burden of their sufferings and sins, in order that he might bear it away with him to the unknown world beyond the grave.

The ancient Greeks were also familiar with the use of a human scapegoat. In Plutarch's native town of Chaeronea a ceremony of this kind was performed by the chief magistrate at the Town Hall, and by each householder at his own home. It was called the "expulsion of hunger." A slave was beaten with rods of the agnus castus, and turned out of doors with the words, "Out with hunger, and in with wealth and health." When Plutarch held the office of chief magistrate of his native town he performed this ceremony at the Town Hall, and he has recorded the discussion to which the custom afterwards gave rise.

But in civilised Greece the custom of the scapegoat took darker forms than the innocent rite over which the amiable and pious Plutarch presided. Whenever Marseilles, one of the busiest and most brilliant of Greek colonies, was ravaged by a plague, a man of the poorer classes used to offer himself as a scapegoat. For a whole year he was maintained at the public expense, being fed on choice and pure food. At the expiry of the year he was dressed in sacred garments, decked with holy branches, and led through the whole city, while prayers were uttered that all the evils of the people might fall on his head. He was then cast out of the city or stoned to death by the people outside of the walls. The Athenians regularly maintained a number of degraded and useless beings at the public expense; and when any calamity, such as plague, drought, or famine, befell the city, they sacrificed two of these outcast scapegoats. One of the victims was sacrificed for the men and the other for the women. The former wore round his neck a string of black, the

latter a string of white figs. Sometimes, it seems, the victim slain on behalf of the women was a woman. They were led about the city and then sacrificed, apparently by being stoned to death outside the city. But such sacrifices were not confined to extraordinary occasions of public calamity; it appears that every year, at the festival of the Thargelia in May, two victims, one for the men and one for the women, were led out of Athens and stoned to death. The city of Abdera in Thrace was publicly purified once a year, and one of the burghers, set apart for the purpose, was stoned to death as a scapegoat or vicarious sacrifice for the life of all the others; six days before his execution he was excommunicated, "in order that he alone might bear the sins of all the people."

Chapter Nine

FIRE FESTIVALS

ALL OVER EUROPE the peasants have been accustomed from time immemorial to kindle bonfires on certain days of the year, and to dance round or leap over them. Customs of this kind can be traced back on historical evidence to the Middle Ages, and their analogy to similar customs observed in antiquity goes with strong internal evidence to prove that their origin must be sought in a period long prior to the spread of Christianity. Indeed the earliest proof of their observance in Northern Europe is furnished by the attempts made by Christian synods in the eighth century to put them down as heathenish rites.

In the Eifel Mountains of Rhenish Prussia, on the first Sunday in Lent young people used to collect straw and brushwood from house to house. These they carried to an eminence and piled up round a tall, slim beech tree, to which a piece of wood was fastened at right angles to form a cross. The structure was known as the "hut" or "castle." Fire was set to it and the young people marched round the blazing "castle" bareheaded, each carrying a lighted torch and praying aloud. Sometimes a straw-man was burned in the "hut." People observed the direction in which the smoke blew from the fire. If it blew towards the corn fields, it was a sign that the harvest would be abundant. On the same day, in some parts of the Eifel, a great wheel was made of straw and dragged by three horses to the top of the hill. Thither the village boys marched at nightfall, set fire to the wheel, and sent it rolling down the slope. At

Opposite: *European fire festivals were recorded in the Middle Ages and are likely to date back to antiquity. The Fire Dragon pageant of Barcelona in Spain.*

Above: *The Boat of the Sun, carrying seven gods along with the sacred symbol of the scarab beetle. Because he rolled his egg into a spherical ball of mud, he was a symbol of the sun and of self-generation to the ancient Egyptians. From the* Book of the Dead Papyrus *of Anhai.*

Oberstattfeld the wheel had to be provided by the young man who was last married. About Echternach in Luxemburg the same ceremony is called "burning the witch." At Voralberg in the Tyrol, on the first Sunday in Lent, a slender young fir tree is surrounded with a pile of straw and firewood. To the top of the tree is fastened a human figure called the "witch," made of old clothes and stuffed with gunpowder. At night the whole is set on

Above: *The Stenness Stone Circle at summer sunset on the island of Orkney, off the coast of Scotland. Thought to date from circa 3,000 B.C.*

Opposite: *Modern Druids performing a ritual at Stonehenge in Wiltshire, England, at the summer solstice sunrise, when the sun can be seen to slide precisely over the sighting-stone, now called the "Heel Stone," outside the circle.*

fire and boys and girls dance round it, swinging torches and singing rhymes in which the words "corn in the winnowing-basket, the plough in the earth" may be distinguished. In Swabia on the first Sunday in Lent a figure called the "witch" or the "old wife" or "winter's grandmother" is made up of clothes and fastened to a pole. This is stuck in the middle of a pile of wood, to which fire is applied. While the "witch" is burning, the young people throw blazing discs into the air. The discs are thin round pieces of wood, a few inches in diameter, with notched edges to imitate the rays of the sun or stars. They have a hole in the middle, by which they are attached to the end of a wand. Before the disc is thrown

it is set on fire, the wand is swung to and fro, and the impetus thus communicated to the disc is augmented by dashing the rod sharply against a sloping board. The burning disc is thus thrown off, and mounting high into the air, describes a long fiery curve before it reaches the ground. The charred embers of the burned "witch" and discs are taken home and planted in the flax-fields the same night, in the belief that they will keep vermin from the fields.

In Switzerland, also, it is or used to be customary to kindle bonfires on high places on the evening of the first Sunday in Lent, and the day is therefore popularly known as Spark Sunday. The custom prevailed, for example, throughout the canton of Lucerne. Boys went about from house to house begging for wood and straw, then piled the fuel on a conspicuous mountain or hill round about a pole, which bore a straw effigy called "the witch." At nightfall the pile was set on fire, and the young folks danced wildly round it, some of them cracking whips or ringing bells; and when the fire burned low enough, they leaped over it. This was called "burning the witch." In some parts of the canton also they used to wrap old wheels in straw and thorns, put a light to them, and send them rolling and blazing down hill. The more bonfires could be seen sparkling and flaring in the darkness, the more fruitful was the year expected to be; and the higher the dancers leaped beside or over the fire, the higher, it was thought, would grow the flax. In some districts it was the last married man or woman who must kindle the bonfire.

In the central Highlands of Scotland bonfires, known as the Beltane fires, were formerly kindled with great ceremony on the first of May, and the traces of human sacrifices at them were particularly clear and unequivocal. The custom of lighting the bonfires lasted in various places far into the eighteenth century, and the descriptions of the ceremony by writers of that period present such a curious and interesting picture of ancient heathendom surviving in our own country that I will reproduce some here. The fullest of the descriptions is the one bequeathed to us by John Ramsay, laird of Ochtertyre, near Crieff, the patron of Burns and the

friend of Sir Walter Scott. He says: "But the most considerable of the Druidical festivals is that of Beltane, or May-day, which was lately observed in some parts of the Highlands with extraordinary ceremonies . . .Like the other public worship of the Druids, the Beltane feast seems to have been performed on hills or eminences. They thought it degrading to him whose temple is the universe, to suppose that he would dwell in any house made with hands. Their sacrifices were therefore offered in the open air, frequently upon the tops of hills, where they were presented with the grandest views of nature, and were nearest the seat of warmth and order. And, according to tradition, such was the manner of celebrating this festival in the Highlands within the last hundred years. But since the decline of superstition, it has been celebrated by the people of each hamlet on some hill or rising ground around which their cattle were pasturing. Thither the young folks repaired in the morning, and cut a trench, on the summit of which a seat of turf was formed for the company. And in the middle a pile of wood or other fuel was placed, which of old they kindled with tein-eigin—i.e., forced-fire or need-fire. Although, for many years past, they have been contented with common fire, yet we shall now describe the process, because ... recourse is still had to the tein-eigin upon extraordinary emergencies.

"The night before, all the fires in the country were carefully extinguished, and next morning the materials for exciting this sacred fire were prepared. The most primitive method seems to be that which was used in the islands of Skye, Mull, and Tiree. A well-seasoned plank of oak was procured, in the midst of which a hole was bored. A wimble of the same timber was then applied, the end of which they fitted to the hole. But in some parts of the mainland the machinery was different. They used a frame of green wood, of a square form, in the centre of which was an axle-tree. In some places three times three persons, in others three times nine, were required for turning round by turns the axle-tree or wimble. If any of them had been guilty of murder, adultery, theft, or other atrocious crime, it was imagined either that the fire would not kindle, or that it

would be devoid of its usual virtue. So soon as any sparks were emitted by means of the violent friction, they applied a species of agaric which grows on old birch-trees, and is very combustible. This fire had the appearance of being immediately derived from heaven and manifold were the virtues ascribed to it."

The Beltane fires seem to have been kindled also in Ireland, for Cormac, "or somebody in his name, says that belltaine, May-day, was so called from the 'lucky fire,' or the 'two fires,' which the druids of Erin used to make on that day with great incantations; and cattle, he adds, used to be brought to those fires, or to be driven between them, as a safeguard against the diseases of the year." The custom of driving cattle through or between fires on May Day or the eve of May Day persisted in Ireland down to a time within living memory.

The first of May is a great popular festival in the more midland and southern parts of Sweden. On the eve of the festival huge bonfires, which should be lighted by striking two flints together, blaze on all the hills and knolls. Every large hamlet has its own fire, round which the young people dance in a ring. The old folk notice whether the flames incline to the north or to the south. In the former case, the spring will be cold and

Above: *The Solstice Fire blazing in the Norwegian town of Bergen.*
Opposite: *Bonfire Night (November 5th). An effigy of the Roman Pope is still burned at Lewes in Sussex, England.*

backward; in the latter, it will be mild and genial. In Bohemia, on the eve of May Day, young people kindle fires on hills and eminences, at crossways, and in pastures, and dance round them. They leap over the glowing embers or even through the flames. The ceremony is called "burning the witches." In some places an effigy representing a witch used to be burnt in the bonfire. We have to remember that the eve of May Day is the notorious Walpurgis Night, when the witches are everywhere speeding unseen through the air on their hellish errands. On this witching night children in Voigtland also light bonfires on the heights and leap over them. Moreover, they wave burning brooms or toss them into the air. So far as the light of the bonfire reaches, so far will a blessing rest on the fields. The kindling of the fires on Walpurgis Night is called "driving away the witches." The custom of kindling fires on the eve of May Day (Walpurgis Night) for the purpose of burning the witches is, or used to be, widespread in the Tyrol, Moravia, Saxony and Silesia.

But the season at which these fire-festivals have been most generally held all over Europe is the summer solstice, that is Midsummer Eve (the twenty-third of June) or Midsummer Day (the twenty-fourth of June). A faint tinge of Christianity has been given to them by naming Midsummer Day after St. John the Baptist, but we cannot doubt that the celebration dates from a time long before the beginning of our era. The summer solstice, or Midsummer Day, is the great turning-point in the sun's career, when, after climbing higher and higher day by day in the sky, the luminary stops and thenceforth retraces his steps down the heavenly road. Such a moment could not but be regarded with anxiety by primitive man so soon as he began to observe and ponder the courses of the great lights across the celestial vault; and having still to learn his own powerlessness in face of the vast cyclic changes of nature, he may have fancied that he could help the sun in his seeming decline—could prop his failing steps and rekindle the sinking flame of the red lamp in his feeble hand.

In some such thoughts as these the midsummer festivals of our European peasantry may perhaps have taken

their rise. Whatever their origin, they have prevailed all over this quarter of the globe, from Ireland on the west to Russia on the east, and from Norway and Sweden on the north to Spain and Greece on the south. According to a mediaeval writer, the three great features of the midsummer celebration were the bonfires, the procession with torches round the fields, and the custom of rolling a wheel. He tells us that boys burned bones and filth of various kinds to make a foul smoke, and that the smoke drove away certain noxious dragons which at this time, excited by the summer heat, copulated in the air and poisoned the wells and rivers by dropping their seed into them; and he explains the custom of trundling a wheel to mean that the sun, having now reached the highest point in the ecliptic, begins thenceforward to descend.

A writer of the first half of the sixteenth century informs us that in almost every village and town of Germany public bonfires were kindled on the Eve of St. John, and young and old, of both sexes, gathered about them and passed the time in dancing and singing. People on this occasion wore chaplets of mugwort and vervain, and they looked at the fire through bunches of larkspur which they held in their hands, believing that this would preserve their eyes in a healthy state throughout the year. As each departed, he threw the mugwort and vervain into the fire, saying, "May all my ill-luck depart and

Above: *A personification of the traditional sacred Druid herb vervain, used in their rituals. It should not be confused with the different plant, lemon verbena, used to make a herbal tea called "vervain" by the French. By A. Grandville, from* Les Fleurs Animées.

Opposite: *The traditional sacred herb mugwort (*Artemisia vulgaris*), said to stimulate the pineal gland and bring psychic insight. In Germany, people wore chaplets of mugwort and vervain on the Eve of St. John.*

be burnt up with these." At Lower Konz, a village situated on a hillside overlooking the Moselle, the midsummer festival used to be celebrated as follows. A quantity of straw was collected on the top of the steep Stromberg Hill. Every inhabitant, or at least every householder, had to contribute his share of straw to the pile. At nightfall the whole male population, men and boys, mustered on the top of the hill; the women and girls were not allowed to join them, but had to take up their position at a certain spring half-way down the slope. On the summit stood a huge wheel completely encased in some of the straw which had been jointly contributed by the villagers; the rest of the straw was made into torches. From each side of the wheel the axle-tree projected

about three feet, thus furnishing handles to the lads who were to guide it in its descent. The mayor of the neighbouring town of Sierck, who always received a basket of cherries for his services, gave the signal; a lighted torch was applied to the wheel, and as it burst into flame, two young fellows, strong-limbed and swift of foot, seized the handles and began running with it down the slope. A great shout went up. Every man and boy waved a blazing torch in the air, and took care to keep it alight so long as the wheel was trundling down the hill. The great object of the young men who guided the wheel was to plunge it blazing into the water of the Moselle; but they rarely succeeded in their efforts, for the vineyards which cover the greater part of the declivity impeded their progress, and the wheel was often burned out before it reached the river. As it rolled past the women and girls at the spring, they raised cries of joy which were answered by the men on the top of the mountain; and the shouts were echoed by the inhabitants of neighbouring villages who watched the spectacle from their hills on the opposite bank of the Moselle. If the fiery wheel was successfully conveyed to the bank of the river and extinguished in the water, the people looked for an abundant vintage that year, and the inhabitants of Konz had the right to exact a waggon-load of white wine from the surrounding vineyards. On the other hand, they believed that, if they neglected to perform the ceremony, the cattle would be attacked by giddiness and convulsions and would dance in their stalls.

Down at least to the middle of the nineteenth century the midsummer fires used to blaze all over Upper Bavaria. They were kindled especially on the mountains, but also far and wide in the lowlands, and we are told that in the darkness and stillness of night the moving groups, lit up by the flickering glow of the flames, presented an impressive spectacle. Cattle were driven through the fire to cure the sick animals and to guard such as were sound against plague and harm of every kind throughout the year. Many a householder on that day put out the fire on the domestic hearth and rekindled it by means of a brand taken from the midsummer bonfire. The people judged of the height to which the

Above: *A Guy Fawkes bonfire, such as are held all over England every November 5th to celebrate the failure of the Catholic "Gunpowder Plot," to blow up the English Houses of Parliament, in Elizabethan times.*

Opposite: *A Swiss spring festival. European herdsmen drive cattle out into the open to fresh grass on the approach of summer. May festivals coincide with this important time in the herdmen's year.*

flax would grow in the year by the height to which the flames of the bonfire rose; and whoever leaped over the burning pile was sure not to suffer from backache in reaping the corn at harvest. In many parts of Bavaria it was believed that the flax would grow as high as the young people leaped over the fire. In others the old folk used to plant three charred sticks from the bonfire in the fields, believing that this would make the flax grow tall. Elsewhere an extinguished brand was put in the roof of the house to protect it against fire. In the towns about Wurzburg the bonfires used to be kindled in the market-places, and the young people who jumped over them wore garlands of flowers, especially of mugwort and vervain, and carried sprigs of larkspur in their hands. They thought that such as looked at the fire holding a bit of larkspur before their face would be troubled by no malady of the eyes throughout the year. Further, it was customary at Wurzburg, in the sixteenth century, for the bishop's followers to throw burning discs of wood into the air from a mountain which overhangs the town. The discs were discharged by means of flexible rods, and in their flight through the darkness presented the appearance of fiery dragons.

Similarly in Swabia, lads and lasses, hand in hand, leap over the midsummer bonfire, praying that the hemp may grow three ells high, and they set fire to wheels of straw and send them rolling down the hill. Sometimes, as the people sprang over the midsummer bonfire they cried out, "Flax, flax! May the flax this year grow seven ells high!" At Rottenburg a rude effigy in human form, called the Angelman, used to be enveloped in flowers and then burnt in the midsummer fire by boys, who afterwards leaped over the glowing embers.

In Austria the midsummer customs and superstitions resemble those of Germany. Thus in some parts of the Tyrol bonfires are kindled and burning discs hurled into the air. In the lower valley of the Inn a tatterdemalion effigy is carted about the village on Midsummer Day and then burned. He is called the Lotter, which has been corrupted into Luther. At Ambras, one of the villages where Martin Luther is thus burned in effigy, they say that if you go through the village between eleven and twelve on St. John's Night and wash yourself in three wells, you will see all who are to die in the following year. At Gratz on St. John's Eve (the twenty-third of June) the common people used to make a puppet called the Tatermann, which they dragged to the bleaching ground, and pelted with burning besoms till it took fire. At Reutte, in the Tyrol, people believed that the flax would grow as high as they leaped over the midsummer bonfire, and they took pieces of charred wood from the fire and stuck them in their flax-fields the same night, leaving them there till the flax harvest had been got in. In Lower Austria bonfires are kindled on the heights, and the boys caper round them, brandishing lighted torches drenched in pitch. Whoever jumps thrice across the fire will not suffer from fever within the year. Cart-wheels are often smeared with pitch, ignited, and sent rolling and blazing down the hillsides.

In many parts of Prussia and Lithuania great fires are kindled on Midsummer Eve. All the heights are ablaze with them, as far as the eye can see. The fires are sup-posed to be a protection against witchcraft, thunder, hail, and cattle disease, especially if next morning the cattle are driven over the places where the fires burned. Above all, the bonfires ensure the farmer against the arts of witches, who try to steal the milk from his cows by charms and spells. That is why next morning you may see the young fellows who lit the bonfire going from house to house and receiving jugfuls of milk. And for the same reason they stick burs and mugwort on the gate or the hedge through which the cows go to pasture, because that is supposed to be a preservative against witchcraft.

In Masuren, a district of Eastern Prussia inhabited by a branch of the Polish family, it is the custom on the evening of Midsummer Day to put out all the fires in the village. Then an oaken stake is driven into the ground and a wheel is fixed on it as on an axle. This wheel the villagers, working by relays, cause to revolve with great rapidity till fire is produced by friction. Everyone takes home a lighted brand from the new fire and with it rekindles the fire on the domestic hearth. In Serbia on Midsummer Eve herdsmen light torches of birch bark and march round the sheepfolds and cattle-stalls; then they climb the hills and there allow the torches to burn out.

Among the Magyars in Hungary the midsummer fire-festival is marked by the same features that meet us in so many parts of Europe. On Midsummer Eve in

many places it is customary to kindle bonfires on heights and to leap over them, and from the manner in which the young people leap the bystanders predict whether they will marry soon. On this day also many Hungarian swineherds make fire by rotating a wheel round a wooden axle wrapt in hemp, and through the fire thus made they drive their pigs to preserve them from sickness.

The Estonians of Russia, who, like the Magyars, belong to the great Turanian family of mankind, also celebrate the summer solstice in the usual way. They think that the St. John's fire keeps witches from the cattle, and they say that he who does not come to it will have his barley full of thistles and his oats full of weeds. In the Estonian island of Oesel, while they throw fuel into the midsummer fire, they call out, "Weeds to the fire, flax to the field," or they fling three billets into the flames, saying, "Flax grow long!" And they take charred sticks from the bonfire home with them and keep them to make the cattle thrive. In some parts of the island the bonfire is formed by piling brushwood and other combustibles round a tree, at the top of which a flag flies. Whoever succeeds in knocking down the flag with a pole before it begins to burn will have good luck. Formerly the festivities lasted till daybreak, and ended in scenes of debauchery which looked doubly hideous by the growing light of a summer morning.

When we pass from the east to the west of Europe we still find the summer solstice celebrated with rites of the same general character. Down to about the middle of the nineteenth century the custom of lighting bonfires at midsummer prevailed so commonly in France that there was hardly a town or a village, we are told, where they were not kindled. People danced round and leaped over them, and took charred sticks from the bonfire home with them to protect the houses against lightning, conflagrations, and spells.

In Brittany, apparently, the custom of the midsummer bonfires is kept up to this day. When the flames have died down, the whole assembly kneels round about the bonfire and an old man prays aloud. Then they all rise and march thrice round the fire; at the third turn they stop and everyone picks up a pebble and throws it on the

burning pile. After that they disperse. In Brittany and Berry it is believed that a girl who dances round nine midsummer bonfires will marry within the year. In the valley of the Orne the custom was to kindle the bonfire just at the moment when the sun was about to dip below the horizon; and the peasants drove their cattle through the fires to protect them against witchcraft, especially against the spells of witches and wizards who attempted to steal the milk and butter. At Jumieges in Normandy, down to the first half of the nineteenth century, the midsummer festival was marked by certain singular features which bore the stamp of a very high antiquity. Every year, on the twenty-third of June, the Eve of St. John, the Brotherhood of the Green Wolf chose a new chief or master, who had always to be taken from the hamlet of Conihout. On being elected, the new head of the brotherhood assumed the title of the Green Wolf, and donned a peculiar costume consisting of a long green mantle and a very tall green hat of a conical shape and without a brim. Thus arrayed he stalked solemnly at the head of the brothers, chanting the hymn of St. John, the crucifix and holy banner leading the way, to a place called Chouquet. Here the procession was met by the priest, precentors, and choir, who conducted the brotherhood to the parish church. After hearing mass the company adjourned to the house of the Green Wolf, where a simple repast was served up to them. At night a bonfire was kindled to the sound of hand-bells by a young man and a young woman, both decked with flowers. Then the Green Wolf and his brothers, with their hoods down on their shoulders and holding each other by the hand, ran round the fire after the man who had been chosen to be the Green Wolf of the following year. Though only the first and the last man of the chain had a hand free, their business was to surround and seize thrice the future Green Wolf, who in his efforts to escape belaboured the brothers with a long wand which he carried. When at last they succeeded in catching him

Opposite: *Masked "green men" feature in many European festivals. Decked out with leaves and foliage, they date back to pagan rites, often associated with fertility. Spring festival in Urnash in Switzerland.*

they carried him to the burning pile and made as if they would throw him on it. This ceremony over, they returned to the house of the Green Wolf, where a supper, still of the most meagre fare, was set before them. Up till midnight a sort of religious solemnity prevailed. But at the stroke of twelve all this was changed. Constraint gave way to license; pious hymns were replaced by Bacchanalian ditties, and the shrill quavering notes of the village fiddle hardly rose above the roar of voices that went up from the merry brotherhood of the Green Wolf. Next day, the twenty-fourth of June or Midsummer Day, was celebrated by the same personages with the same noisy gaiety. One of the ceremonies consisted in parading, to the sound of musketry, an enormous loaf of consecrated bread, which, rising in tiers, was surmounted by a pyramid of verdure adorned with ribbons. After that the holy hand-bells, deposited on the step of the altar, were entrusted as insignia of office to

Above: *People in China celebrate a torch festival.*

Opposite: *Japanese temple festival during which the celebrants wear animal masks and circle the temple ground, holding burning torches to light their path.*

the man who was to be the Green Wolf next year.

Bonfires were lit in almost all the hamlets of Poitou on the Eve of St. John. People marched round them thrice, carrying a branch of walnut in their hand. Shepherdesses and children passed sprigs of mullein (verbascum) and nuts across the flames; the nuts were supposed to cure toothache, and the mullein to protect the cattle from sickness and sorcery. When the fire died down people took some of the ashes home with them, either to keep them in the house as a preservative against thunder or to scatter them on the fields for the purpose of destroying corn-cockles and darnel. In Poitou also it used to be customary on the Eve of St.

John to trundle a blazing wheel wrapt in straw over the fields to fertilise them.

In Provence the midsummer fires are still popular. Children go from door to door begging for fuel, and they are seldom sent empty away. Formerly the priest, the mayor, and the aldermen used to walk in procession to the bonfire, and even deigned to light it; after which the assembly marched thrice round the burning pile. At Aix a nominal king, chosen from among the youth for his skill in shooting at a popinjay, presided over the midsummer festival. He selected his own oficiers, and escorted by a brilliant train marched to the bonfire, kindled it, and was the first to dance round it. Next day he distributed largesse to his followers. His reign lasted a year, during which he enjoyed certain privileges. He was allowed to attend the mass celebrated by the commander of the Knights of St. John on St. John's Day; the right of hunting was accorded to

him, and soldiers might not be quartered in his house. At Marseilles also on this day one of the guilds chose a king of the badache or double axe; but it does not appear that he kindled the bonfire, which is said to have been lighted with great ceremony by the prefet and other authorities.

The custom of lighting bonfires at midsummer has been observed in many parts of our own country, and as usual people danced round and leaped over them. In Wales three or nine different kinds of wood and charred faggots carefully preserved from the last midsummer were deemed necessary to build the bonfire, which was generally done on rising ground. In the Vale of Glamorgan a cart-wheel swathed in straw used to be ignited and sent rolling down the hill. If it kept alight all the way down and blazed for a long time, an abundant harvest was expected.

On Midsummer Eve people in the Isle of Man were

wont to light fires to the windward of every field, so that the smoke might pass over the corn; and they folded their cattle and carried blazing furze or gorse round them several times. In Ireland cattle, especially barren cattle, were driven through the midsummer fires, and the ashes were thrown on the fields to fertilise them, or live coals were carried into them to prevent blight. In Scotland the traces of midsummer fires are few; but at that season in the highlands of Perthshire cowherds used to go round their folds thrice, in the direction of the sun, with lighted torches. This they did to purify the flocks and herds and to keep them from falling sick.

From the foregoing survey we may infer that among the heathen forefathers of the European peoples the most popular and widespread fire-festival of the year was the great celebration of Midsummer Eve or Midsummer Day. The coincidence of the festival with the summer solstice can hardly be accidental. Rather we must suppose that our pagan ancestors purposely timed the ceremony of fire on earth to coincide with the arrival of the sun at the highest point of his course in the sky. If that was so, it follows that the old founders of the midsummer rites had observed the solstices or turning-points of the sun's apparent path in the sky, and that they accordingly regulated their festal calendar to some extent by astronomical considerations.

But while this may be regarded as fairly certain for what we may call the aborigines throughout a large part of the continent, it appears not to have been true of the Celtic peoples who inhabited the Land's End of Europe, the islands and promontories that stretch out into the Atlantic Ocean on the north-west. The principal fire-festivals of the Celts, which have survived, though in a restricted area and with diminished pomp, to modern times and even to our own day, were seemingly timed without any reference to the position of the sun in the heaven. They were two in number, and fell at an interval of six months, one being celebrated on the eve of May Day and the other on Allhallow Even or Hallowe'en, as it is now commonly called, that is, on the thirty-first of October, the day preceding All Saints' or Allhallows' Day. These dates coincide with none of the four great hinges on which the solar year revolves, to wit, the solstices and the equinoxes. Nor do they agree with the

principal seasons of the agricultural year, the sowing in spring and the reaping in autumn. For when May Day comes, the seed has long been committed to the earth; and when November opens, the harvest has long been reaped and garnered, the fields lie bare, the fruit-trees are stripped, and even the yellow leaves are fast fluttering to the ground. Yet the first of May and the first of November mark turning-points of the year in Europe; the one ushers in the genial heat and the rich vegetation of summer, the other heralds, if it does not share, the cold and barrenness of winter. Now these particular points of the year, as has been well pointed out by a learned and ingenious writer, while they are of comparatively little moment to the European husbandman, do deeply concern the European herdsman; for it is on the approach of summer that he drives his cattle out into the open to crop the fresh grass, and it is on the approach of winter that he leads them back to the safety and shelter of the stall. Accordingly it seems not improbable that the Celtic bisection of the year into two halves at the beginning of May and the beginning of November dates from a time when the Celts were mainly a pastoral people, dependent for their subsistence on their herds, and when accordingly the great epochs of the year for them were the days on which the cattle went forth from the homestead in early summer and returned to it again in early winter. Even in Central Europe, remote from the region now occupied by the Celts, a similar bisection of the year may be clearly traced in the great popularity, on the one hand, of May Day and its Eve (Walpurgis Night), and, on the other hand, of the Feast of All Souls at the beginning of November, which under a thin Christian cloak conceals an ancient pagan festival of the dead. Hence we may conjecture that everywhere throughout Europe the celestial division of the year according to the solstices was preceded by what we may call a terrestrial division of the year according to the beginning of summer and the beginning of winter.

Be that as it may, the two great Celtic festivals of May Day and the first of November or, to be more accurate, the Eves of these two days, closely resemble each other in the manner of their celebration and in the

Above: *Midsummer Eve coincides with the summer solstice which was the greatest festival of the year.* Painting by Edward Robert Hughes.

Opposite: *Hallowe'en falls on the same day as the great Celtic fire festivals.* Painting by James H. Edgar, 1864.

superstitions associated with them, and alike, by the antique character impressed upon both, betray a remote and purely pagan origin. If the heathen of ancient Europe celebrated, as we have good reason to believe, the season of Midsummer with a great festival of fire, of which the traces have survived in many places down to our own time, it is natural to suppose that they should have observed with similar rites the corresponding season of Midwinter; for Midsummer and Midwinter, or, in more technical language, the summer solstice and the winter solstice, are the two great turning-points in the sun's apparent course through the sky, and from the standpoint of primitive man nothing might seem more

appropriate than to kindle fires on earth at the two moments when the fire and heat of the great luminary in heaven begin to wane or to wax.

In modern Christendom the ancient fire-festival of the winter solstice appears to survive, or to have survived down to recent years, in the old custom of the Yule log, clog, or block, as it was variously called in England. The custom was widespread in Europe, but seems to have flourished especially in England, France, and among the southern Slavs; at least the fullest accounts of the custom come from these quarters. That the Yule log was only the winter counterpart of the midsummer bonfire, kindled within doors instead of in the open air on account of the cold and inclement weather of the season, was pointed out long ago by our English antiquary John Brand, and the view is supported by the many quaint superstitions attaching to the Yule log, superstitions which have no apparent connexion with Christianity but carry their heathen origin plainly stamped upon them. But while the two solstitial celebrations were both festivals of fire, the necessity or desirability of holding the winter celebration within doors lent it the character of a private or domestic festivity, which contrasts strongly with the publicity of the summer celebration, at which the people gathered on some open space or conspicuous height, kindled a huge bonfire in common, and danced and made merry round it together.

Down to about the middle of the nineteenth century the old rite of the Yule log was kept up in some parts of Central Germany. Thus in the valleys of the Sieg and Lahn the Yule log, a heavy block of oak, was fitted into the floor of the hearth, where, though it glowed under the fire, it was hardly reduced to ashes within a year. When the new log was laid next year, the remains of the old one were ground to powder and strewed over the fields during the Twelve Nights, which was supposed to promote the growth of the crops. In some villages of Westphalia, the practice was to withdraw the Yule log (Christbrand) from the fire so soon as it was slightly charred; it was then kept carefully to be replaced on the fire whenever a thunderstorm broke, because the peo-

Above: *The solstice sunset seen over the so-called "winter solstice monolith" at Mystery Hill, North Salem, New Hampshire, United States. Known as the "American Stonehenge," it consists of a large complex of stone constructions.*

Opposite: *Prometheus stole fire from heaven and brought it to men concealed in a stalk of the Giant Fennel, a plant of the Libyan coast. Prometheus Carrying Fire by Jan Cossters, seventeenth century.*

ple believed that lightning would not strike a house in which the Yule log was smouldering. In other villages of Westphalia the old custom was to tie up the Yule log in the last sheaf cut at harvest.

In several provinces of France, and particularly in Provence, the custom of the Yule log or trefoir, as it was called in many places, was long observed. A French writer of the seventeenth cenury denounces as superstitious "the belief that a log called the trefoir or Christmas brand, which you put on the fire for the first time on Christmas Eve and continue to put on the fire for a little while every day till Twelfth Night, can, if kept under

Above: *The Yule log being dragged into the house for Christmas festivities. The yule log was lit at Christmas and burned slowly throughout the year, protecting the house from fire and lightning.* Engraving from Chamber's *Book of Days*, London, 1862.

the bed, protect the house for a whole year from fire and thunder; that it can prevent the inmates from having chilblains on their heels in winter; that it can cure the cattle of many maladies; that if a piece of it be steeped in the water which cows drink it helps them to calve; and lastly that if the ashes of the log be strewn on the fields it can save the wheat from mildew."

In some parts of Flanders and France the remains of the Yule log were regularly kept in the house under a bed as a protection against thunder and lightning; in Berry, when thunder was heard, a member of the family used to take a piece of the log and throw it on the fire, which was believed to avert the lightning. Again, in Perigord, the charcoal and ashes are carefully collected and kept for healing swollen glands; the part of the trunk which has not been burnt in the fire is used by ploughmen to make the wedge for their plough, because they allege that it causes the seeds to thrive better; and the women keep pieces of it till Twelfth Night for the sake of their chickens. Some people imagine that they will have as many chickens as there are sparks that fly out of the brands of the log when they shake them; and others place the extinct brands under the bed to drive away vermin. In various parts of France the charred log is thought to guard the house against sorcery as well as against lightning.

In England the customs and beliefs concerning the Yule log used to be similar. On the night of Christmas Eve, says the antiquary John Brand, "our ancestors were wont to light up candles of an uncommon size, called Christmas Candles, and lay a log of wood upon the fire, called a Yule-clog or Christmas-block, to illuminate the house, and, as it were, to turn night into day." The old custom was to light the Yule log with a fragment of its predecessor, which had been kept throughout the year for the purpose; where it was so kept, the fiend could do no mischief. The remains of the log were also supposed to guard the house against fire and lightning.

To this day the ritual of bringing in the Yule log is observed with much solemnity among the southern Slavs, especially the Serbians. The log is usually a block of oak, but sometimes of olive or beech. They seem to think that they will have as many calves, lambs, pigs, and kids as they strike sparks out of the burning log. Some people carry a piece of the log out to the fields to protect them against hail. In Albania down to recent years it was a common custom to burn a Yule log at Christmas, and the ashes of the fire were scattered on the fields to make them fertile. The Huzuls, a Slavonic people of the Carpathians, kindle fire by the friction of wood on Christmas Eve (Old Style, the fifth of January) and keep it burning till Twelfth Night.

It is remarkable how common the belief appears to have been that the remains of the Yule log, if kept throughout the year, had power to protect the house against fire and especially against lightning. As the Yule log was frequently of oak, it seems possible that this belief may be a relic of the old Aryan creed which associated the oak tree with the god of thunder. Whether the curative and fertilising virtues ascribed to the ashes of the Yule log, which are supposed to heal cattle as well as men, to enable cows to calve, and to promote the fruitfulness of the earth, may not be derived from the same ancient source, is a question which deserves to be considered.

The foregoing survey of the popular fire-festivals of Europe suggests some general observations. In the first place we can hardly help being struck by the resemblance which the ceremonies bear to each other, at whatever time of the year and in whatever part of Europe they are celebrated. The custom of kindling great bonfires, leaping over them, and driving cattle through or round them would seem to have been practically universal throughout Europe, and the same may be said of the processions or races with blazing torches round fields, orchards, pastures, or cattle-stalls. Less widespread are the customs of hurling lighted discs into the air and trundling a burning wheel down hill. The ceremonial of the Yule log is distinguished from that of the other fire-festivals by the privacy and domesticity which characterise it; but this distinction may well be due simply to the rough weather of midwinter, which is apt not only to render a public assembly in the open air disagreeable, but also at any moment to defeat the object of the assembly by extinguishing the all-important fire under a downpour of rain or a fall of snow. Apart from these local or seasonal differences, the general resemblance between the fire-festivals at all times of the year and in all places is tolerably close. And as the ceremonies themselves resemble each other, so do the benefits which the people expect to reap from them. Whether applied in the form of bonfires blazing at fixed points, or of torches carried about from place to place, or of embers and ashes taken from the smouldering heap of fuel, the fire is believed to promote the growth of the crops and the welfare of man and beast, either positively by stimulating them, or negatively by averting the dangers and calamities which threaten them from such causes as thunder and lightning, conflagration, blight, mildew, vermin, sterility, disease, and not least of all witchcraft.

But we naturally ask, How did it come about that benefits so great and manifold were supposed to be attained by means so simple? In what way did people imagine that they could procure so many goods or avoid so many ills by the application of fire and smoke, of embers and ashes? In regard to the dates of the festivals it can be no mere accident that two of the most important and widely spread of the festivals are timed to coincide more or less exactly with the summer and winter solstices, that is, with the two turning-points in the sun's apparent course in the sky when he reaches respectively his highest and his lowest elevation at noon. Indeed with respect to the midwinter celebration of Christmas we are not left to conjecture; we know from the express testimony of the ancients that it was instituted by the church to supersede an old heathen festival of the birth of the sun, which was apparently conceived to be born again on the shortest day of the year, after which his light and heat were seen to grow till they attained their full maturity at midsummer. Therefore it is no very far-fetched conjecture to suppose that the Yule log, which figures so prominently in the popular celebration of Christmas, was originally designed to help the labouring sun of midwinter to rekindle his seemingly expiring light.

Not only the date of some of the festivals but the manner of their celebration suggests a conscious imitation of the sun. The custom of rolling a burning wheel down a hill, which is often observed at these ceremonies, might well pass for an imitation of the sun's course in the sky, and the imitation would be especially appropriate on Midsummer Day when the sun's annual declension begins. Indeed the custom has been thus interpreted by some of those who have recorded it. Not less graphic, it may be said, is the mimicry of his apparent revolution by swinging a burning tar-barrel round a pole. Again, the common practice of throwing fiery discs, sometimes expressly said to be shaped like suns, into the air at the festivals may well be a piece of imitative magic. In these, as in so many cases, the magic force may be supposed to take effect through mimicry or sympathy: by imitating the desired result you actually produce it; by counterfeiting the sun's progress through the heavens you really help the luminary to pursue his celestial journey with punctuality and despatch. The name "fire of heaven," by which the midsummer fire is sometimes popularly known, clearly implies a consciousness of a connexion between the earthly and the heavenly flame.

Again, the manner in which the fire appears to have been originally kindled on these occasions has been alleged in support of the view that it was intended to be a mock-sun. As some scholars have perceived, it is highly probable that at the periodic festivals in former times fire was universally obtained by the friction of two pieces of wood. It is still so procured in some places both at the Easter and the midsummer festivals, and it is expressly said to have been formerly so procured at the Beltane celebration both in Scotland and Wales. But what makes it nearly certain that this was once the invariable mode of kindling the fire at these periodic festivals is the analogy of the need-fire, which has almost always been produced by the friction of wood, and sometimes by the revolution of a wheel. It is a plausible conjecture that the wheel employed for this purpose represents the sun, and if the fires at the regularly recurring celebrations were formerly produced in the same way, it might be regarded as a confirmation of the view that they were originally sun-charms. In point of fact there is, as Kuhn has indicated, some evidence to show that the midsummer fire was originally thus produced. We have seen that many Hungarian swine-herds make fire on Midsummer Eve by rotating a wheel round a wooden axle wrapt in hemp, and that they drive their

Opposite: *The Sun Chariot of Apollo.* Painting by Odilon Redon, 1907-10. Musée des Beaux-Arts, Bordeaux, France.

pigs through the fire thus made. At Ober-medlingen, in Swabia, the "fire of heaven," as it was called, was made on St. Vitus's Day (the fifteenth of June) by igniting a cart-wheel, which, smeared with pitch and plaited with straw, was fastened on a pole twelve feet high, the top of the pole being inserted in the nave of the wheel. This fire was made on the summit of a mountain, and as the flame ascended, the people uttered a set form of words, with eyes and arms directed heavenward. Here the fixing of a wheel on a pole and igniting it suggests that originally the fire was produced, as in the case of the need-fire, by the revolution of a wheel. The day on which the ceremony takes place (the fifteenth of June)

is near midsummer; and in Masuren fire is, or used to be, actually made on Midsummer Day by turning a wheel rapidly about an oaken pole, though it is not said that the new fire so obtained is used to light a bonfire.

Further, the influence which these fires, whether periodic or occasional, are supposed to exert on the weather and vegetation may be cited in support of the view that they are sun-charms, since the effects ascribed to them resemble those of sunshine. Thus, the French belief that in a rainy June the lighting of the midsummer bonfires will cause the rain to cease appears to assume that they can disperse the dark clouds and make the sun to break out in radiant glory,

drying the wet earth and dripping trees. Similarly the
use of the need-fire by Swiss children on foggy days for
the purpose of clearing away the mist may very naturally be interpreted as a sun-charm. In the Vosges
Mountains the people believe that the midsummer fires
help to preserve the fruits of the earth and ensure good
crops. In Sweden the warmth or cold of the coming
season is inferred from the direction in which the
flames of the May Day bonfire are blown; if they blow
to the south, it will be warm, if to the north, cold. No
doubt at present the direction of the flames is regarded
merely as an augury of the weather, not as a mode of
influencing it. But we may be pretty sure that this is one
of the cases in which magic has dwindled into divination. So in the Eifel Mountains, when the smoke blows
towards the corn-fields, this is an omen that the harvest
will be abundant. But the older view may have been not
merely that the smoke and flames prognosticated, but
that they actually produced an abundant harvest, the
heat of the flames acting like sunshine on the corn.
Perhaps it was with this view that people in the Isle of
Man lit fires to windward of their fields in order that
the smoke might blow over them. So in South Africa,
about the month of April, the Matabeles light huge fires
to the windward of their gardens, "their idea being that
the smoke, by passing over the crops, will assist the
ripening of them." Among the Zulus also "medicine is
burned on a fire placed to windward of the garden, the
fumigation which the plants in consequence receive
being held to improve the crop." Again, the idea of our
European peasants that the corn will grow well as far as
the blaze of the bonfire is visible, may be interpreted as
a remnant of the belief in the quickening and fertilising
power of the bonfires. The same belief, it may be
argued, reappears in the notion that embers taken from
the bonfires and inserted in the fields will promote the
growth of the crops, and it may be thought to underlie
the customs of sowing flax-seed in the direction in

which the flames blow, of mixing the ashes of the bonfire with the seed-corn at sowing, of scattering the
ashes by themselves over the field to fertilise it, and of
incorporating a piece of the Yule log in the plough to
make the seeds thrive. The opinion that the flax or
hemp will grow as high as the flames rise or the people
leap over them belongs clearly to the same class of
ideas. Again, at Konz, on the banks of the Moselle, if the
blazing wheel which was trundled down the hillside
reached the river without being extinguished, this was
hailed as a proof that the vintage would be abundant. So
firmly was this belief held that the successful perfor-
mance of the ceremony entitled the villagers to levy a
tax upon the owners of the neighbouring vineyards.
Here the unextinguished wheel might be taken to represent an unclouded sun, which in turn would portend
an abundant vintage. So the waggon-load of white wine
which the villagers received from the vineyards round
about might pass for a payment for the sunshine which
they had procured for the grapes. Similarly in the Vale
of Glamorgan a blazing wheel used to be trundled
down hill on Midsummer Day, and if the fire were
extinguished before the wheel reached the foot of the
hill, the people expected a bad harvest; whereas if the
wheel kept alight all the way down and continued to
blaze for a long time, the farmers looked forward to
heavy crops that summer. Here, again, it is natural to
suppose that the rustic mind traced a direct connection
between the fire of the wheel and the fire of the sun, on
which the crops are dependent.

But in popular belief the quickening and fertilising
influence of the bonfires is not limited to the vegetable
world; it extends also to animals. This plainly appears
from the Irish custom of driving barren cattle through
the midsummer fires, from the French belief that the
Yule log steeped in water helps cows to calve, from the
French and Serbian notion that there will be as many
chickens, calves, lambs, and kids as there are sparks
struck out of the Yule log, from the French custom of
putting the ashes of the bonfires in the fowls' nests to
make the hens lay eggs, and from the German practice
of mixing the ashes of the bonfires with the drink of

Above: *The Hatherleigh Fire Carnival in Devonshire, England, is held every year on the Wednesday nearest to November 5th.*

Opposite: *A panel of the silver Gundestrup cauldron, which is Celtic in origin, but was taken by the Vikings as plunder. Taranis the thunder god hurls a wheel of fire.* Detail from the inside of the cauldron. National Museum, Copenhagen.

cattle in order to make the animals thrive. Further, there are clear indications that even human fecundity is supposed to be promoted by the genial heat of the fires. In Morocco the people think that childless couples can obtain offspring by leaping over the midsummer bonfire. It is an Irish belief that a girl who jumps thrice over the midsummer bonfire will soon marry and become the mother of many children; in Flanders women leap over the midsummer fires to ensure an easy delivery; in various parts of France they think that if a girl dances round nine fires she will be sure to marry within the year, and in Bohemia they fancy that she will do so if she merely sees nine of the bonfires. On the other hand, in Lechrain people say that if a young man and woman, leaping over the midsummer fire together, escape unsmirched, the young woman will not become a mother within twelve months; the flames have not touched and fertilised her. In parts of

Switzerland and France the lighting of the Yule log is accompanied by a prayer that the women may bear children, the she-goats bring forth kids, and the ewes drop lambs. The rule observed in some places that the bonfires should be kindled by the person who was last married seems to belong to the same class of ideas, whether it be that such a person is supposed to receive from, or to impart to, the fire a generative and fertilising influence. The common practice of lovers leaping over the fires hand in hand may very well have originated in a notion that thereby their marriage would be blessed with offspring; and the like motive would explain the custom which obliges couples married within the year to dance to the light of torches. And the scenes of profligacy which appear to have marked the midsummer celebration among the Estonians, as they once marked the celebration of May Day among ourselves, may have sprung, not from the mere licence of holiday-makers, but from a crude notion that such orgies were justified, if not required, by some mysterious bond which linked the life of man to the courses of the heavens at this turning-point of the year.

At the festivals which we are considering the custom of kindling bonfires is commonly associated with a custom of carrying lighted torches about the fields, the orchards, the pastures, the flocks and the herds; and we can hardly doubt that the two customs are only two different ways of attaining the same object, namely, the benefits which are believed to flow from the fire, whether it be stationary or portable. Accordingly if we accept the solar theory of the bonfires, we seem bound to apply it also to the torches; we must suppose that the practice of marching or running with blazing torches about the country is simply a means of diffusing far and wide the genial influence of the sunshine of which these flickering flames are a feeble imitation.

We have still to ask, What is the meaning of burning effigies in the fire at these festivals? After the preceding investigation the answer to the question seems obvious. As the fires are often alleged to be kindled for the purpose of burning the witches, and as the effigy burnt in them is sometimes called "the Witch," we might naturally be disposed to conclude that all the effigies consumed in the flames on these occasions represent witches or warlocks, and that the custom of burning them is merely a substitute for burning the wicked men and women themselves, since on the principle of imitative magic you effectively destroy the witch herself in destroying her effigy. Yet it may be that this explanation does not apply to all the cases, and that certain of them may admit and even require another interpretation.

In the popular customs connected with the fire-festivals of Europe there are certain features which appear to point to a former practice of human sacrifice. We have reasons for believing that in Europe living persons have often acted as representatives of the tree-spirit and corn-spirit and have suffered death as such. Of human sacrifices offered on these occasions the most unequivocal traces, as we have seen, are those which, about a hundred years ago, still lingered at the Beltane fires in the Highlands of Scotland, that is, among a Celtic people who, situated in a remote cor-

Above: *The Mexican gods Tezcatlipoca and Huitzilopochtli are featured on this Aztec bas relief. Tezcatlipoca represents the summer sun, needed for the harvest but also bringing the risk of drought.* National Anthropological Museum, Mexico City.

Opposite: *According to Roman historians, the British Celts made giant wicker men in which prisoners were placed and burned alive as sacrifices.*

ner of Europe and almost completely isolated from foreign influence, had till then conserved their old heathenism better perhaps than any other people in the West of Europe. It is significant, therefore, that human sacrifices by fire are known, on unquestionable evidence, to have been systematically practised by the Celts. The earliest description of these sacrifices has been bequeathed to us by Julius Caesar. As conqueror of the hitherto independent Celts of Gaul, Caesar had ample opportunity of observing the national Celtic religion and manners, while these were still fresh and crisp from the native mint and had not yet been fused in the melting-pot of Roman civilisation. With his own notes Caesar appears to have incorporated the observations of a Greek explorer, by name Posidonius, who travelled in Gaul about fifty years before Caesar carried the Roman arms to the English Channel. The Greek geographer Strabo and the historian Diodorus seem also to have derived their descriptions of the Celtic sacrifices from the work of Posidonius, but independently of each other, and of Caesar, for each of

the three derivative accounts contain some details which are not to be found in either of the others. By combining them, therefore, we can restore the original account of Posidonius with some probability, and thus obtain a picture of the sacrifices offered by the Celts of Gaul at the close of the second century before our era. The following seem to have been the main outlines of the custom. Condemned criminals were reserved by the Celts in order to be sacrificed to the gods at a great festival which took place once in every five years. The more there were of such victims, the greater was believed to be the fertility of the land. If there were not enough criminals to furnish victims, captives taken in war were immolated to supply the deficiency.

When the time came the victims were sacrificed by the Druids or priests. Some they shot down with arrows, some they impaled, and some they burned alive in the following manner. Colossal images of wicker work or of wood and grass were constructed; these were filled with live men, cattle, and animals of other kinds; fire was then applied to the images, and they were burned with their living contents.

Thus it appears that the sacrificial rites of the Celts of ancient Gaul can be traced in the popular festivals of modern Europe. Naturally it is in France, or rather in the wider area comprised within the limits of ancient Gaul, that these rites have left the clearest traces in the customs of burning giants of wickerwork and animals enclosed in wickerwork or baskets. These customs, it will have been remarked, are generally observed at or about midsummer. From this we may infer that the original rites of which these are the degenerate successors were solemnised at midsummer. This inference harmonises with the conclusion suggested by a general survey of European folk custom, that the midsummer festival must on the whole have been the most widely diffused and the most solemn of all the yearly festivals celebrated by the primitive Aryans in Europe.

Chapter Ten

THE WANDERING SOUL

IN AN EARLIER part of this work (see p.105) we saw that, in the opinion of primitive people, the soul may temporarily absent itself from the body without causing death. Such temporary absences of the soul are often believed to involve considerable risk, since the wandering soul is liable to a variety of mishaps at the hands of enemies, and so forth. But there is another aspect to this power of disengaging the soul from the body. If only the safety of the soul can be ensured during its absence, there is no reason why the soul should not continue absent for an indefinite time; indeed a man may, on a pure calculation of personal safety, desire that his soul should never return to his body. Unable to conceive of life abstractly as a "permanent possibility of sensation" or a "continuous adjustment of internal arrangements to external relations," the savage thinks of it as a concrete material thing of a definite bulk, capable of being seen and handled, kept in a box or jar, and liable to be bruised, fractured, or smashed in pieces. It is not needful that the life, so conceived, should be in the man; it may be absent from his body and still continue to animate him by virtue of a sort of sympathy or action at a distance. So long as this object which he calls his life or soul remains unharmed, the man is well; if it is injured, he suffers; if it is destroyed, he dies. Or, to put it otherwise, when a man is ill or dies, the fact is explained by saying that the material object called his life or soul, whether it be in his body or out of it, has either sustained injury or been

Above: *A scene from the epic poem Ramayana in which the heroic Indian prince, Rama, is searching for his beloved Sita.* Indian painting of 1780. National Museum of India, New Delhi.

Opposite: *Serket, one of four goddesses who protected the dead, guarding the canopic chest containing the viscera of the young pharoah Tutankhamen.* Gilded wood. Cairo Museum, Egypt.

destroyed. But there may be circumstances in which, if the life or soul remains in the man, it stands a greater chance of sustaining injury than if it were stowed away in some safe and secret place. Accordingly, in such circumstances, primitive man takes his soul out of his body and deposits it for security in some snug spot, intending to replace it in his body when the danger is past. Or if he should discover some place of absolute security, he may be content to leave his soul there permanently. The advantage of this is that, so long as the soul remains unharmed in the place where he has deposited it, the man himself is immortal; nothing can kill his body, since his life is not in it.

Evidence of this primitive belief is furnished by a class of folk tales of which the Norse story of "The giant who had no heart in his body" is perhaps the best-known example. Stories of this kind are widely diffused over the world, and from their number and the variety of incident and of details in which the leading idea is embodied, we may infer that the conception of an external soul is one which has had a powerful hold on the minds of men at an early stage of history. For folk tales are a faithful reflection of the world as it appeared to the primitive mind; and we may be sure that any idea which commonly occurs in them, however absurd it may seem to us, must once have been an ordinary article of belief. This assurance, so far as it concerns the supposed power of disengaging the soul from the body for a longer or shorter time, is amply corroborated by a comparison of the folk tales in question with the actual beliefs and practices of savages. To this we shall return after some specimens of the tales have been given. The specimens will be selected with a view of illustrating both the characteristic features and the wide diffusion of this class of tales.

In the first place, the story of the external soul is told, in various forms, by all Aryan peoples from Hindoostan to the Hebrides. A very common form of it is this: a warlock, giant, or other fairyland being is invulnerable and immortal because he keeps his soul hidden far away in some secret place; but a fair princess, whom he holds enthralled in his enchanted castle, wiles his secret from him and reveals it to the hero, who seeks out the warlock's soul, heart, life, or death (as it is variously called), and by destroying it, simultaneously kills the warlock. Thus a Hindoo story tells how a magician called Punchkin held a queen captive for twelve years, and would fain marry her, but she would not have him. At last the queen's son came to rescue her, and the two plotted together to kill Punchkin. So the queen spoke the magician fair, and pretended that she had at last made up her mind to marry him. "And do tell me," she said, "are you quite

immortal? Can death never touch you? And are you too great an enchanter ever to feel human suffering?" "It is true," he said, "that I am not as others. Far, far away, hundreds of thousands of miles from this, there lies a desolate country covered with thick jungle. In the midst of the jungle grows a circle of palm trees, and in the centre of the circle stand six chattees full of water, piled one above another: below the sixth chattee is a small cage, which contains a little green parrot;—on the life of the parrot depends my life;—and if the parrot is killed I must die. It is, however," he added, "impossible that the parrot should sustain any injury, both on account of the inaccessibility of the country, and because, by my appointment, many thousand genii surround the palm trees, and kill all who approach the place." But the queen's young son overcame all difficulties, and got possession of the parrot. He brought it to the door of the magician's palace, and began playing with it. Punchkin, the magician, saw him, and, coming out, tried to persuade the boy to give him the parrot. "Give me my parrot!" cried Punchkin. Then the boy took hold of the parrot and tore off one of his wings; and as he did so the magician's right arm fell off. Punchkin then stretched out his left arm, crying, "Give me my parrot!" The prince pulled off the parrot's second wing, and the magician's left arm tumbled off. "Give me my parrot!" cried he, and fell on his knees. The prince pulled off the parrot's right leg, the magician's right leg fell off; the prince pulled off the parrot's left leg, down fell the magician's left. Nothing remained of him except the trunk and the head; but still he rolled his eyes, and cried, "Give me my parrot!" "Take your parrot, then," cried the boy; and with that he wrung the bird's neck, and threw it at the magician; and, as he did so, Punchkin's head twisted round, and, with a fearful groan, he died! In another Hindoo tale an ogre is asked by his daughter, "Papa, where do you keep your soul?" "Sixteen miles away from this place," he said, "is a tree. Round the tree are tigers, and bears, and scorpions, and snakes; on the top of the tree is a very great fat snake; on his head is a little cage; in the cage is a bird; and my soul is in that bird." The end of the ogre is like that of the magician in the previous tale. As the bird's wings and legs are torn off, the ogre's arms and legs drop off; and when its neck is wrung he falls down dead. In a Bengali story it is said that all the ogres dwell in Ceylon, and that all their lives are in a single lemon. A boy cuts the lemon in pieces, and all the ogres die.

In a Siamese or Cambodian story, probably derived from India, we are told that Thossakan or Ravana, the King of Ceylon, was able by magic art to take his soul out of his body and leave it in a box at home, while he went to the wars. Thus he was invulnerable in battle. When he was about to give battle to Rama, he deposited his soul with a hermit called Fire-eye, who was to keep it safe for him. So in the fight Rama was astounded to see that his arrows struck the king without wounding him. But one of Rama's allies, knowing the secret of the king's invulnerability, transformed himself

Below: *A Minoan fresco from the Palace of Knossos on Crete, showing someone balancing on the back of a bull, in a acrobatic pose.* The "Toreador's Fresco," circa 1500 B.C. National Archaeological Museum, Athens.

by magic into the likeness of the king, and going to the hermit asked back his soul. On receiving it he soared up into the air and flew to Rama, brandishing the box and squeezing it so hard that all the breath left the King of Ceylon's body, and he died.

In a Bengali story a prince going into a far country planted with his own hands a tree in the courtyard of his father's palace, and said to his parents, "This tree is my life. When you see the tree green and fresh, then know that it is well with me; when you see the tree fade in some parts, then know that I am in an ill case; and when you see the whole tree fade, then know that I am dead and gone." In another Indian tale a prince, setting forth on his travels, left behind him a barley plant, with instructions that it should be carefully tended and watched; for if it flourished, he would be alive and well, but if it drooped, then some mischance was about to happen to him. And so it fell out. For the prince was beheaded, and as his head rolled off, the barley plant snapped in two and the ear of barley fell to the ground.

In Greek tales, ancient and modern, the idea of an external soul is not uncommon. When Meleager was

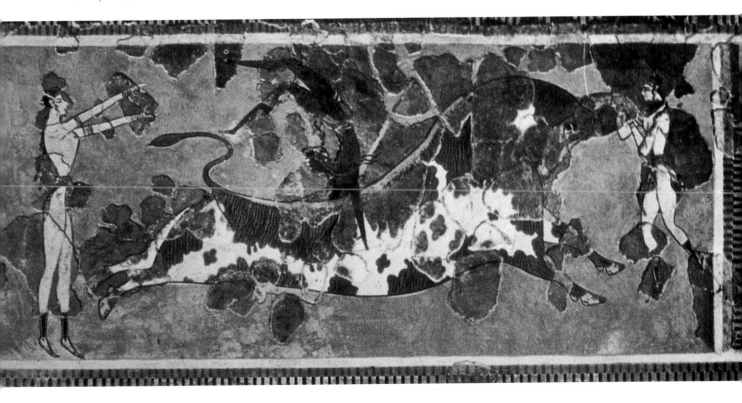

seven days old, the Fates appeared to his mother and told her that Meleager would die when the brand which was blazing on the hearth had burnt down. So his mother snatched the brand from the fire and kept it in a box. But in after-years, being enraged at her son for slaying her brothers, she burnt the brand in the fire and Meleager expired in agonies, as if flames were preying on his vitals.

Again, Nisus King of Megara had a purple or golden hair on the middle of his head, and it was fated that whenever the hair was pulled out the king should die. When Megara was besieged by the Cretans, the king's daughter Scylla fell in love with Minos, their king, and pulled out the fatal hair from her father's head. So he died. In a modern Greek folk tale a man's strength lies in three golden hairs on his head. When his mother pulls them out, he grows weak and timid and is slain by his enemies. In another modern Greek story the life of an enchanter is bound up with three doves which are in the belly of a wild boar. When the first dove is killed, the magician grows sick; when the second is killed, he grows very sick; and when the third is killed, he dies. In another Greek story of the same sort an ogre's strength is in three singing birds which are in a wild boar. The hero kills two of the birds, and then coming to the ogre's house finds him lying on the ground in great pain. He shows the third bird to the ogre, who begs that the hero will either let it fly away or give it to him to eat. But the hero wrings the bird's neck, and the ogre dies on the spot.

In a modern Roman version of "Aladdin and the Wonderful Lamp," the magician tells the princess, whom he holds captive in a floating rock in mid-ocean, that he will never die. The princess reports this to the prince her husband, who has come to rescue her. The prince replies, "It is impossible but that there should be some one thing or other that is fatal to him; ask him what that one fatal thing is." So the princess asked the magician, and he told her that in the wood was a hydra with seven heads; in the middle head of the hydra was a leveret, in the head of the leveret was a bird, in the bird's head was a precious

stone, and if this stone were put under his pillow he would die. The prince procured the stone, and the princess laid it under the magician's pillow. No sooner did the enchanter lay his head on the pillow than he gave three terrible yells, turned himself round and round three times, and died.

Stories of the same sort are current among Slavonic peoples. Thus a Russian story tells how a warlock called Koshchei the Deathless carried off a princess and kept her prisoner in his golden castle. However, a prince made up to her one day as she was walking alone and disconsolate in the castle garden, and cheered by the prospect of escaping with him she went to the warlock and coaxed him with false and flattering words, saying, "My dearest friend, tell me, I pray you, will you never die?" "Certainly not," says he. "Well," says she, "and where is your death? Is it in your dwelling?" "To be sure it is," says he, "it is in the broom under the threshold." Thereupon the princess seized the broom and threw it on the fire, but although the broom burned, the deathless Koshchei remained alive; indeed not so much as a hair of him was singed. Balked in her first attempt, the artful hussy pouted and said, "You do not love me true, for you have not told me where your death is; yet I am not angry, but love you with all my heart." With these fawning words she besought the warlock to tell her truly where his death was. So he laughed and said, "Why do you wish to know? Well then, out of love I will tell you where it lies. In a certain field there stand three green oaks, and under the roots of the largest oak is a worm, and if ever this worm is found and crushed, that instant I shall die." When the princess heard these words, she went straight to her lover and told him all; and he searched till he found the oaks and dug up the worm and crushed it. Then he hurried to the warlock's castle, but only to learn from the princess that the warlock was still alive. Then she fell to wheedling and coaxing Koshchei once more, and this time, overcome by her wiles, he opened his heart to her and told her the truth. "My death," said he, "is far from here and hard to find, on

Above: *An illustration from* Aladdin and the Wonderful Lamp.

the wide ocean. In that sea is an island, and on the island there grows a green oak, and beneath the oak is an iron chest, and in the chest is a small basket, and in the basket is a hare, and in the hare is a duck, and in the duck is an egg; and he who finds the egg and breaks it, kills me at the same time." The prince naturally procured the fateful egg and with it in his hands he confronted the deathless warlock. The monster would have killed him, but the prince began to squeeze the egg. At that the warlock shrieked with pain, and turning to the false princess, who stood by smirking and smiling, "Was it not out of love for you," said he, "that I told you where my death was? And is this the return you make to me?" With that he grabbed at his sword, which hung from a peg on the wall; but before he could reach it, the prince had crushed the egg, and sure enough the deathless warlock found his death at the same moment. "In one of the descriptions of Koshchei's death, he is said to be killed by a blow on the forehead inflicted by the mys-

185

"The King stepped out
and the fight began"
THE SOULLESS KING

terious egg—that last link in the magic chain by which his life is darkly bound. In another version of the same story, but told of a snake, the fatal blow is struck by a small stone found in the yolk of an egg, which is inside a duck, which is inside a hare, which is inside a stone, which is on an island."

Amongst peoples of the Teutonic stock stories of the external soul are not wanting. In a tale told by the Saxons of Transylvania it is said that a young man shot at a witch again and again. The bullets went clean through her but did her no harm, and she only laughed and mocked at him. "Silly earthworm," she cried, "shoot as much as you like. It does me no harm. For know that my life resides not in me but far, far away. In a mountain is a pond, on the pond swims a duck, in the duck is an egg, in the egg burns a light, that light is my life. If you could put out that light, my life would be at an end. But that can never, never be." However, the young man got hold of the egg, smashed it, and put out the light, and with it the witch's life went out also.

In a German story a cannibal called Body without Soul or Soulless keeps his soul in a box, which stands on a rock in the middle of the Red Sea. A soldier gets possession of the box and goes with it to Soulless, who begs the soldier to give him back his soul. But the soldier opens the box, takes out the soul, and flings it backward over his head. At the same moment the cannibal drops dead to the ground.

In another German story an old warlock lives with a damsel all alone in the midst of a vast and gloomy wood. She fears that being old he may die and leave her alone in the forest. But he reassures her. "Dear child," he said, "I cannot die, and I have no heart in my breast." But she importuned him to tell her where his heart was. So he said, "Far, far from here in an unknown and lonesome land stands a great church. The church is well secured with iron doors, and round about it flows a broad deep moat. In the church flies a bird and in the bird is my heart. So long as the bird lives, I live. It can-

Opposite *"The King stepped out and the fight began."* Illustration of the Soulless King, from *The Golden Bough*, London, 1925.

not die of itself, and no one can catch it; therefore I cannot die, and you need have no anxiety." However the young man, whose bride the damsel was to have been before the warlock spirited her away, contrived to reach the church and catch the bird. He brought it to the damsel, who stowed him and it away under the warlock's bed. Soon the old warlock came home. He was ailing, and said so. The girl wept and said, "Alas, daddy is dying; he has a heart in his breast after all." "Child," replied the warlock, "hold your tongue. I can't die. It will soon pass over." At that the young man under the bed gave the bird a gentle squeeze; and as he did so, the old warlock felt very unwell and sat down. Then the young man gripped the bird tighter, and the warlock fell senseless from his chair. "Now squeeze him dead," cried the damsel. Her lover obeyed, and when the bird was dead, the old warlock also lay dead on the floor.

In the Norse tale of "The giant who had no heart in his body," the giant tells the captive princess, "Far, far away in a lake lies an island, on that island stands a church, in that church is a well, in that well swims a duck, in that duck there is an egg, and in that egg there lies my heart." The hero of the tale, with the help of some animals to whom he had been kind, obtains the egg and squeezes it, at which the giant screams piteously and begs for his life. But the hero breaks the egg in pieces and the giant at once bursts. In another Norse story a hill-ogre tells the captive princess that she will never be able to return home unless she finds the grain of sand which lies under the ninth tongue of the ninth head of a certain dragon; but if that grain of sand were to come over the rock in which the ogres live, they would all burst "and the rock itself would become a gilded palace, and the lake green meadows." The hero finds the grain of sand and takes it to the top of the high rock in which the ogres live. So all the ogres burst and the rest falls out as one of the ogres had foretold.

In a Celtic tale, recorded in the West Highlands of Scotland, a giant is questioned by a captive queen as to where he keeps his soul. At last, after deceiving her several times, he confides to her the fatal secret: "There is a great flagstone under the threshold. There is a wether

under the flag. There is a duck in the wether's belly, and an egg in the belly of the duck, and it is in the egg that my soul is." On the morrow when the giant was gone, the queen contrived to get possession of the egg and crushed it in her hands, and at that very moment the giant, who was coming home in the dusk, fell down dead.

In another Celtic tale, a sea beast has carried off a king's daughter, and an old smith declares that there is no way of killing the beast but one. "In the island that is in the midst of the loch is Eillid Chaisfhion—the white-footed hind, of the slenderest legs, and the swiftest step, and though she should be caught, there would spring a hoodie out of her, and though the hoodie should be caught, there would spring a trout out of her, but there is an egg in the mouth of the trout, and the soul of the beast is in the egg, and if the egg breaks, the beast is dead." As usual the egg is broken and the beast dies.

In an Irish story we read how a giant kept a beautiful damsel a prisoner in his castle on the top of a hill, which was white with the bones of the champions who had tried in vain to rescue the fair captive. At last the hero, after hewing and slashing at the giant all to no purpose, discovered that the only way to kill him was to rub a mole on the giant's right breast with a certain egg, which was in a duck, which was in a chest, which lay locked and bound at the bottom of the sea. With the help of some obliging animals, the hero made himself master of the precious egg and slew the giant by merely striking it against the mole on his right breast. Similarly in a Breton story there figures a giant whom neither fire nor water nor steel can harm. He tells his seventh wife, whom he has just married after murdering all her predecessors, "I am immortal, and no one can hurt me unless he crushes on my breast an egg, which is in a pigeon, which is in the belly of a hare; this hare is in the belly of a wolf, and this wolf is in the belly of my brother, who dwells a thousand leagues from here. So I am quite easy on that score." A soldier contrived to obtain the egg and crush it on the breast of the giant, who immediately expired. In another Breton tale the life of a giant resides in an old box tree which grows in his castle garden; and to kill him it is necessary to sever the tap-root of the tree at a single blow of an axe without injuring any of the lesser roots. This task the hero, as usual, successfully accomplishes, and at the same moment the giant drops dead.

The notion of an external soul has now been traced in folk tales told by Aryan peoples from India to Ireland. We have still to show that the same idea occurs commonly in the popular stories of peoples who do not belong to the Aryan stock. In the ancient Egyptian tale of "The Two Brothers," which was written down in the reign of Rameses II, about 1300 B.C., we read how one of the brothers enchanted his heart and placed it in the flower of an acacia tree, and how, when the flower was cut at the instigation of his wife, he immediately fell down dead, but revived when his brother found the lost heart in the berry of the acacia and threw it into a cup of fresh water.

In the story of Seyf el-Mulook in the Arabian Nights the jinnee tells the captive daughter of the King of India, "When I was born, the astrologers declared that the destruction of my soul would be effected by the hand of one of the sons of the human kings. I therefore took my soul, and put it into the crop of a sparrow, and I imprisoned the sparrow in a little box, and put this into another small box, and this I put within seven other small boxes, and I put these within seven chests, and the chests I put into a coffer of marble within the verge of this circumambient ocean; for this part is

Above: *The descent of Aeneas to the Underworld to consult the spirits of the dead about the future, as described in Book VI of Virgil's* Aeneid. *Jan Breughel the Elder. Museum of Fine Arts, Budapest.*

Opposite: *When Orpheus' wife, Eurydice, died of a snake-bite, he followed her to the Underworld and charmed its inhabitants with his singing. Orpheus and His Muse by Edmond Aman-Jean.*

remote from the countries of mankind, and none of mankind can gain access to it." But Seyf el-Mulook got possession of the sparrow and strangled it, and the jinnee fell upon the ground a heap of black ashes.

In a Kabyle story an ogre declares that his fate is far away in an egg, which is in a pigeon, which is in a camel, which is in the sea. The hero procures the egg and crushes it between his hands, and the ogre dies. In a Magyar folk tale, an old witch detains a young prince called Ambrose in the bowels of the earth. At last she confided to him that she kept a wild boar in a silken meadow, and if it were killed, they would find a hare inside, and inside the hare a pigeon, and inside the

pigeon a small box, and inside the box one black and one shining beetle; the shining beetle held her life, and the black one held her power; if these two beetles died, then her life would come to an end also. When the old hag went out, Ambrose killed the wild boar, and took out the hare; from the hare he took the pigeon, from the pigeon the box, and from the box the two beetles; he killed the black beetle, but kept the shining one alive. So the witch's power left her immediately, and when she came home, she had to take to her bed. Having learned from her how to escape from his prison to the upper air, Ambrose killed the shining beetle, and the old hag's spirit left her at once.

In a Kalmuck tale we read how a certain khan challenged a wise man to show his skill by stealing a precious stone on which the khan's life depended. The sage contrived to purloin the talisman while the khan and his guards slept; but not content with this he gave a further proof of his dexterity by bonneting the slumbering potentate with a bladder. This was too much for the khan. Next morning he informed the sage that he could overlook everything else, but that the indignity of being bonneted with a bladder was more than he could bear; and he ordered his facetious friend to instant execution. Pained at this exhibition of royal ingratitude, the sage dashed to the ground the talisman which he still held in his hand; and at the same instant blood flowed from the nostrils of the khan, and he gave up the ghost.

Another story of an external soul comes from Nias, an island to the west of Sumatra. Once upon a time a chief was captured by his enemies, who tried to put him to death but failed. Water would not drown him nor fire burn him nor steel pierce him. At last his wife revealed the secret. On his head he had a hair as hard as a copper wire; and with this wire his life was bound up. So the hair was plucked out, and with it his spirit fled.

A West African story from southern Nigeria relates how a king kept his soul in a little brown bird, which perched on a tall tree beside the gate of the palace. The king's life was so bound up with that of the bird that whoever should kill the bird would simultaneously kill the king and succeed to the kingdom. The secret was betrayed by the queen to her lover, who shot the bird with an arrow and thereby slew the king and ascended the vacant throne.

A tale told by the Ba-Ronga of South Africa sets forth how the lives of a whole family were contained in one cat. When a girl of the family, named Titishan, married a husband, she begged her parents to let her take the precious cat with her to her new home. But they refused, saying, "You know that our life is attached to it," and they offered to give her an antelope or even an elephant instead of it. But nothing would satisfy her but the cat. So at last she carried it off with her and shut it up in a place where nobody saw it; even her husband knew nothing about it. One day, when she went to work in the fields, the cat escaped from its place of concealment, entered the hut, put on the warlike trappings of the husband, and danced and sang. Some children, attracted by the noise, discovered the cat at its antics, and when they expressed their astonishment, the animal only capered the more and insulted them besides. So they went to the owner and said, "There is somebody dancing in your house, and he insulted us." "Hold your tongues," said he, "I'll soon put a stop to your lies." So he went and hid behind the door and peeped in, and there sure enough was the cat prancing about and singing. He fired at it, and the animal dropped down dead. At the same moment his wife fell to the ground in the field where she was at work; said she, "I have been killed at home." But she had strength enough left to ask her husband to go with her to her parents' village, taking with him the dead cat wrapt up in a mat. All her relatives assembled, and bitterly they reproached her for having insisted on taking the animal with her to her husband's village. As soon as the mat was unrolled and they saw the dead cat, they all fell down lifeless one after the other. So the Clan of the Cat was destroyed; and the bereaved husband closed the gate of the village with a branch, and returned home, and told his friends how in killing the cat he had killed the whole clan, because their lives depended on the life of the cat.

Ideas of the same sort meet us in stories told by the North American Indians. Thus the Navajoes tell of a certain mythical being called "the Maiden that becomes a Bear," who learned the art of turning herself into a bear from the prairie wolf. She was a great warrior and quite invulnerable; for when she went to war she took out her vital organs and hid them, so that no one could kill her; and when the battle was over she put the organs back in their places again. The Kwakiutl Indians of British Columbia tell of an ogress, who could not be killed because her life was in a hemlock branch. A brave boy met her in the woods, smashed her head with a stone, scattered her brains, broke her bones, and threw them into the water. Then, thinking he had disposed of the ogress, he went into her house. There he saw a woman rooted to the floor, who warned him, saying, "Now do not stay long. I know that you have tried to kill the ogress. It is the fourth time that somebody has tried

to kill her. She never dies; she has nearly come to life. There in that covered hemlock branch is her life. Go there, and as soon as you see her enter, shoot her life. Then she will be dead." Hardly had she finished speaking when sure enough in came the ogress, singing as she walked. But the boy shot at her life, and she fell dead to the floor. Thus the idea that the soul may be deposited for a longer or shorter time in some place of security outside the body, or at all events in the hair, is found in the popular tales of many races. It remains to show that the idea is not a mere figment devised to adorn a tale, but is a real article of primitive faith, which has given rise to a corresponding set of customs.

We have seen that in folk tales a man's soul or strength is sometimes represented as bound up with his hair, and that when his hair is cut off he dies or grows weak. So the natives of Amboyna used to think that their strength was in their hair and would desert them if it were shorn. A criminal under torture in a Dutch court of that island persisted in denying his guilt till his hair

was cut off, when he immediately confessed. One man, who was tried for murder, endured without flinching the utmost ingenuity of his torturers till he saw the surgeon standing with a pair of shears. On asking what this was for, and being told that it was to cut his hair, he begged they would not do it, and made a clean breast. In subsequent cases, when torture failed to wring a confession from a prisoner, the Dutch authorities made a practice of cutting off his hair.

Here in Europe it used to be thought that the maleficent powers of witches and wizards resided in their hair, and that nothing could make any impression on the miscreants so long as they kept their hair on. Hence in France it was customary to shave the whole bodies of persons charged with sorcery before handing them over to the torturer. Millaeus witnessed the torture of some persons at Toulouse, from whom no confession could be wrung until they were stripped and completely shaven, when they readily acknowledged the truth of the charge. A woman also, who apparently led a pious life, was put to the torture on suspicion of witchcraft, and bore her agonies with incredible constancy, until complete depilation drove her to admit her guilt. The noted inquisitor Sprenger contented himself with shaving the head of the suspected witch or wizard; but his more thoroughgoing colleague Cumanus shaved the whole bodies of forty-seven women before committing them all to the flames. He had high authority for this rigorous scrutiny, since Satan himself, in a sermon preached from the pulpit of North Berwick church, comforted his many servants by assuring them that no harm could befall them "sa lang as their hair wes on, and sould newir latt ane teir fall fra thair ene." Similarly in Bastar, a province of India, "if a man is adjudged guilty of witchcraft, he is beaten by the crowd, his hair is shaved, the hair being supposed to constitute his power of mischief, his front teeth are knocked out, in order, it is said, to prevent him from muttering incantations. Women suspected of sorcery have to undergo the same ordeal; if found guilty, the same punishment is awarded, and after being shaved, their hair is attached to a tree in some public place."

Above: *A death "celebration," where everyone tries to climb onto the recently deceased man's roof. The Dogon tribe of Mali in West Africa.*

Opposite: *In Greek mythology Charon was the ferryman of the Underworld who rowed the shades of the dead across the River Styx.* Painting by Joachim Patinir, sixteenth century. Prado, Madrid.

So among the Bhils of India, when a woman was convicted of witchcraft and had been subjected to various forms of persuasion, such as hanging head downwards from a tree and having pepper put into her eyes, a lock of hair was cut from her head and buried in the ground, "that the last link between her and her former powers of mischief might be broken." In like manner among the Aztecs of Mexico, when wizards and witches "had done their evil deeds, and the time came to put an end to their detestable life, someone laid hold of them and cropped the hair on the crown of their heads,

which took from them all their power of sorcery and enchantment, and then it was that by death they put an end to their odious existence."

But in practice, as in folk tales, it is not merely with inanimate objects and plants that a person is occasionally believed to be united by a bond of physical sympathy. The same bond, it is supposed, may exist between a man and an animal, so that the welfare of the one depends on the welfare of the other, and when the animal dies the man dies also. The analogy between the custom and the tales is all the closer because in both of them the power of thus removing the soul from the body and stowing it away in an animal is often a special privilege of wizards and witches.

The Yakuts of Siberia believe that every shaman or wizard keeps his soul, or one of his souls, incarnate in an animal which is carefully concealed from all the world. "Nobody can find my external soul," said one famous wizard, "it lies hidden far away in the stony mountains of Edzhigansk." Only once a year, when the last snows melt and the earth turns black, do these external souls of wizards appear in the shape of animals among the dwellings of men. They wander everywhere, yet none but wizards can see them. The strong ones sweep roaring and noisily along, the weak steal about quietly and furtively. Often they fight, and then the wizard whose external soul is beaten, falls ill or dies. The weakest and most cowardly wizards are they whose souls are incarnate in the shape of dogs, for the dog gives his human double no peace, but gnaws his heart and tears his body. The most powerful wizards are they whose external souls have the shape of stallions, elks, black bears, eagles, or boars. Again, the Samoyeds of the Turukhinsk region hold that every shaman has a familiar spirit in the shape of a boar, which he leads about by a magic belt. On the death of the boar the shaman himself dies; and stories are told of battles between wizards who send their spirits to fight before they encounter each other in person. The Malays believe that "the soul of a person may pass into another person or into an animal, or rather that such a mysterious relation can arise between the two that the fate of the one is wholly dependent on that of the other."

It has been shown that in folk tales the life of a person is sometimes so bound up with the life of a plant that the withering of the plant will immediately follow or be followed by the death of the person. Among the M'Bengas in western Africa, about the Gabon, when two children are born on the same day, the people plant two trees of the same kind and dance round them. The life of each of the children is believed to be bound up with the life of one of the trees; and if the tree dies or is thrown down, they are sure that the child will soon die. In the Cameroons, also, the life of a person is believed to be sympathetically bound up with that of a tree. The chief of Old Town in Calabar kept his soul in a sacred grove near a spring of water. When some Europeans, in frolic or ignorance, cut down part of the grove, the spirit was most indignant and threatened the perpetrators of the deed, according to the king, with all manner of evil.

Some of the Papuans unite the life of a new-born babe sympathetically with that of a tree by driving a pebble into the bark of the tree. This is supposed to give them complete mastery over the child's life; if the tree is cut down, the child will die. After a birth the Maoris used to bury the navel-string in a sacred place and plant a young sapling over it. As the tree grew, it was a tohu oranga or sign of life for the child; if it flourished, the child would prosper; if it withered and died, the parents augured the worst for the little one. In some parts of Fiji the navel-string of a male infant is planted together with a cocoanut or the slip of a breadfruit-tree, and the child's life is supposed to be intimately connected with that of the tree.

Amongst the Dyaks of Landak and Tajan, districts of Dutch Borneo, it is customary to plant a fruit-tree for a baby, and henceforth in the popular belief the fate of the child is bound up with that of the tree. If the tree shoots up rapidly, it will go well with the child; but if the tree is dwarfed or shrivelled, nothing but misfortune can be expected for its human counterpart.

It is said that there are still families in Russia, Germany, England, France, and Italy who are accustomed to plant a tree at the birth of a child. The tree, it is hoped, will grow with the child, and it is tended with special care. The custom is still pretty general in the canton of Aargau in Switzerland; an apple tree is planted for a boy and a pear tree for a girl, and the people think that the child will flourish or dwindle with the tree. In Mecklenburg the afterbirth is thrown out at the foot of a young tree, and the child is then believed to grow with the tree. Near the Castle of Dalhousie, not far from Edinburgh, there grows an oak tree, called the Edgewell Tree, which is popularly believed to be linked to the fate of the family by a mysterious tie; for they say that when one of the family dies, or is about to die, a branch falls from the Edgewell Tree. Thus, on seeing a great bough drop from the tree on a quiet, still day in July 1874, an old forester exclaimed, "The laird's deid noo!" and soon after news came that Fox Maule, eleventh Earl of Dalhousie, was dead.

The residing of a soul in a plant is fundamental to the myth of the Norse god Balder. He was a deity whose life might in a sense be said to be neither in heaven nor on earth but between the two, the good and beautiful god, the son of the great god Odin, and himself the wisest, mildest, and best beloved of all the immortals. The story

of his death, as it is told in the younger or prose Edda, runs thus. Once on a time Balder dreamed heavy dreams which seemed to forebode his death. Thereupon the gods held a council and resolved to make him secure against every danger. So the goddess Frigg took an oath from fire and water, iron and all metals, stones and earth, from trees, sicknesses and poisons, and from all four-footed beasts, birds, and creeping things, that they would not hurt Balder. When this was done Balder was deemed invulnerable; so the gods amused themselves by setting him in their midst, while some shot at him, others hewed at him, and others threw stones at him. But

Above: *Rowing with a tree branch fixed to the prow of the boat, on Sagnefjord, Norway. This was one of the bays in which the god Balder had his great sanctuary in Viking times. Happy Journey, painting by Hans Dahl.*

whatever they did, nothing could hurt him; and at this they were all glad. Only Loki, the mischief-maker, was displeased, and he went in the guise of an old woman to Frigg, who told him that the weapons of the gods could not wound Balder, since she had made them all swear not to hurt him. Then Loki asked, "Have all things sworn to spare Balder?" She answered, "East of Valhalla grows a plant called the mistletoe; it seemed to me too young to swear." So Loki went and pulled the mistletoe and took it to the assembly of the gods.

There he found the blind god Hother standing at the outside of the circle. Loki asked him, "Why do you not shoot at Balder?" Hother answered, "Because I do not see where he stands; besides I have no weapon." Then said Loki, "Do like the rest and show Balder honour, as they all do. I will show you where he stands, and do you shoot at him with this twig." Hother took the mistletoe and threw it at Balder, as Loki directed him. The mistletoe struck Balder and pierced him through and through, and he fell down dead. And that was the greatest misfortune that ever befell gods and men. For a while the gods stood speechless, then they lifted up their voices and wept bitterly. They took Balder's body and brought it to the seashore. There stood Balder's ship; it was called Ringhorn, and was the hugest of all ships. The gods wished to launch the ship and to burn Balder's body on it, but the ship would not stir. So they sent for a giantess called Hyrrockin. She came riding on a wolf and gave the ship such a push that fire flashed from the rollers and all the earth shook. Then Balder's body was taken and placed on the funeral pile upon his ship. When his wife Nanna saw that, her heart burst for sorrow and she died. So she was laid on the funeral pile with her husband, and fire was put to it. Balder's horse, too, with all its trappings, was burned on the pile.

Whether he was a real or merely a mythical personage, Balder was worshipped in Norway. On one of the bays of the beautiful Sogne Fjord, which penetrates far into the depths of the solemn Norwegian mountains, with their sombre pineforests and their lofty cascades dissolving into spray before they reach the dark water of the fjord far below, Balder had a great sanctuary. It was called Balder's Grove. A palisade enclosed the hallowed ground, and within it stood a spacious temple with the images of many gods, but none of them was worshipped with such devotion as Balder. So great was the awe with which the heathen regarded the place that no man might harm another there, nor steal his cattle, nor defile himself with women. But women cared for

Above: *A druid in an oak grove near Stonehenge carries a sickle and mistletoe.* Vignette by Francis Grose, *Antiquities of England and Wales*, London, 1773-87.

the images of the gods in the temple; they warmed them at the fire, anointed them with oil, and dried them with cloths.

From time immemorial the mistletoe has been the object of superstitious veneration in Europe. It was worshipped by the Druids, as we learn from a famous passage of Pliny. After enumerating the different kinds of mistletoe, he proceeds: "In treating of this subject, the admiration in which the mistletoe is held throughout Gaul ought not to pass unnoticed. The Druids, for so they call their wizards, esteem nothing more sacred than the mistletoe and the tree on which it grows, provided only that the tree is an oak. But apart from this they choose oak woods for their sacred groves and perform no sacred rites without oak leaves; so that the very name of Druids may be regarded as a Greek appellation derived from their worship of the oak (drus is oak in Greek). For they believe that whatever grows on these trees is sent from heaven, and is a sign that the tree has been chosen by the god himself. The mistletoe is very rarely to be met with; but when it is found, they gather it with solemn ceremony. This they do above all on the sixth day of the moon, from whence they date the beginnings of their months, of their years, and of their thirty years' cycle, because by the sixth day the moon has plenty of vigour and has not run half its course. After due preparations have been made for a sacrifice and a feast under the tree, they hail it as the universal healer and bring to the spot two white bulls, whose horns have never been bound before. A priest clad in a white robe climbs the tree and with a golden sickle cuts the mistletoe, which is caught in a white cloth. Then they sacrifice the victims, praying that God may make his own gift to prosper with those upon whom he has bestowed it. They believe that a potion prepared from mistletoe will make barren animals to bring forth, and that the plant is a remedy against all poison."

The Druidical belief, reported by Pliny, was that whatever grew on an oak was sent from heaven and was a sign that the tree had been chosen by the god himself. Such a belief explains why the Druids cut the mistletoe not with a common knife, but with a golden sickle, and why, when cut, it was not suffered to touch the earth; probably they thought that the celestial plant would have been profaned and its marvellous virtue lost by contact with the ground.

Both in France and Sweden special virtues are ascribed to mistletoe gathered at Midsummer.

The rule in Sweden is that "mistletoe must be cut on the night of Midsummer Eve when sun and moon stand in the sign of their might." Again, in Wales it was believed that a sprig of mistletoe gathered on St. John's Eve (Midsummer Eve), or at any time before the berries appeared, would induce dreams of omen, both good and bad, if it were placed under the pillow of the sleeper. Thus mistletoe is one of the many plants whose magical or medicinal virtues are believed to culminate with the culmination of the sun on the longest day of the year. Hence it seems reasonable to conjecture that in the eyes of the Druids, also, who revered the plant so highly, the sacred mistletoe may have acquired a double portion of its mystic qualities at the solstice in June, and that accordingly they may have regularly cut it with solemn ceremony on Midsummer Eve.

Be that as it may, certain it is that the mistletoe, the instrument of Balder's death, has been regularly gathered for the sake of its mystic qualities on Midsummer Eve in Scandinavia, Balder's home. The plant is found commonly growing on pear trees, oaks, and other trees in thick damp woods throughout the more temperate parts of Sweden. Thus one of the two main incidents of Balder's myth is reproduced in the great midsummer festival of Scandinavia. But the other main incident of the myth, the burning of Balder's body on a pyre, has also its counterpart in the bonfires which still blaze, or blazed till lately, in Denmark, Norway, and Sweden on Midsummer Eve. It does not appear, indeed, that any effigy is burned in these bonfires; but the burning of an effigy is a feature which might easily drop out after its meaning was forgotten. And the name of Balder's bale-fires (Balder's Balar), by which these midsummer fires were formerly known in Sweden, puts their connexion with Balder beyond the reach of doubt, and makes it probable that in former times either a living representative or an effigy of Balder was annually burned in them. Midsummer was the season sacred to Balder, and the Swedish poet Tegner, in placing the burning of Balder at midsummer, may very well have followed an old tradition that the summer solstice was the time when the good god came to his untimely end.

Thus it has been shown that the leading incidents of the Balder myth have their counterparts in those fire-festivals of our European peasantry which undoubtedly date from a time long prior to the introduction of Christianity. The pretence of throwing the victim chosen by lot into the Beltane fire, and the similar treat-

Above: *Balder lies dead, killed by mistletoe, the only plant to which he was not immune.* Illustration from Dorothy Hardy's *Myths and Norsemen*, London.

Opposite: *Loki, the embodiment of deceit and trickery, bound and fettered after contriving the death of Balder.* Viking cross at Kirkby Stephen, Cumbria, England.

ment of the man, the future Green Wolf, at the midsummer bonfire in Normandy, may naturally be interpreted as traces of an older custom of actually burning human beings on these occasions; and the green dress of the Green Wolf, coupled with the leafy envelope of the young fellow who trod out the midsummer fire,

seems to hint that the persons who perished at these festivals did so in the character of tree-spirits or deities of vegetation.

From all this we may reasonably infer that in the Balder myth on the one hand, and the fire-festivals and custom of gathering mistletoe on the other hand, we have, as it were, the two broken and dissevered halves of an original whole. In other words, we may assume with some degree of probability that the myth of Balder's death was not merely a myth, that is, a description of physical phenomena in imagery borrowed from human life, but that it was at the same time the story which people told to explain why they annually burned a human representative of the god

Above: *The Green Man of English mythology sprouts foliage from his face.* Norwich Cathedral, circa late fourteenth century.

Opposite: *Copy of murals from the ancient city of Teotihuacan in Mexico, showing the afterlife as imagined in Tlalocan, Paradise of the Dead.* National Anthropological Museum, Mexico City.

and cut the mistletoe with solemn ceremony. If I am right, the story of Balder's tragic end formed, so to say, the text of the sacred drama which was acted year by year as a magical rite to cause the sun to shine, trees to grow, crops to thrive, and to guard man and beast from the baleful arts of fairies and trolls, of witches and warlocks. The tale belonged, in short, to that class of nature myths which are meant to be supplemented by ritual; here, as so often, myth stood to magic in the relation of theory to practice.

But if the victims—the human Balders—who died by fire, whether in spring or at midsummer, were put to death as living embodiments of tree-spirits or deities of vegetation, it would seem that Balder himself must have

been a tree-spirit or deity of vegetation. It becomes desirable, therefore, to determine, if we can, the particular kind of tree or trees, of which a personal representative was burned at the fire-festivals. For we may be quite sure that it was not as a representative of vegetation in general that the victim suffered death. The idea of vegetation in general is too abstract to be primitive. Most probably the victim at first represented a particular kind of sacred tree. But of all European trees none has such claims as the oak to be considered as preeminently the sacred tree of the Aryans. We have seen that its worship is attested for all the great branches of the Aryan stock in Europe; hence we may certainly conclude that the tree was venerated by the Aryans in common before the dispersion, and that their primitive home must have lain in a land which was clothed with forests of oak.

Now, considering the primitive character and remarkable similarity of the fire-festivals observed by all the branches of the Aryan race in Europe, we may infer that these festivals form part of the common stock of religious observances which the various peoples carried with them in their wanderings from their old home. But, if I am right, an essential feature of those primitive fire-festivals was the burning of a man who represented the tree-spirit. In view, then, of the place occupied by the oak in the religion of the Aryans, the presumption is that the tree so represented at the fire-festivals must originally have been the oak. So far as the Celts and Lithuanians are concerned, this conclusion will perhaps hardly be contested. But both for them and for the Germans it is confirmed by a remarkable piece of religious conservatism. The most primitive method known to man of producing fire is by rubbing two pieces of wood against each other till they ignite; and this method is still used in Europe for kindling sacred fires such as the need-fire, and most probably it was formerly resorted to at all the fire-festivals under discussion.

Now it is sometimes required that the need-fire, or other sacred fire, should be made by the friction of a particular kind of wood; and when the kind of wood is prescribed, whether among Celts, Germans, or Slavs, that wood appears to be generally the oak. But if the sacred fire was regularly kindled by the friction of oak-wood, we may infer that originally the fire was also fed with the same material. In point of fact, it appears that the perpetual fire of Vesta at Rome was fed with oak-wood, and that oak-wood was the fuel consumed in the perpetual fire which burned under the sacred oak at the great Lithuanian sanctuary of Romove. Further, that oak-wood was formerly the fuel burned in the midsummer fires may perhaps be inferred from the custom, said to be still observed by peasants in many mountain districts of Germany, of making up the cottage fire on Midsummer Day with a heavy block of oak-wood. The block is so arranged that it smoulders slowly and is not finally reduced to charcoal till the expiry of a year. Then upon next Midsummer Day the charred embers of the old log are removed to make room for the new one, and are mixed with the seed-corn or scattered about the garden. This is believed to guard

the food cooked on the hearth from witchcraft, to preserve the luck of the house, to promote the growth of the crops, and to keep them from blight and vermin. Thus the custom is almost exactly parallel to that of the Yule-log, which in parts of Germany, France, England, Serbia, and other Slavonic lands was commonly of oak-wood. The general conclusion is, that at those periodic or occasional ceremonies

Above: *The ancient oak forests in the Aber Valley of North Wales are much as they were in the Iron Age.*

the ancient Aryans both kindled and fed the fire with the sacred oak-wood.

But if at these solemn rites the fire was regularly made of oak-wood, it follows that any man who was burned in it as a personification of the tree-spirit could have represented no tree but the oak. The sacred oak was thus burned in duplicate; the wood of the tree was consumed in the fire, and along with it was consumed a living man as a personification of the oak-spirit. The conclusion thus drawn for the European Aryans in general is confirmed in its special application to the Scandinavians by the relation in which amongst them the mistletoe appears to have stood to the burning of the victim in the midsummer fire. We have seen that among Scandinavians it has been customary to gather the mistletoe at midsummer. But so far as appears on the face of this custom, there is nothing to connect it with the midsummer fires in which human victims or effigies of them were burned. Even if the fire, as seems probable, was originally always made with oak-wood, why should it have been necessary to pull the mistletoe?

The last link between the midsummer customs of gathering the mistletoe and lighting the bonfires is supplied by Balder's myth, which can hardly be disjoined from the customs in question. The myth suggests that a vital connexion may once have been believed to subsist between the mistletoe and the human representative of the oak who was burned in the fire. According to the myth, Balder could be killed by nothing in heaven or earth except the mistletoe; and so long as the mistletoe remained on the oak, he was not only immortal but invulnerable. Now, if we suppose that Balder was the oak, the origin of the myth becomes intelligible. The mistletoe was viewed as the seat of life of the oak, and so long as it was uninjured nothing could kill or even wound the oak. The conception of the mistletoe as the seat of life of the oak would naturally be suggested to primitive people by the observation that while the oak is deciduous, the mistletoe which grows on it is evergreen. In winter the sight of its fresh foliage among the bare branches must have been hailed by the worshippers of the tree as a sign that the divine life which had ceased to animate the branches yet survived in the mistletoe, as the heart of a sleeper still beats when his body is motionless. Hence when the god had to be killed—when the sacred tree had to be burnt—it was necessary to begin by breaking off the mistletoe. For so long as the mistletoe remained intact, the oak (so people might think) was invulnerable; all the blows of their knives and axes would glance harmless from its surface. But once tear from the oak its sacred heart—the mistletoe—and the tree nodded to its fall. And when in later times the spirit of the oak came to be represented by a living man, it was logically necessary to suppose that, like the tree he personated, he could neither be killed nor wounded so long as the mistletoe remained uninjured. The pulling of the mistletoe was thus at once the signal and the cause of his death.

On this view the invulnerable Balder is neither more nor less than a personification of a mistletoe-bearing oak. The interpretation is confirmed by what seems to have been an ancient Italian belief, that the mistletoe can be destroyed neither by fire nor water; for if the parasite is thus deemed indestructible, it might easily be supposed to communicate its own indestructibility to the tree on which it grows, so long as the two remain in conjunction. Or, to put the same idea in mythical form, we might tell how the kindly god of the oak had his life securely deposited in the imperishable mistletoe which grew among the branches; how accordingly so long as the mistletoe kept its place there, the deity himself remained invulnerable; and how at last a cunning foe, let into the secret of the god's invulnerability, tore the mistletoe from the oak, thereby killing the oak-god and afterwards burning his body in a fire which could have made no impression on him so long as the incombustible parasite retained its seat among the boughs.

The idea of a being whose life is thus, in a sense, outside himself, must be strange to many readers, but has, by the examples drawn both from story and custom which we have given above, been amply illustrated. I hope that the result has been to show that, in assuming this idea as the explanation of Balder's relation to the mistletoe, we assume a principle which is deeply engraved on the mind of primitive man. The further significance of the mistletoe as the golden bough is not unconnected with this, and it will be recounted in our final chapter.

Chapter Eleven

THE GOLDEN BOUGH

FROM WHAT WE have learned about the external soul, we can see that the view that Balder's life was in the mistletoe of the sacred tree is entirely in harmony with primitive modes of thought. It may indeed sound like a contradiction that, if his life was in the mistletoe, he should nevertheless have been killed by a blow from the plant. But when a person's life is conceived as embodied in a particular object, with the existence of which his own existence is inseparably bound up, and the destruction of which involves his own, the object in question may be regarded and spoken of indifferently as his life or his death, as happens in the fairy tales.

Hence if a man's death is in an object, it is perfectly natural that he should be killed by a blow from it. In the fairy tales Koshchei the Deathless is killed by a blow from the egg or the stone in which his life or death is secreted; the ogres burst when a certain grain of sand—doubtless containing their life or death—is carried over their heads; the magician dies when the stone in which his life or death is contained is put under his pillow; and the Tartar hero is warned that he may be killed by the golden arrow or golden sword in which his soul has been stowed away.

The idea that the life of the oak was in the mistletoe was probably suggested by the observation that in winter the mistletoe growing on the oak remains green while the oak itself is leafless. But the position of the plant—growing not from the ground but from the

Above: *A chief druid in his judicial habit.* Nineteenth century aquatint by R. Havell.

Opposite: *Mistletoe, the "golden bough," was regarded by the Druids as being particularly sacred when found growing on oak trees.*

205

trunk or branches of the tree—might confirm this idea. Primitive man might think that, like himself, the oak-spirit had sought to deposit his life in some safe place, and for this purpose had pitched on the mistletoe, which, being in a sense neither on earth nor in heaven, might be supposed to be fairly out of harm's way. We can understand why it has been a rule both of ancient and of modern folk-medicine that the mistletoe should not be allowed to touch the ground; were it to touch the ground, its healing virtue would be gone. This may be a survival of the old superstition that the plant in which the life of the sacred tree was concentrated should not be exposed to the risk incurred by contact with the earth.

In an Indian legend, which offers a parallel to the Balder myth, Indra swore to the demon Namuci that he would slay him neither by day nor by night, neither with staff nor with bow, neither with the palm of the hand nor with the fist, neither with the wet nor with the dry. But he killed him in the morning twilight by sprinkling over him the foam of the sea. The foam of the sea is just such an object as a savage might choose to put his life in, because it occupies that sort of intermediate or nondescript position between earth and sky or sea and sky in which primitive man sees safety. It is therefore not surprising that the foam of the river should be the totem of a clan in India.

Again, the view that the mistletoe owes its mystic character partly to its not growing on the ground is confirmed by a parallel superstition about the mountain-ash or rowan tree. In Jutland a rowan that is found growing out of the top of another tree is esteemed "exceedingly effective against witchcraft: since it does not grow on the ground witches have no power over it; if it is to have its full effect it must be cut on Ascension Day." Hence it is placed over doors to prevent the ingress of witches. In Sweden and Norway, also, magical properties are ascribed to a "flying-rowan" (flogrönn), that is to a rowan which is found growing not in the ordinary fashion on the ground but on another tree, or on a roof, or in a cleft of the rock, where it has sprouted from seed scattered by birds. They say that a man who is out in the dark should have a bit of "flying-rowan" with him to chew; else he runs a risk of being bewitched and of being unable to stir from the spot.

Just as in Scandinavia the parasitic rowan is deemed a countercharm to sorcery, so in Germany the parasitic mistletoe is still commonly considered a protection against witchcraft, and in Sweden the mistletoe which is gathered on Midsummer Eve is attached to the ceiling of the house, the horse's stall or the cow's crib, in the belief that this renders the Troll powerless to injure man or beast.

The view that the mistletoe was not merely the instrument of Balder's death, but that it contained his life, is countenanced by the analogy of a Scottish superstition. Tradition ran that the fate of the Hays of Errol, an estate in Perthshire, near the Firth of Tay, was bound up with the mistletoe that grew on a certain great oak. A member of the Hay family has recorded the old belief as follows:

"Among the low country families the badges are now almost generally forgotten; but it appears by an ancient manuscript, and the tradition of a few old people in Perthshire, that the badge of the Hays was the mistletoe. There was formerly in the neighbourhood of Errol, and not far from the Falcon stone, a vast oak of an unknown age, and upon which grew a profusion of the plant: many charms and legends were considered to be connected with the tree, and the duration of the family of Hay was said to be united with its existence. It was believed that a sprig of the mistletoe cut by a Hay on Allhallowmas eve, with a new dirk, and after surrounding the tree three times sunwise, and pronouncing a certain spell, was a sure charm against all glamour or witchery, and an infallible guard in the day of battle. A spray gathered in the same manner was placed in the cradle of infants, and thought to defend them from being changed for elf-bairns by the fairies. Finally, it was affirmed, that when the root of the oak had per-

Opposite: *The foam of the sea occupies an intermediate position between the sea and sky and is the kind of place in which primitive man might have chosen to put his life.* Painting by David James, 1897.

ished, 'the grass should grow in the hearth of Errol, and a raven should sit in the falcon's nest.' The two most unlucky deeds which could be done by one of the name of Hay was to kill a white falcon, and to cut down a limb from the oak of Errol. When the old tree was destroyed I could never learn. The estate has been sold out of the family of Hay, and of course it is said that the fatal oak was cut down a short time before." The old superstition is recorded in verses which are traditionally ascribed to Thomas the Rhymer:

While the mistletoe bats on Errol's aik,
And that aik stands fast,
The Hays shall flourish, and their good grey hawk
Shall nocht flinch before the blast.

But when the root of the aik decays,
And the mistletoe dwines on its withered breast,
The grass shall grow on Errol's hearthstane,
And the corbie roup in the falcon's nest.

It is not a new opinion that the Golden Bough was the mistletoe. True, Virgil does not identify but only compares it with mistletoe. But this may be only a poetical device to cast a mystic glamour over the humble plant. Or, more probably, his description was based on a popular superstition that at certain times the mistletoe blazed out into a supernatural golden glory. The poet tells how two doves, guiding Aeneas to the gloomy vale in whose depth grew the Golden Bough, alighted upon a tree, "whence shone a flickering gleam of gold. As in the woods in winter cold the mistletoe—a plant not native to its tree—is green with fresh leaves and twines its yellow berries about the boles; such seemed upon the shady holm-oak the leafy gold, so rustled in the gentle breeze the golden leaf." Here Virgil definitely describes the Golden Bough as growing on a holm-oak, and compares it with the mistletoe. The inference is almost inevitable that the Golden Bough was nothing but the mistletoe seen through the haze of poetry or of popular superstition.

Grounds have been shown for believing that the priest of the Arician grove at Nemi—the King of the Wood—personified the tree on which grew the Golden Bough. Hence if that tree was the oak, the King of the Wood must have been a personification of the oak-spirit. It is, therefore, easy to understand why, before he could be slain, it was necessary to break the Golden Bough. As an oak-spirit, his life or death was in the mistletoe on the oak, and so long as the mistletoe remained intact, he, like Balder, could not die. To slay him, therefore, it was necessary to break the mistletoe, and probably, as in the case of Balder, to throw it at him. And to complete the parallel, it is only necessary to suppose that the King of the Wood was formerly burned, dead or alive, at the midsummer fire festival which, as we have seen, was annually celebrated in the Arician grove. The perpetual fire which burned in the grove,

like the perpetual fire which burned in the temple of Vesta at Rome and under the oak at Romove in Lithuania, was probably fed with the sacred oak-wood; and thus it would be in a great fire of oak that the King of the Wood formerly met his end.

At a later time, as I have suggested, his annual tenure of office was lengthened or shortened, as the case might be, by the rule which allowed him to live so long as he could prove his divine right by the strong hand. But he only escaped the fire to fall by the sword.

Thus it seems that at a remote age in the heart of Italy, beside the sweet Lake of Nemi, the same fiery tragedy was annually enacted which Italian merchants and soldiers were afterwards to witness among their rude kindred, the Celts of Gaul, and which, if the Roman eagles had ever swooped on Norway, might have been found repeated with little difference among the barbarous Aryans of the North. The rite was probably an essential feature in the ancient Aryan worship of the oak.

It only remains to ask, Why was the mistletoe called the Golden Bough? The whitish-yellow of the mistletoe berries is hardly enough to account for the name, for Virgil says that the bough was altogether golden, stems as well as leaves. Perhaps the name may be derived from the rich golden yellow which a bough of mistletoe assumes when it has been cut and kept for some months; the bright tint is not confined to the leaves, but spreads to the stalks as well, so that the whole branch appears to be indeed a Golden Bough. Breton peasants hang up great bunches of mistletoe in front of their cottages, and in the month of June these bunches are conspicuous for the bright golden tinge of their foliage. In some parts of Brittany, especially about Morbihan, branches of mistletoe are hung over the doors of stables and byres to protect the horses and cattle, probably against witchcraft.

The yellow colour of the withered bough may partly explain why the mistletoe has been sometimes supposed to possess the property of disclosing treasures in the earth; for on the principles of similarity magic there is a natural affinity between a yellow bough and yellow gold. This suggestion is confirmed by the analogy of the

Above: *The Guizer Jarl of Lerwick stands before a blazing longboat pyre. In this annual re-enactment of a Viking ceremony in Lerwick in the Shetland Isles off the coast of Scotland, the ceremonies of fire festival and chieftain's burial are combined.*

Opposite: *The mysterious and rare plant Moonwort (Botrychium lunaria) is the world's smallest fern, no higher than a blade of grass. In ancient times it was a favourite of witches and necromancers because of its lunar symbolism. For alchemists it was sigificant because it resembled the curious crystalline structure called "golden shrub."*

marvellous properties popularly ascribed to the mythical fern-seed, which is popularly supposed to bloom like gold or fire on Midsummer Eve. Thus in Bohemia it is said that "on St. John's Day fern-seed blooms with golden blossoms that gleam like fire." Now it is a property of this mythical fern-seed that whoever has it, or will ascend a mountain holding it in his hand on Midsummer Eve, will discover a vein of gold or will see the treasures of the earth shining with a bluish flame. In Russia they say that if you succeed in catching the wondrous bloom of the fern at midnight on Midsummer Eve, you have only to throw it up into the air, and it will fall like a star on the very spot where a treasure lies hidden. In Brittany treasure-seekers gather fern-seed at midnight on Midsummer Eve, and keep it till Palm Sunday of the following year; then they strew the seed on the ground where they think a treasure is concealed. Tyrolese peasants imagine that hidden treasures can be seen glowing like flame on Midsummer Eve, and that fern-seed, gathered at this mystic season, with the usual precautions, will help to bring the buried gold to the surface. In the

Æneas finds the Golden Bough

unfailing supply of gold. But while the fern-seed is described as golden, it is equally described as glowing and fiery. Hence, when we consider that two great days for gathering the fabulous seed are Midsummer Eve and Christmas—that is, the two solstices (for Christmas is nothing but an old heathen celebration of the winter solstice)—we are led to regard the fiery aspect of the fern-seed as primary, and its golden aspect as secondary and derivative. Fern-seed, in fact, would seem to be an emanation of the sun's fire at the two turning-points of its course, the summer and winter solstices. This view is confirmed by a German story in which a hunter is said to have procured fern-seed by shooting at the sun on Midsummer Day at noon; three drops of blood fell down, which he caught in a white cloth, and these blood-drops were the fern-seed. Here the blood is clearly the blood of the sun, from which the fern-seed is thus directly derived. Thus it may be taken as probable that fern-seed is golden, because it is believed to be an emanation of the sun's golden fire.

Now, like fern-seed, the mistletoe is gathered either at Midsummer or at Christmas—that is, either at the summer or at the winter solstice—and, like fern-seed, it is supposed to possess the power of revealing treasures in the earth. On Midsummer Eve people in Sweden make divining-rods of mistletoe, or of four different kinds of wood, one of which must be mistletoe. The treasure-seeker places the rod on the ground after sundown, and when it rests directly over treasure, the rod begins to move as if it were alive. Now, if the mistletoe discovers gold, it must be in its character of the Golden Bough; and if it is gathered at the solstices, must not the Golden Bough, like the golden fern-seed, be an emanation of the sun's fire? The question cannot be answered with a simple affirmative. We have seen that the old Aryans perhaps kindled the solstitial and other ceremonial fires in part as sun-charms, that is, with the intention of supplying the sun with fresh fire; and as these fires were usually made by the friction or combustion of oak-wood, it may have appeared to the ancient Aryan that the sun was periodically recruited from the fire which resided in the sacred oak. In other words, the oak

Swiss canton of Freiburg people used to watch beside a fern on St. John's night in the hope of winning a treasure, which the devil himself sometimes brought to them. In Bohemia they say that he who procures the golden bloom of the fern at this season has thereby the key to all hidden treasures; and that if maidens will spread a cloth under the fast-fading bloom, red gold will drop into it. And in the Tyrol and Bohemia if you place fern-seed among money, the money will never decrease, however much of it you spend. Sometimes the fern-seed is supposed to bloom on Christmas night, and whoever catches it will become very rich. In Styria they say that by gathering fern-seed on Christmas night you can force the devil to bring you a bag of money.

Thus, on the principle of like by like, fern-seed is supposed to discover gold because it is itself golden; and for a similar reason it enriches its possessor with an

may have seemed to him the original storehouse or reservoir of the fire which was from time to time drawn out to feed the sun. But if the life of the oak was conceived to be in the mistletoe, the mistletoe must on that view have contained the seed or germ of the fire which was elicited by friction from the wood of the oak. Thus, instead of saying that the mistletoe was an emanation of the sun's fire, it might be more correct to say that the sun's fire was regarded as an emanation of the mistletoe. No wonder, then, that the mistletoe shone with a golden splendour, and was called the Golden Bough. Probably, however, like fern-seed, it was thought to assume its golden aspect only at those stated times,

Opposite: *In the forest Aeneas finds the Golden Bough, which he will carry with him through the Underworld to light his way. Oracular doves flutter around his head.* From the 1925 illustrated edition of *The Golden Bough.*

Below: *The head on the handle of this decorative Celtic bronze bucket represents the Celtic god associated with the Tree of Life. The curved detail on the head is mistletoe.* First century B.C. Found at Aylesford, Kent, in England. British Museum, London.

especially midsummer, when fire was drawn from the oak to light up the sun.

At Pulverbatch, in Shropshire, it was believed within living memory that the oak tree blooms on Midsummer Eve and the blossom withers before daylight. A maiden who wishes to know her lot in marriage should spread a white cloth under the tree at night, and in the morning she will find a little dust, which is all that remains of the flower. She should place the pinch of dust under her pillow, and then her future husband will appear to her in her dreams. This fleeting bloom of the oak, if I am right, was probably the mistletoe in its character of the Golden Bough. The conjecture is confirmed by the observation that in Wales a real sprig of mistletoe gathered on Midsummer Eve is similarly placed under the pillow to induce prophetic dreams; and further the mode of catching the imaginary bloom of the oak in a white cloth is exactly that which was employed by the Druids to catch the real mistletoe when it dropped from the bough of the oak, severed by the golden sickle. As Shropshire borders on Wales, the belief that the oak blooms on Midsummer Eve may be Welsh in its immediate origin, though probably the belief is a fragment of the primitive Aryan creed.

In some parts of Italy, as we saw, peasants still go out on Midsummer morning to search the oak-trees for the "oil of St. John," which, like the mistletoe, heals all wounds, and is, perhaps, the mistletoe itself in its glorified aspect. Thus it is easy to understand how a title like the Golden Bough, so little descriptive of its usual appearance on the tree, should have been applied to the seemingly insignificant parasite. Further, we can perhaps see why in antiquity mistletoe was believed to possess the remarkable property of extinguishing fire, and why in Sweden it is still kept in houses as a safeguard against conflagration. Its fiery nature marks it out, on the principles of similarity-magic, as the best possible cure or preventive of injury by fire.

These considerations may partially explain why Virgil makes Aeneas carry a glorified bough of mistletoe with him on his descent into the gloomy subterranean world. The poet describes how at the very gates of hell there

211

stretched a vast and gloomy wood, and how the hero, following the flight of two doves that lured him on, wandered into the depths of the immemorial forest till he saw afar off through the shadows of the trees the flickering light of the Golden Bough illuminating the matted boughs overhead. If the mistletoe, as a yellow withered bough in the sad autumn woods, was conceived to contain the seed of fire, what better companion could a forlorn wanderer in the nether shades take with him than a bough that would be a lamp to his feet as well as a rod and staff to his hands? Armed with it he might boldly confront the dreadful spectres that would cross his path on his adventurous journey. Hence when

Aeneas, emerging from the forest, comes to the banks of Styx, winding slow with sluggish stream through the infernal marsh, and the surly ferryman refuses him passage in his boat, he has but to draw the Golden Bough from his bosom and hold it up, and straightway the blusterer quails at the sight and meekly receives the hero into his crazy bark, which sinks deep in the water

Opposite: *Sunlight streaming from behind an oak. The heavenly fire and power of the sun could embody itself in the sacred oak and its mistletoe.*

Below: *A flash of lightning, which could bring the heavenly fire into a tree, where it would appear as mistletoe.*

under the unusual weight of the living man. Even in recent times, as we have seen, mistletoe has been deemed a protection against witches and trolls, and the ancients may well have credited it with the same magical virtue. And if the parasite can, as some of our peasants believe, open all locks, why should it not have served as an "open Sesame" in the hands of Aeneas to unlock the gates of death?

Now, too, we can conjecture why Virbius at Nemi came to be confounded with the sun. If Virbius was, as I have tried to show, a tree-spirit, he must have been the spirit of the oak on which grew the Golden Bough; for tradition represented him as the first of the Kings of the Wood. As an oak-spirit he must have been supposed periodically to re-kindle the sun's fire, and might therefore easily be confounded with the sun itself. Similarly we can explain why Balder, an oak-spirit, was described as "so fair of face and so shining that a light went forth from him," and why he should have been so often taken to be the sun. And in general we may say that in primitive society, when the only known way of making fire is by the friction of wood, the savage must necessarily conceive of fire as a property stored away, like sap or juice, in trees, from which he has laboriously to extract it.

The Senal Indians of California "profess to believe that the whole world was once a globe of fire, whence that element passed up into the trees, and now comes out whenever two pieces of wood are rubbed together." Similarly the Maidu Indians of California hold that "the earth was primarily a globe of molten matter, and from that the principle of fire ascended through the roots into the trunk and branches of trees, whence the Indians can extract it by means of their drill."

In Namoluk, one of the Caroline Islands, they say that the art of making fire was taught men by the gods. Olofaet, the cunning master of flames, gave fire to the bird *mwi* and bade him carry it to earth in his bill. So the bird flew from tree to tree and stored away the slumbering force of the fire in the wood, from which men can elicit it by friction. In the ancient Vedic hymns of India the fire-god Agni "is spoken of as born in wood, as the embryo of plants, or as distributed in plants. He is also said to have entered into all plants or to strive after them. When he is called the embryo of trees or of trees as well as plants, there may be a side-glance at the fire produced in forests by the friction of the boughs of trees."

A tree which has been struck by lightning is naturally regarded by the savage as charged with a double or triple portion of fire; for has he not seen the mighty flash enter into the trunk with his own eyes? Hence perhaps we may explain some of the many superstitious beliefs concerning trees that have been struck by lightning. When the Thompson Indians of British Columbia wished to set fire to the houses of their enemies, they shot at them arrows which were either made from a tree that had been struck by lightning or had splinters of such wood attached to them. Wendish peasants of Saxony refuse to burn in their stoves the wood of trees that have been struck by lightning; they say that with such fuel the house would be burnt down. In like manner the Thonga of South Africa will not use such wood as fuel nor warm themselves at a fire which has been kindled with it. On the contrary, when lightning sets fire to a tree, the Winamwanga of Northern Rhodesia put out all the fires in the village and plaster the fireplaces afresh, while the head men convey the lightning-kindled fire to the chief, who prays over it. The chief then sends out the new fire to all his villages, and the villagers reward his messengers for the boon. This shows that they look upon fire kindled by lightning with reverence, and the reverence is intelligible, for they speak of thunder and lightning as God himself coming down to earth. Similarly the Maidu Indians of California believe that a Great Man created the world and all its inhabitants, and that lightning is nothing but the Great Man himself descending swiftly out of heaven and rending the trees with his flaming arms.

It is a plausible theory that the reverence which the ancient peoples of Europe paid to the oak, and the connexion which they traced between the tree and their sky-god, were derived from the much greater frequency with which the oak appears to be struck by lightning than any other tree of our European forests. This peculiarity of the tree has seemingly been established by a series of observations instituted within recent years by scientific enquirers who have no mythological theory to maintain. However we may explain it, whether by the easier passage of electricity through oak-wood than through any other timber, or in some other way, the fact itself may well have attracted the notice of our rude forefathers, who dwelt in the vast forests which then covered a large part of Europe; and they might naturally account for it in their simple religious way by supposing that the great sky-god, whom they worshipped and whose awful voice they heard in the roll of thunder, loved the oak above all the trees of the wood and often

Opposite: *The thunder god Thor was believed by some to be second only to the warlike Teutonic god Wotan (Odin), shown here on horseback, accompanied by ravens.* From a painting by Max Koch, 1905.

Above: *The Hindu god Vishnu Visvarupa, represented as the whole world.* An Indian painting from Jaipur, early nineteenth century. Victoria and Albert Museum, London.

Opposite: *A symbolical depiction of the ancient Egyptian view of the Universe. The long-limbed goddess Nut, representing the celestial vault, stretches from horizon to horizon as the stars twinkle above her. Nut, the twin sister of the earth god, Geb, was the mother of Isis and Osiris.*

descended into it from the murky cloud in a flash of lightning, leaving a token of his presence or of his passage in the riven and blackened trunk and the blasted foliage. Such trees would thenceforth be encircled by a nimbus of glory as the visible seats of the thundering sky-god. Certain it is that, like some savages, both Greeks and Romans identified their great god of the sky and of the oak with the lightning flash which struck the ground; and they regularly enclosed such a stricken spot

and treated it thereafter as sacred. It is not rash to suppose that the ancestors of the Celts and Germans in the forests of Central Europe paid a like respect for like reasons to a blasted oak.

This explanation of the Aryan reverence for the oak and of the association of the tree with the great god of the thunder and the sky, was suggested or implied long ago by Jacob Grimm, and has been in recent years powerfully reinforced by Mr. W. Warde Fowler. It appears to be simpler and more probable than the explanation which I formerly adopted, namely, that the oak was worshipped primarily for the many benefits which our rude forefathers derived from the tree, particularly for the fire which they drew by friction from its wood; and that the connexion of the oak with the sky was an afterthought based on the belief that the flash of lightning was nothing but the spark which the sky-god up aloft elicited by rubbing two pieces of oak-wood against each other, just as his savage worshipper kindled fire in the forest on earth.

On that theory the god of the thunder and the sky was derived from the original god of the oak; on the present theory, which I now prefer, the god of the sky and the thunder was the great original deity of our Aryan ancestors, and his association with the oak was merely an inference based on the frequency with which the oak was seen to be struck by lightning. If the Aryans, as some think, roamed the wide steppes of Russia or Central Asia with their flocks and herds before they plunged into the gloom of the European forests, they may have worshipped the god of the blue or cloudy firmament and the flashing thunderbolt long before they thought of associating him with the blasted oaks in their new home.

Perhaps the new theory has the further advantage of throwing light on the special sanctity ascribed to mistletoe which grows on an oak. The mere rarity of such a growth on an oak hardly suffices to explain the extent and the persistence of the superstition. A hint of its real origin is possibly furnished by the statement of Pliny that the Druids worshipped the plant because they believed it to have fallen from heaven and to be a token that the tree on which it grew was chosen by the god himself. Can they have thought that the mistletoe dropped on the oak in a flash of lightning? The conjecture is confirmed by the name thunder-besom which is applied to mistletoe in the Swiss canton of Aargau, for the epithet clearly implies a close connexion between the parasite and the thunder; indeed "thunder-besom" is a popular name in Germany for any bushy nest-like excrescence growing on a branch, because such a parasitic growth is actually believed by the ignorant to be a product of lightning.

If there is any truth in this conjecture, the real reason why the Druids worshipped a mistletoe-bearing oak above all other trees of the forest was a belief that every such oak had not only been struck by lightning but bore among its branches a visible emanation of the celestial fire; so that in cutting the mistletoe with mystic rites they were securing for themselves all the magical properties of a thunderbolt. If that was so, we must appar-

ently conclude that the mistletoe was deemed an emanation of the lightning rather than, as I have thus far argued, of the midsummer sun. Perhaps, indeed, we might combine the two seemingly divergent views by supposing that in the old Aryan creed the mistletoe descended from the sun on Midsummer Day in a flash of lightning. But such a combination is artificial and unsupported, so far as I know, by any positive evidence. Whether on mythical principles the two interpretations can really be reconciled with each other or not,

I will not presume to say; but even should they prove to be discrepant, the inconsistency need not have prevented our rude forefathers from embracing both of them at the same time with an equal fervour of conviction; for like the great majority of mankind the savage is above being hidebound by the trammels of a pedantic logic. In attempting to track his devious thought through the jungle of crass ignorance and blind fear, we must always remember that we are treading enchanted

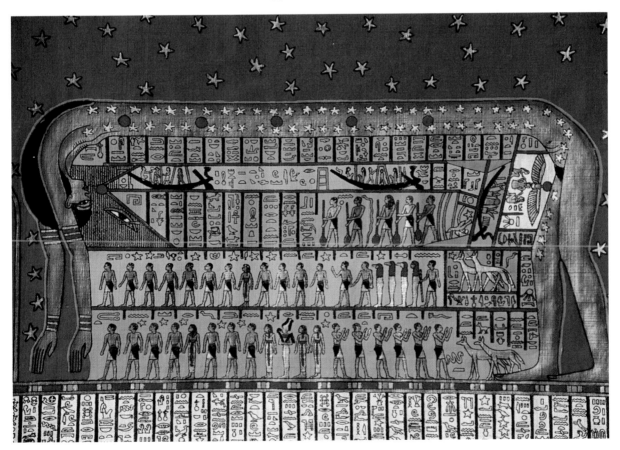

ground, and must beware of taking for solid realities the cloudy shapes that cross our path or hover and gibber at us through the gloom. We can never completely replace ourselves at the standpoint of primitive man, see things with his eyes, and feel our hearts beat with the emotions that stirred his. All our theories concerning him and his ways must therefore fall far short of certainty; the utmost we can aspire to in such matters is a reasonable degree of probability.

To conclude these enquiries we may say that if Balder was indeed, as I have conjectured, a personification of a mistletoe-bearing oak, his death by a blow of the mistletoe might on the new theory be explained as a death by a stroke of lightning. So long as the mistletoe, in which the flame of the lightning smouldered, was suffered to remain among the boughs, so long no harm could befall the good and kindly god of the oak, who kept his life stowed away for safety between earth and heaven in the mysterious parasite; but when once that seat of his life, or of his death, was torn from the branch and hurled at the trunk, the tree fell—the god died—smitten by a thunderbolt.

And what we have said of Balder in the oak forests of Scandinavia may perhaps, with all due diffidence in a question so obscure and uncertain, be applied to the priest of Diana, the King of the Wood, at Aricia in the oak forests of Italy. He may have personated in flesh and blood the great Italian god of the sky, Jupiter, who had kindly come down from heaven in the lightning flash to dwell among men in the mistletoe—the thunder-besom—the Golden Bough—growing on the sacred oak in the dells of Nemi. If that was so, we need not wonder that the priest guarded with drawn sword the mystic bough which contained the god's life and his own. The goddess whom he served and married was herself, if I am right, no other than the Queen of Heaven, the true wife of the sky-god. For she, too, loved the solitude of the woods and the lonely hills, and sailing overhead on clear nights in the likeness of the silver moon looked down with pleasure on her own fair image reflected on the calm, the burnished surface of the lake, Diana's Mirror.

As we draw now to our close, let us contemplate the lessons we have learned from a contemplation of the modes of thought of our forebears and compare them with our own. Every great advance in knowledge has extended the sphere of order and correspondingly restricted the sphere of apparent disorder in the world, till now we are ready to anticipate that even in regions where chance and confusion appear still to reign, a fuller knowledge would everywhere reduce the seeming chaos to cosmos. Thus the keener minds, still pressing forward to a deeper solution of the mysteries of the universe, come to reject the religious theory of nature as inadequate, and to revert in a measure to the older standpoint of magic by postulating explicitly, what in magic had only been implicitly assumed, to wit, an inflexible regularity in the order of natural events, which, if carefully observed, enables us to foresee their course with certainty and to act accordingly. In short, religion, regarded as an explanation of nature, is displaced by science.

But while science has this much in common with magic, that both rest on a faith in order as the underlying principle of all things, readers of this work will hardly need to be reminded that the order presupposed by magic differs widely from that which forms the basis of science. The difference flows naturally from the different modes in which the two orders have been reached. For whereas the order on which magic reckons is merely an extension, by false analogy, of the order in which ideas present themselves to our minds, the order laid down by science is derived from patient and exact observation of the phenomena themselves. The abundance, the solidity, and the splendour of the results already achieved by science are well fitted to inspire us with a cheerful confidence in the soundness of its method. Here at last, after groping about in the dark for countless ages, man has hit upon a clue to the labyrinth, a golden key that opens many locks in the treasury of nature. It is probably not too much to say that the hope of progress—moral and intellectual as well as material—in the future is bound up with the fortunes of science, and that every obstacle placed in the way of scientific dis-

Above: *In Frazer's words, "the advance of knowledge is an infinite progression towards a goal that forever recedes." Earth is but a tiny part of a universe that is itself threatened by great forces we have yet to fully understand.*

covery is a wrong to humanity.

Yet the history of thought should warn us against concluding that because the scientific theory of the world is the best that has yet been formulated, it is necessarily complete and final. We must remember that at bottom the generalisations of science or, in common parlance, the laws of nature are merely hypotheses devised to explain that ever-shifting phantasmagoria of thought which we dignify with the high-sounding names of the world and the universe. In the last analysis magic, religion, and science are nothing but theories of thought; and as science has supplanted its predecessors, so it may hereafter be itself superseded by some more perfect hypothesis, perhaps by some totally different way of looking at the phenomena—of registering the shadows on the screen—of which we in this generation can form no idea. The advance of knowledge is an infinite progression towards a goal that forever recedes. We need not murmur at the

endless pursuit. Great things will come of that pursuit, though we may not enjoy them. Brighter stars will rise on some voyager of the future—some great Ulysses of the realms of thought—than shine on us. The dreams of magic may one day be the waking realities of science. But a dark shadow lies athwart the far end of this fair prospect. For however vast the increase of knowl-edge and of power which the future may have in store for man, he can scarcely hope to stay the sweep of those great forces which seem to be making silently but relentlessly for the destruction of all this starry universe in which our earth swims as a speck or mote.

In the ages to come man may be able to predict, perhaps even to control, the wayward courses of the winds and clouds, but hardly will his puny hands have strength to speed afresh our slackening planet in its orbit or rekindle the dying fire of the sun. Yet the philosopher who trembles at the idea of such distant catastrophes may console himself by reflecting that these gloomy apprehensions, like the earth and the sun themselves, are only parts of that unsubstantial world which thought has conjured up out of the void, and that the phantoms which the subtle enchantress has evoked today she may ban tomor-

Above: *Frazer compares the differing threads of magic, religion and science, which weave themselves through human history, with those of dew-covered spider's webs on a cluster of reeds.*

Opposite: *The lake and grove of Nemi.* Detail of *The Golden Bough* by Turner. Tate Gallery, London.

row. They too, like so much that to common eyes seems solid, may melt into air, into thin air.

Without dipping so far into the future, we may illustrate the course which thought has hitherto run by likening it to a web woven of three different threads—the black thread of magic, the red thread of religion, and the white thread of science, if under science we may include those simple truths, drawn from observation of nature, of which men in all ages have possessed a store. Could we then survey the web of thought from the beginning, we should probably perceive it to be at first a chequer of black and white, a patchwork of true and false notions, hardly tinged as yet by the red thread of religion. But carry your eye far-

ther along the fabric and you will remark that, while the black and white chequer still runs through it, there rests on the middle portion of the web, where religion has entered most deeply into its texture, a dark crimson stain, which shades off insensibly into a lighter tint as the white thread of science is woven more and more into the tissue. To a web thus chequered and stained, thus shot with threads of diverse hues, but gradually changing colour the farther it is unrolled, the state of modern thought, with all its divergent aims and conflicting tendencies, may be compared. Will the great movement which for centuries has been slowly altering the complexion of thought be continued in the near future? Or will a reaction set in which may arrest progress and even undo much that has been done? To keep up our parable, what will be the colour of the web which the Fates are now weaving on the humming loom of time? Will it be white or red? We cannot tell. A faint glimmering light illumines the backward portion of the web. Clouds and thick darkness hide the other end.

Our long voyage of discovery is over and our bark has drooped her weary sails in port at last. Once more we take the road to Nemi. It is evening, and as we climb the long slope of the Appian Way up to the Alban Hills, we look back and see the sky aflame with sunset, its golden glory resting like the aureole of a dying saint over Rome and touching with a crest of fire the dome of St. Peter's. The sight once seen can never be forgotten, but we turn from it and pursue our way darkling along the mountain side, till we come to Nemi and look down on the lake in its deep hollow, now fast disappearing in the evening shadows. The place has changed but little since Diana received the homage of her worshippers in the sacred grove. The temple of the sylvan goddess, indeed, has vanished and the King of the Wood no longer stands sentinel over the Golden Bough. But Nemi's woods are still green, and as the sunset fades above them in the west, there comes to us, borne on the swell of the wind, the sound of the church bells of Aricia ringing the Angelus. Ave Maria! Sweet and solemn they chime out from the distant town and die lingeringly away across the wide Campagnan marshes. Le roi est mort, vive le roi! Ave Maria!

INDEX

ACKNOWLEDGMENTS

Picture Research: Jan Croot for Image Select International (London)

A-Z Botanical: 208.
AKG: 10, 12, 13 (bottom), 18, 19, 24, 100, 101, 131, 136, 138, 139, 174, 205.
Bridgeman Art Library: Back cover, Half title page, 8, 11, 13 top; 16, 17, 27?; 56, 59, 66, 82, 88, 97, 104, 124, 151 168, 173, 181, 183, 189, 190, 192, 221.
Collections/Robert Hallmann: 51 top, Brian Shuel 156, 160, 170, 176, 209.
Corbis: 130.
Jan Croot: 22, 44, 185, 186, 210.

ET Archive: Contents page, 13 bottom, 17, 21, 22, 57, 68, 83, 132, 159, 216.
Robert Estall: 54, 155, 109.
Mary Evans: 62, 75, 79, 89, 118, 194, 199.
Fine Art Photographic Library: 78, 79, 81, 125, 135, 137, 166, 167, 188, 196, 207.
Werner Forman Archive: 4, 14, 15, 26, 27, 28, 30, 33, 34, 38, 41, 43, 47, 48, 49, 51 bottom, 58, 61, 71, 72, 73, 91, 92, 98, 110, 111, 116, 119, 128, 133, 144, 147, 149, 150, 178, 179, 198, 202, 203, 211.
Fortean Picture Library: 134.
Robert Francis 84, 120, 126, 140.
Giraudon: 11.

Robert Harding: 29.
Michael Holford: 9, 42, 62, 64, 105, 122.
Hutchison: 20, 25, 31 (right); 52, 67, 76, 77, 80, 85, 109, 120, 121, 126, 127, 140, 141, 193.
Images Colour Library: 23, 31 (left), 32, 36, 40, 45, 50, 65, 69, 73 (right), 74, 86, 87, 90, 95, 99, 103, 106, 108, 114, 115, 142, 146, 148, 153, 164, 183, 177, 179, 197, 200, 201, 212.
Image Select: 180, 217.
Frank Lane Picture Agency: 158, 204, 220.
Panos: 53, 96, 113, 117, 129, 145.

Science Photo Library: 219.
Stills Pictures: 26, 37, 53, 60, 93, 143.
Robert K. G. Temple: 6.
Charles Tair: 154.
Trip: 112.
Zefa: 35, 151, 157, 161, 163, 165, 213.

PUBLISHER'S NOTE: The publishers have made every effort to locate and credit the copyright holders of material reproduced in this book, and they regret any omissions that have occurred.